PENGUIN BOOKS

GETTING TO US

Seth Davis is the author of the *New York Times* bestsellers *Wooden: A Coach's Life* and *When March Went Mad: The Game That Transformed Basketball*. He is an on-air studio analyst for CBS Sports and CBS Sports Network during coverage of college basketball and the NCAA tournament, and he is also the managing editor of the national college basketball platform at *The Athletic*. Before joining *The Athletic*, Davis spent twenty-two years covering college basketball for *Sports Illustrated*. A graduate of Duke University, he lives with his family in Los Angeles.

GETTING TO US

HOW GREAT COACHES MAKE GREAT TEAMS

SETH DAVIS

PENGUIN BOOKS

PENGUIN BOOKS

An imprint of Penguin Random House LLC

penguinrandomhouse.com

First published in the United States of America by Penguin Press,
an imprint of Penguin Random House LLC, 2018
Published in Penguin Books 2019

ISBN 9780735222724 (hardcover)
ISBN 9780735222748 (paperback)
ISBN 9780735222731 (ebook)

Printed in the United States of America
1   3   5   7   9   10   8   6   4   2

DESIGNED BY AMANDA DEWEY

For my home team—
Melissa, Zachary, Noah, Gabriel, and Clarence

Contents

BRAD STEVENS 217
"All the good ones want to be coached."

DABO SWINNEY 246
"God never says, 'Oops.'"

Introduction

A man paces the sidelines, arms folded, jaw set, eyes ablaze. Wheels turn in his mind, stress rips up his gut. He stomps, he gesticulates, he barks orders, he bitches at referees. In preparation for this moment, he hires a staff, chooses his roster, devises game plans, studies video, makes substitutions, diagrams plays, perorates in the locker room, builds a culture.

And his teams win. Not always, for even the greatest of coaching minds cannot avoid losses. Over time, however, his excellence shines through, not so much because of anything he himself does, but because of the mysterious process by which he is able to stir his players to reach their potential as individuals and as a unit, a team. It is a delicate task, requiring an ability to set standards and apply them, and to manage a diverse group of egos. A team begins as a collection of *mes, hims,* and *yous.* It is the job of the coach to figure out a way to get to *Us.*

It is not easy to do, nor is it easily explained.

During my quarter century as a journalist working for outlets like *Sports Illustrated*, CBS Sports, and *The Athletic*, I have had the privilege of observing from close range many of the greatest coaches in sports, particularly in football and basketball. I have been to their games, sat in on their meetings and practices, interviewed them at length in private settings. I've found many athletes intensely interesting. But when it comes to fascinating characters, there is nothing like highly successful coaches. They are a writer's dream—multihued, paradoxical characters, by turns brilliant, driven, tortured, compulsive, and philosophical. By rule, seemingly, they are all at least a little bit weird. They are laser-focused yet absentminded. They are often gratified, but rarely do I get the sense that they are deeply, truly happy.

My desire to demystify this vocation was what inspired me to write this book. The intent here is not to add to what is commonly referred to as the "cult of the coach." There is already more than enough idolatry in our sporting culture. These are men, not gods, and they will be the first to tell you that much of their success is rooted in the good fortune to coach great players at great organizations or universities. My purpose is simply to examine these men in the hope of figuring out how they get to *Us*. I set out to trace their steps, all the way back to their early years, in hopes of developing an understanding of the forces that have formed their character and taught them the skills they apply to their craft. I didn't want just to assess their leadership methods, though I did learn a lot about how they go about their jobs. I also wanted to know *why* they go about their jobs.

You will find in these portraits a wide variety of life experiences and leadership philosophies. However, I have isolated four personal qualities that I believe to be the core requirements all great coaches must have in order to get a group of individuals to *Us*. They form what I call the PEAK profile:

Persistence. We all know that great coaches are passionate and competitive. They burn with intensity. Many look for perceived slights or contrived conspiracies to provide extra motivation. But those forces are ephemeral. Persistence is the strain of character one leans upon during those quiet moments when self-doubt creeps in. It is both tested and manufactured during childhood and early-adulthood adversity. It is evinced in the day-to-day mundane routines, the unglamorous aspects that make up the bulk of the time spent on the job. Those tasks are performed in solitude when the fans are gone and the cameras are nowhere in sight. Yet they are vital. It takes persistence to get them done, and done right.

What I learned is that if a coach lacks sufficient persistence, he will be unable to complete the critical task of finding growth opportunities out of adversity. If the setbacks do not enable him to mature and learn, he will ultimately fail. More important, he will be unable to persuade his players to cohere during the tough times. Persistence is the mortar that holds the bricks together when the high winds blow. Without it, the ethos of *Us* will collapse against the force of high-level competition.

Empathy. It is important to understand the difference between *sympathy* and *empathy.* Sympathy involves feeling sad for another person's dire condition. Empathy requires feeling whatever that person is feeling. And so a great coach must find ways to learn about his players, taking time to acquire the critical information that will lead him to understand how the player's mind, heart, and guts operate.

If I were ranking the PEAK qualities in order of importance, empathy would come first. Like snowflakes, no two athletes are alike. The one thing that great coaches have most in common is the ability to discern the different ways to motivate each guy. Some players need a soft touch. Others need a firm kick. All have individual goals—and they are entitled to that—so a coach cannot get them to *Us* unless he can persuade them to act in a way that serves the team's best interests as well as their own. Empathy is an indispensable trait in great leaders. There is no getting to *Us* without it.

Authenticity. Some coaches scream a lot, berate their players, and are unable to get through a declarative sentence without profanity.

Others are quiet, reserved, maybe a little pious. In the end, it doesn't matter what they believe or how they behave. What matters is that they remain true to themselves and act accordingly.

Tom Izzo and Dabo Swinney are as congenial as it gets. Jim Boeheim and Urban Meyer tend to be standoffish, and they can be real tools when they want to be. Jim Harbaugh is a raving maniac on the sideline. Brad Stevens barely has a pulse. What makes them great coaches is their refusal to be something they're not. Players can spot a phony in an instant. Trust may be an important component in any team, but there is no trust without authenticity. The guys on the team must have full confidence that their coach will remain authentic, particularly in those critical moments when the team must function as a single unit or suffer defeat.

Moreover, authenticity plays a part in every decision a coach makes, and that includes the type of system he wants to run. Far too often, our assessment of a coach's performance centers on game strategy. It is more important for the coach to recognize his own strengths and weaknesses, and acknowledge that they often come from the same place. Only then can he build a system that best suits his skill set and personality profile. His players will execute their tasks as long as they know he will never deviate from his fundamental belief set. That authenticity must be on display every hour of every day.

Knowledge. A surgeon may have a lot of personal qualities you admire, but you wouldn't want her to operate on you unless she has the proper medical training. The same is true for coaches. Acquiring this knowledge takes time and passion. It is accrued during late, lonely nights spent poring over videos, not to mention a lifetime of reading books and articles, attending clinics, and picking the brains of mentors who came before.

The acquisition of expertise is a lifetime pursuit. Knowledge without adaptability will eventually diminish a leader's effective-

ness. People change, games change, times change. Like authenticity, knowledge is an important step on the pathway to trust. We
often think about trust as a synonym for integrity, but a player also
needs to trust that a coach has the knowledge to justify his instructions. Good people with good intentions can give bad advice if they
do not know enough about their craft. Thus it requires a level of
knowledge for the coach to persuade his players to commit totally to
what he is asking them to do. Without that commitment, there is no
getting to *Us*.

The point of this book is not to uncover every secret about why the
teams these men coach win so much, though that will become
evident enough as their stories unfurl. The real secret is that there
are no secrets. There is no magic key that unlocks the door to winning. Rather, the ability to get to *Us* results from a lifetime of practice, the accumulation of a lot of small, important wins that accrue
to the point where a coach can pass along his persistence, empathy,
authenticity, and knowledge to his players. In examining some of
the best coaches working in sports—who they are, where they came
from, how and why they do their jobs so well, I trained my focus on
one question above all, that of how they got to *Us*.

For me, this journey, this inquiry, has been the capstone of my
two and a half decades spent hanging around arenas and stadiums,
searching for morsels of wisdom that might enrich my own life and
enable me to do my job better. At heart, all of these men are united
in their dedication to the art of excellence. I found a great deal to
learn from them, and I hope you will, too.

Urban Meyer

The story has changed a little over the years, so let's start with what we know.

It was May 1982, and Urban Meyer was a senior shortstop playing for St. John High School in Ashtabula, Ohio. The team was trailing by one run against its rival, Harbor High, when Urban came to the plate in the last inning with two outs and two men on base. The pitcher had been throwing him curves and knuckleballs all game, which was smart considering Urban was one of the best power hitters in the state. When the count reached 2-2, Urban naturally expected another off-speed pitch, so he was caught off guard when the pitcher fired a fastball right down the middle. The ump rang him up. Game over.

It was a pretty horrific transgression. This was blue-collar northeast Ohio, where men were men, losing was a failure, and striking out without swinging was out of the question. After the game, Urban walked over to the car of his buddy who had given him a ride to the game, tossed his baseball cleats into the backseat, and said, "Get these back to me tomorrow. I'm running home."

And so he did. It was a good eight miles.

The friend who drove him, Dean Hood, who was a student at Harbor High, distinctly remembers Urban saying, "My father is making me run home." Another childhood chum, Tom Penna, recalls driving by Urban as he ran and wanting to pick him up, but declining to do so because "we were too afraid. We didn't want Bud to see us bring him home." Bud was Urban's dad's nickname. His real name was Urban Jr. They were both named for a pope.

Urban has told the story often over the years, and he has usually indicated that running home was Bud's idea. In an interview with *Sports Illustrated* writer S.L. Price in 2009, Meyer, who at the time was the head football coach at the University of Florida, claimed that he ran as a result of an argument he and his dad were having. "We were getting into it and I just didn't want to hear it," Meyer said. "He said, 'Go run home.' And it wasn't, like, across the street. [It was] about eight miles."

When Meyer published his book *Above the Line* in 2015, however, he claimed that running home was his idea. "I had to run. I had to do something," he wrote. "I'd just stood there with the game on the line, star shortstop turned statue, as useless as a freighter stuck on the shoals of nearby Lake Erie." He later added that "some people had the idea that my father, Bud Meyer, a tough guy who was old school even by old school standards, ordered me to run home as punishment for coming up small. . . . The run home had nothing to do with my father, though. It had completely to do with how much I hate to lose and how upset I was that I had let the team down."

When I visited Meyer in his office at the Woody Hayes Center on the campus of Ohio State in the spring of 2017, he stuck to his story. "My idea," he said. When I read to him quotes from his friends in Ashtabula who thought it was Bud's, he shook his head and said, "Yeah, they're out of their minds. I don't know where they got that." He added, "I think part of it was I didn't want to have to listen about that third strike in the car. I was pissed. I went home and hit for an hour. So [running] was my way of saying, *I have to get the hell out of here and get this right.*"

"Did you fear your dad?" I asked.

"Oh, yeah. Everybody did. Still fear him to this day, and he's been gone six years."

Could it be that as a result of that never-dying fear, Meyer is now shading the oft-told story to put his dad in a better light? Is his memory playing tricks on him? Or was he just misunderstood all these years? I like that we'll never know for sure, because the mystery goes a long way toward explaining how Urban Meyer gets to *Us*. It lies in that sweet spot where a magic transference was made that day—from a father making his son do something hard to the son *wanting* to do something hard. That is the same thing Meyer does with the players on his football teams. That transference marks a special connection. If a coach can achieve that connection with all the players in his locker room, or at least enough of them, then he has something special.

In his three decades coaching college football, during which time he has won three national championships as a head coach at two different schools, Meyer has proven to be one of the most masterful tacticians in the game's history. His spread option offense has literally changed the way college football in America is played. Yet that only begins to explain his effectiveness as a coach. "He has a great ability to push buttons on people, whether it's players or assistant coaches," says Dan Mullen, who was an assistant with Meyer for seven years at three different schools and is now the head coach at Mississippi State. "There's no one better when it comes to motivating you to want to give him your best."

You can see the seeds of Meyer's PEAK profile taking root during that eight-mile run. You can also see the stirrings of the inner turmoil that would later threaten his career, not to mention his health. There's no problem in wanting to run hard, long, and fast. The problems come when you don't know how to stop.

There's another story about Bud that has likewise become part of the Urban legend. It happened a few months later, in the summer of 1982, when Urban was struggling while playing rookie baseball in Bradenton, Florida. The Atlanta Braves had selected him in the 13th round of the 1982 Major League Baseball draft. At seventeen years old, he was the youngest player selected in the entire draft, and he was starting to realize how overmatched he was. One night, he took a nasty grounder to the face. His eye was swollen shut. The next day, a tearful Urban called home and told his father he wanted to quit.

"That's fine," Bud said evenly. "Just know that you will not be welcome in this house. We don't let any quitters in here."

At first, Urban thought he was kidding. Then Bud said, "Be sure to call your mother on Christmas. I'm sure she'll want to hear from you." And he hung up.

Urban's feelings were hurt badly that day, but that conversation marked the moment his coaching empathy was born. "I just shared that story with a player the other day. I use that all the time," Meyer told me. "Every athlete I've ever coached reaches a point where he says, *I'm out, this is too much.* So I share that with them, and I share it with the parents. It helps because they look at me and say, 'Wow, you know exactly what I'm going through.'"

As the middle child between two academically proficient sisters, Urban was raised to believe that high achievement was a requirement, not an option. If one of Bud's kids brought home an unacceptable grade, he would order them to run laps around the house. Urban showed promise in football and baseball, and eventually he set up his weights in the dining room. Bud gave out compliments even less frequently than he gave out hugs. But he never missed a game.

"I didn't get a whole lot of 'I love you' from my dad," Urban says. "That generation wasn't warm and fuzzy. But when I went out there to play shortstop, I knew right where he was, and that meant the world to me. It's like that old saying. How do you spell love? T-I-M-E."

When Urban was in second grade, his younger sister, Erika, came home crying because two of his classmates were picking on her. Bud gave his son clear instructions that when he went to school the next morning, he had better take care of the situation. Urban was afraid to fight, but fight he did. That night Bud invited him to sit at the head of the dinner table and said, "You became a man today." Thus were imbued two important values that Urban would later bring to his football teams: toughness and brotherhood.

Bud was brilliant in his own right. His job as a chemical engineer afforded a comfortable living, with access to private school and membership at the local boating club. When the kids were in grade school, Bud gave them lessons in Latin, German, and trigonometry. His wife, Gisela, had some grit of her own, having escaped Hitler's Germany as a refugee at the age of thirteen before emigrating to the United States when she was twenty-three. Gisela, however, was more of the nurturing kind, which suited her as a professional chef at the fancy hotel in town. When Urban was a boy, she filled his head with dreams of becoming the head football coach at Notre Dame, the ultimate ascension for a nice Catholic boy who was named for a pope.

Like everyone else in the state, Urban was an Ohio State Buckeyes fan. He wore No. 45 as an homage to the great Ohio State running back Archie Griffin, the only player to win back-to-back Heisman Trophies. At that time, the state was under the sway of the legendary coach Woody Hayes, who was known as much for his intemperateness as his tactical brilliance. The coaches Urban grew up playing for were just like Woody—loud, demanding, and mean. "When I was in Ohio in the 1970s, it was not uncommon for the football coach to grab your facemask and kick you right square," he told me. "This was back in the Woody Hayes era. Football was a tough, violent game, and putting your hands on players was acceptable. When I was a young coach coming up, the louder you were, the harder you were, the better the coach you were."

Meyer was pretty popular in high school, but he was serious too, old beyond his years. He went to his share of parties, but he didn't get wasted or get into trouble. Hood recalls Meyer as a young man with "presence," but he adds, "Urban has always been guarded. He wasn't easy to get to know at first. You had to spend some time with him before he would loosen up." His focus was heavily on sports. Meyer was a pretty good fullback and defensive back, but his real talents were on the diamond. After the Braves drafted him, he skipped his senior prom so he could board a flight to Florida and get a head start on rookie ball.

After that fateful phone call to his father, Urban finished out his first season. He hit a whopping .170. The average ticked up to .193 the following season. It was especially frustrating to Urban, since he always tried to eat right, get his sleep, and practice until his hands bled.

He realized he wasn't cut out for baseball one night when his roommate came home late and stinking drunk. The next morning, the guy ripped two homers while Urban went hitless and made a couple of errors at shortstop. "Maybe you should try it my way," the guy cracked. At the end of the season, the Braves cut him. Urban got the bad news via a letter signed by the great Hank Aaron. He still has that letter framed.

As difficult as it was to accept his failure at baseball, the setback provided an opportunity to develop his persistence. So he went home and enrolled at the University of Cincinnati. Though he dabbled in some semipro baseball, he signed up to play defensive back for the

Bearcats' football team. The team was terrible, but Meyer still wasn't good enough to start. Because he was already thinking about a career in coaching, he decided to major in psychology, figuring the knowledge he gained would someday make him a good motivator.

During his senior year at Cincinnati, Meyer interned as a defensive backs coach at local St. Xavier High School. After graduation he got a job as a graduate assistant at Ohio State and enrolled in the university's sports administration program. He was joined in Columbus by his college girlfriend, Shelley Mather. Shelley was also a psychology major, working toward a career in the mental health field.

The two years that Urban spent in Columbus brought him into the orbit of Buckeyes coach Earle Bruce, who would become like a second father to him. Bruce succeeded Woody Hayes, and he very much followed in Hayes's fierce tradition. He got to *Us* by berating his players, enforcing strict discipline, and insisting they meet his high standards. Bruce could be merciless to his guys during practice, but he also routinely invited players over to his house so he could get to know them in a more relaxed setting. When Urban introduced Bruce to his own father, it was like they had known each other their whole lives. Bruce paid Bud the ultimate compliment when he called him a "nasty ass."

"They were clones," Urban says. "They believed there's no such thing as a gray area. There's a right way and a wrong way to do things. I'm so grateful they were there to teach me that."

After completing his two-year master's degree, Meyer accepted a part-time position as linebackers coach at Illinois State University. He worked day and night, seven days a week, for a whopping $6,000 salary. Shelley supported them as a full-time psychiatric nurse. The question of providing for a family is never a trivial one, and Urban briefly found himself wondering whether he should be a lawyer instead. Shelley helped him stay the course. "I could see how good he was and how much he loved it," she says.

They were all in—he with coaching, she with him. Urban and Shelley got married on July 8, 1989, during a brief window between recruiting and summer camps. (Over the years, Shelley would notice that a lot of coaches shared an anniversary during that same week.) The following year, at twenty-six, he moved on to take a position as wide receivers coach at Colorado State, where Bruce had recently taken over as head coach. While Urban was coaching, Shelley completed her graduate degree at the University of Colorado in Denver while raising their two young daughters—Nicki, who was born in 1990, and Gigi, who came along three years later.

Four years after the Meyers arrived in Fort Collins, Colorado State fired Bruce, accusing him of hitting at least nine players "with a closed fist in unprotected areas of their bodies" and creating "a climate of intimidation and fear." Meyer was initially swept out the door with the rest of the staff, but Bruce's replacement, Sonny Lubick, brought him back.

Meyer was grateful to be able to keep his job, but he had serious misgivings about what he perceived as Lubick's lax approach. After Meyer drove one of his receivers to quit the team, Lubick let him know that if he wanted to keep his job, he had better lighten up. Urban did as he was told. To his surprise, Lubick's methods proved to be effective as the Rams went on to win back-to-back Western Athletic Conference titles.

The three years that Meyer spent under Lubick provided a critical addition to his knowledge. Sure, intensity and drive were important, but a coach could also get to *Us* using a gentle touch, if that was authentically of a piece with his personality. "His way of getting to the final product was different, but deep to the core he's very similar to Earle Bruce," Meyer says. "I don't believe I would still be coaching if it weren't for him."

That was an important lesson for Meyer. Unfortunately, he didn't learn it well enough.

. . .

He doesn't remember exactly what set him off, only that he was coaching a "nonfunctional group" and saw something on the screen that he obviously didn't like. This was 1996, and Meyer was in his first season as the wide receivers coach at Notre Dame. When he spied the unpardonable sin, he exploded in rage and tossed the remote control at the television. The glass shattered. Notre Dame's head coach, Lou Holtz, later joked in front of the team that he would charge his wide receivers coach the cost of replacing the television.

This was the only way he knew how to coach, and the occasional damage to electronics aside, it was becoming very clear that he was good at it. He may have been coaching a finesse position, but he was determined to turn his kids into football players, Ashtabula-style. A typical two-hour workout would include ninety minutes of physical pounding, blocking, and hitting, over and over again. Only during the last thirty minutes would he use a football to actually work on receiving. "It was extremely unconventional," says Mickey Marotti, who was Notre Dame's strength coach at the time and has followed Meyer to Florida and Ohio State. "I looked at Urban as using an offensive line coach mentality to coach wideouts. He was all about teaching toughness."

In Meyer's view, there were no small problems. His nickname around the team was "Captain Emergency." Some of the players called him "Lunatic." Yet, staying true to what he learned from Earle Bruce, he would still welcome his players over to his house several times a week to eat, watch TV, and hang out. Oftentimes they would go there even when he was out of town recruiting. They liked hanging with Shelley better anyway. "I really enjoyed talking to those young men. It was like having your own kids," Shelley says. "At first, he just wanted to coach X's and O's, but he learned early on you can't just get on the field and start running plays. You've got to deal with the whole player."

Alas, his body would prove to be unsuited to the hard-core way he lived his job. Meyer was working the sidelines during a Notre Dame game in 1998 when he was overcome by a sharp pain in his head. He visited a doctor, who told him it was the result of a benign cyst in his brain. The cyst didn't require any surgery or treatment, but the doctor warned Meyer that the pain could flare up again if he got too stressed.

Bud and Gisela made it to South Bend for every home game, each time throwing a huge tailgate party for family and friends, with Gisela creating a theme for each party, cooking up a storm, and serving champagne. Sure, they were proud Catholic parents, but they didn't start making that kind of effort just for Notre Dame. When Urban was at Illinois State they once drove ten hours each way to watch the team play a road game at Indiana State.

Gisela's dream was for her son to become a head college football coach, but she didn't live long enough to see it happen. In 2000, she died from cancer. A year later, her dream came true when Meyer became the head coach at Bowling Green State University.

The program had just endured six consecutive losing seasons, including a 2–9 record the previous year. Within the first few weeks of his tenure, Meyer learned that twenty-seven players had skipped study hall. He saw an immediate opportunity to instill a new culture, and he seized it. He called for a 5 a.m. workout at the team's indoor practice facility. It was a frigid winter morning, and he had lined up trash cans around the field so the players could puke in them while he ran them ragged. That workout came to be known as Black Wednesday, but according to Meyer, it was the least of his cruel and unusual tactics. "I was a thirty-six-year-old raving lunatic," he says. "I did things at Bowling Green that should've gotten me let go. I needed to be at a place where I could make mistakes, where not many people cared and it certainly wasn't in the lime-light."

Nearly two dozen players quit the team as a result. The ones who remained were his type of guys, in mentality if not in talent. Meyer and his staff oversaw all aspects of the program. That included academics; Urban proctored some study halls and tutored his guys in math. But he knew that discipline and effort could take his team only so far. At some point they would have to figure out a way to beat more talented teams.

So he and his assistants bunkered themselves over the summer in an effort to come up with a fresh offensive scheme. The idea was to create a system that no one else was running. Dan Mullen, who was a graduate assistant at Notre Dame, came with Meyer to Bowling Green as quarterbacks coach, and they talked about how Holtz and his staff used to get freaked out the week they were preparing to go up against Navy's wishbone offense. That was the psychological advantage of wielding an anomaly.

While they were at Notre Dame, Mullen and Meyer had spent some time at Louisville with Scott Linehan, the team's offensive coordinator, who was doing some creative things with the I formation. That system was normally designed to feature tough, hard straightaway running, but Louisville was doing some innovative things to open things up. Mullen and Meyer experienced an epiphany when they asked Linehan what he did to counter a blitz from a cornerback or safety. Smith explained that because they regularly deployed four or five wide receivers, "we never see a corner or safety blitz, ever." It was a powerful concept: If you use the entire field, you won't have to feel any pressure.

As part of their Bowling Green experiment, Meyer, Mullen, and offensive coordinator Gregg Brandon studied what had come to be called the "spread option offense," a modern scheme that called for the quarterback to operate from a shotgun formation and fire a lot of short, pinpoint passes. The spread had been used in the past by Kansas State's Bill Snyder, but a young, up-and-coming coach named Rich Rodriguez, who had just taken over at West Virginia, was pushing the concept even further. Meyer liked the spread, but he didn't want to get away from his mind-set that football was a tough-man's game. His solution was to take the tactics of the spread and combine them with some elements of traditional power football.

Meyer sat in a room with Mullen and his offensive coordinator, and they doodled and dabbled for three months, not sure what they were doing. "It was awesome," Meyer says with a big grin. To further keep defenses off guard, they devised an intricate set of calls and audibles that gave the quarterback lots of leeway in decision making. They went through every possible scenario, figuring out how they would counter the counters to their counters. The goal was that they would never run a play where they had to cross their fingers that the defense wasn't in a certain formation.

Meyer took a player named Josh Harris, who had been converted from quarterback to running back, and put him back under center—or at least, in the shotgun. Then he went to work teaching him the offense. Harris thought he was working hard, but his coach let him know early on that he was selling himself short. "You're a great kid and a good student," Meyer told him. "I just don't understand how you cannot be a fanatic about this game." Harris responded well—evolving from responding well to being told to work hard to *wanting* to work hard—and the rest of the team followed suit.

Thus did Meyer successfully apply his PEAK profile to his very first job. He showed his players the value of persistence even as he ran them until they puked. He had to convince them that he understood what they were going through, no doubt telling and retelling the story of that phone call with his dad. He needed to demonstrate that he was being authentic with them, and that he was making his choices for the right reasons. And they needed to trust that he knew what he was talking about. Otherwise they would never fully commit to running this weird, newfangled offense.

The season opener at Missouri presented a major challenge, to say the least. Meyer had one big advantage: Missouri's coaching staff could not have prepared their team to defend the spread option, since no one had ever run it before. Most of Bowling Green's offensive plays had four or five wide receivers. Only one or two of them could catch, but the Missouri defenders didn't know that. They had no choice but to defend the whole field, which hampered their ability to put pressure on Harris. Bowling Green won a shocking 20–13 victory. The score reverberated around college football, forcing observers to ask a pair of questions that would be asked many times again: Who is this guy coaching this team? And what the hell is he running?

H e was too big of a talent for Bowling Green to hold. The Falcons finished that first season with an 8–3 record, the biggest turnaround any team in America enjoyed that season. They went 9–3 the next. Just like that, Meyer was scooped up by the University of Utah, which signed him to a five-year contract worth $400,000 per year.

Once again, Meyer brought down his cultural hammer. He did the trash can trick again, put the Utes through military-style boot camp, turned weight room workouts into a test of wills. He faced his own cultural challenge because many of the players were from a Polynesian background. They shied away from eye contact and bristled at his penchant for confrontation. He had to adjust intelligently and empathetically.

Several assistants, most importantly Mullen, followed Meyer to Utah and helped him teach the spread option. They were met with a once-in-a-lifetime stroke of luck that Alex Smith, a tall, gangly quarterback out of Bremerton, Washington, was on the roster. Smith only had one other major scholarship offer, Louisville, and started off as the team's third-string quarterback. He was skinny as hell but possessed a beautiful mind. Smith entered college with so many advanced placement credits that he was able to earn an economics degree from Utah in two years. He was also a quick study when it came to the spread option, devouring the complex array of audibles and split-second decisions the quarterback was required to make. He loved discussing the intricate details with Meyer.

Meyer considered himself a keen evaluator of talent, but he had no idea how good Smith was until Smith was pressed into duty after the team's starter, Brett Elliott, broke his wrist in the second game of the season. The next week, Smith led Utah to a 31–24 victory over a California team that was led by another underrecruited quarterback named Aaron Rodgers. Two weeks later, Smith piloted the Utes to a four-point win over No. 19 Oregon. By the time Utah finished the season with a 10–2 record, Smith knew the playbook as well as any of his coaches. Meyer trusted him to call most of the plays himself.

Smith was the marquee talent, but in many ways another player had a more profound effect on the head coach and his wife. He was Marty Johnson, a gifted but deeply troubled running back from Sacramento. Johnson had a previous drunk driving conviction before Meyer got to Utah, so when he was arrested for DUI again during the 2003 season, Meyer's instinct was to dismiss him. Shelley, however, prevailed upon him to give Johnson another chance. Unlike Urban, she understood the powers of addiction. She worked with addicts all the time, particularly adolescents, her specialty at the University of Utah's psychiatric hospital. She also taught classes in the school's nursing program. Shelley pointed out that if Johnson didn't get his problem under control, someday he could do serious damage, to himself as well as others.

Urban decided to give it a try. Both of them visited Johnson during the month he spent in jail, and after his release he spent a lot of time at the Meyers' house. He became like a big brother to their three children. Urban did what he could to help the kid, but he didn't empathize with him the way Shelley did. "My attitude was, if you have an addiction to smoking, stop smoking. If you have an addiction to alcohol, stop drinking," he says.

Shelley understood that her husband didn't have the highest regard for her profession. "He was raised to be really strong, so you don't need help with anything," Shelley says. "I think it was hard for him to see that people might need help dealing with emotions, stress, loss, addiction—that people could have difficulty dealing with those things to the point where they would try to commit suicide or need to be in a hospital."

With Johnson and Smith back in the fold, Utah embarked on a season for the ages. Having begun with high expectations, they entered November with a perfect record. They had become one of the biggest stories in college football. Because Utah played in the Mountain West Conference, the only way it would have a chance to play for a national championship was to go undefeated, and even then it was far from a sure thing. A single loss and the season was over.

For the first time in his career, Meyer was faced with the challenges of celebrity, scrutiny, and colossal expectations. The stress started to wear on him. He confessed to his younger sister, Erika, that he was "petrified" of losing. "Now we're all like that—petrified of him losing," she said. That was especially concerning since Meyer was still trying to contain the benign cyst in his head. During that upset of Oregon the previous season, he was hit by a blinding pain that brought him to his knees. The next week, he went to a doctor to get a CAT scan. When he came in to view the results, he saw the large, dark mass blotting out the image of his brain. *Holy shit,* he thought. *I've got a brain tumor.* The doctor assured Meyer he did not have a tumor, but that the cyst appeared to have grown. He would have to make doubly sure that he kept his stress to a minimum. That was easier said than done.

The dreaded loss never came, but even though Utah finished the season with an 11–0 record, due to its weak schedule it was denied an opportunity to participate in the Bowl Championship Series National Championship Game. The Utes capped off the season with a win over Pittsburgh in the Fiesta Bowl. Smith went on to become the No. 1 pick in the 2005 NFL draft, and Meyer became the hottest ticket in the sport.

As it happened, two of the most prestigious programs in the country, Notre Dame and Florida, had vacancies. Meyer's abilities were so obvious that there was no suspense as to whether those schools would offer him the job. The only question was which one he would accept. Dozens of media outlets followed every wrinkle in the competition to land him. Despite his sentimental ties to Notre Dame, Meyer chose Florida because he believed he would have a better chance to win a national championship there. So once again he picked up his family, which now included a sixteen-year-old son named Nate, and moved them to another part of the country. He was officially off and running, and the pace was only going to get quicker.

For the first time in his career, Meyer was the head coach at a place where winning wasn't so much appreciated as expected. It was also the third time in five years that he took on the exhausting grind of taking over a program and instilling a culture. His persistence would be tested—and developed—like never before.

If Meyer was going to get to *Us* at Florida the way he did in his previous two jobs, he would need another first-rate staff. Mullen and several others who were with him in the past came along, but he also hired two people who would become invaluable—Mick Marotti, the strength coach whom he had befriended at Notre Dame, and Steve Addazio, the tight ends coach at Notre Dame who had gone on to become offensive coordinator at Indiana. One of the staples of Meyer's leadership was his ability to teach assistants what he needed them to know and then empower them to pass that knowledge to the players. Crucially, Addazio came up with the concept of "Nine Units." Meyer loved it. From that point on, the team would not have coordinators, it would have "unit leaders." At various times during the season, Meyer would call on one of the leaders without warning and ask him to speak to the team. "You've got fifteen minutes," he would say. "Make us better." This created a foxhole mentality within the team. The players got to be so close with the head of their unit that if he ever got dressed down by Captain Emergency for something they did, they would feel awful and want to redeem the unit immediately.

Meyer inherited a capable quarterback in Chris Leak, but he was not nearly as mobile as Josh Harris at Bowling Green. Nor did his mind work as quickly as Smith's. The Gators went 9–3 in that first season—good, but not good enough. Once again, Meyer's culture took hold in his second year. With Leak growing into the offense, the Gators went through the season winning 12 of their 13 games and were granted a slot in the BCS National Championship Game. There they met Meyer's childhood team, Ohio State, and prevailed easily, 41–14.

That championship vaulted Meyer into the stratosphere, a perch he did not occupy comfortably. He was still in many ways the same guarded kid from Ashtabula, Ohio. Gainesville is a relatively small college town, and the folks there are obsessed with their football team. Meyer was only forty-two years old. Life was coming at him fast. Every move he made was dissected by the public and scrutinized by the press.

As long as he had good players to coach, his team would always have a chance to win a national championship. That was especially true at quarterback, which required a unique skill set, intellect, and level of determination to run his offense. Meyer had been fortunate to work with great quarterbacks in the past, but he was about to partner with one whose physical gifts and mental makeup would prove to be the perfect complement. Too perfect, perhaps.

In many ways, Tim Tebow was a better version of a young Urban Meyer. He was bigger, stronger, faster, more talented, more handsome, more outgoing, more pious, and, if possible, more determined. Meyer noticed that Tebow was a different breed of cat as soon as he stepped on campus in January 2006. "We did rope pulls, tug-of-war, weight lifting. Any competitive drills we did, he was going to win it," Meyer recalls. If Tebow wasn't in the weight room or the practice field, he was in the head coach's office. He and his coach typically spent eight hours a day together, having long talks about football, life, whatever came to mind. Tebow practically lived in the facility, so much so that Marotti, who is no shrinking violet himself, had to order the quarterback to leave. "I would have to tell him, 'Tim, get out of here, go be a kid,'" Marotti says.

Tebow played a minor role as the backup quarterback during the 2006 championship season. Once he became the starter, he grew into one of the truly iconic players in the history of the college game. At 6′3″, 245 pounds, he was basically a fullback who could throw a little. But he was a winner. The rest of the players fed off his confidence. Tebow finished the 2007 regular season with the second-highest passing efficiency in the nation while averaging 4.3 yards per carry and rushing for 20 touchdowns. He led the Gators to a win over rival Florida State with a fractured bone in his right (nonthrowing) hand. On December 8, 2007, Tebow was awarded the ultimate individual prize in his sport, the Heisman Trophy.

And yet the Gators finished with a disappointing 9–4 record. Meyer cursed himself for relaxing his micromanaging tendencies, delegating more responsibilities to his staff, and trying to spend a little more time with his family. This was the first time in his head coaching career that he was in his third season at a single place, so he thought he could ease up just a hair. The correlation between those modifications and the team's record is suspect to say the least, but in Meyer's mind, the lesson was clear: He could not ease off, ever, for any reason, even just a little. If he wasn't all in, all the time, the program would suffer.

Tebow returned for his junior season, and though Meyer said he would lighten his quarterback's load in hopes of preserving him physically, Tebow broke Emmitt Smith's school career rushing touchdown record—an astounding accomplishment for a quarterback. He did not win another Heisman Trophy (he finished third in the voting), but he did lead the Gators to another national championship, this time a 24–14 win over Oklahoma in the BCS National Championship Game.

It was remarkable. Meyer was only forty-four years old. He had been a head coach for all of eight seasons. But he owned two titles in three years. He should have felt like he was on top of the world, but he had long before stopped taking the time to enjoy his success. As soon as the win over Oklahoma was over, he went right into a back office and started calling recruits. Shelley noticed he was more preoccupied than ever. He even sent text messages while they were in church.

Meyer had organized a victory meal during the season for his players after every win, but he stopped going after a few weeks because he preferred to study video of the next opponent. He went back some time later, only to discover that very few players were there. When Meyer asked Marotti where everyone was, Marotti told him that once the head coach stopped coming, the players figured it was okay to skip it as well. Meyer was running hard now, and fast, but not necessarily in the right direction. "Winning stopped being fun," Mullen says. "Losing was miserable and winning was a relief. That can really wear on you. Where's the joy in what you're doing?"

Few people knew just how badly the pressure was getting to him. Meyer had always been a great sleeper, but he started having trouble during his first season at Florida. Now that problem was getting worse. He had an unhealthy tendency to stop eating during the season. He also skipped his daily workouts, which Shelley found perplexing. "I'd tell him every day, 'What, you can't skip thirty minutes of film to work out? Just get on a treadmill,'" she says.

Even more frightening, Urban found himself experiencing mysterious chest pains. He thought about other coaches who had died suddenly from heart attacks, like his friend Randy Walker, the football coach at Northwestern, or Wake Forest basketball coach Skip Prosser. He went to a cardiologist on multiple occasions, but each time the doctor found no irregularities. Yet the pains would not subside. The specter of a serious heart problem added to his anxiety, which, in a diabolical cycle, made his anxiety even worse.

Tebow surprised everyone by turning down the NFL draft and returning for his senior season. In many ways, that was just about the worst thing that could have happened to Meyer. It was as if he were an alcoholic whose drinking buddy said he was going to live with him for another year. The Gators began the season ranked No. 1 by the largest margin in the history of the Associated Press's preseason poll, but that wasn't good enough for Meyer and Tebow.

They wanted to accomplish something that had never been done at Florida: an undefeated season.

It's hard to imagine a more foolish decision. Instead of staying in the moment—setting daily goals like having a good practice, a good film session, a good workout, a good night's rest—Meyer and Tebow pushed the goalposts farther away and made the thought of losing even more frightening. At the same time, Meyer was taking on more responsibility for running the program because he had lost several assistants, including Mullen and Addazio, who had been hired away as head coaches. When I brought this up to him, I half apologized for using the word *foolish,* but he cut me off. "*Foolish* is the appropriate word," he said. "You're talking about two very driven personalities. Go undefeated? Here's what you need to do. Sleep's not necessary. Don't need to eat, don't need to work out, let's just see if we can get there."

They almost did, remaining perfect through October and November and strengthening their hold on the No. 1 ranking. Meyer was grinding himself past the point of no return. He was taking two Ambien pills and drinking a can of beer just to get three or four hours of sleep. Despite the efforts of his wife and staff to get him to eat, or at least drink protein shakes during the day, he was too wound up to ingest anything. He dropped nearly forty pounds. His pants sagged off him so badly that Marotti called him "Poopy Drawers." Shelley knew her husband was having a hard time, but she was in denial about how bad things were. "You don't really see that physical change when you're with somebody every day," she says. "I didn't think it was really bad."

Urban, on the other hand, knew full well he was on a downward spiral. He just felt there was nothing he could do to stop the momentum. "I wasn't oblivious to what was happening. I lost thirty-seven pounds, I was unhealthy, I wasn't working out," he says. "It's just, when do you find time to stop it in this profession? Are you gonna take that time during recruiting? No. Will you take time during spring practice? No. You take time during the month of July, but then you're getting ready for the ship to pull away in August."

The Gators finished the regular season 12–0, setting up a titanic clash with No. 2 Alabama in the SEC championship game. Four days before the game, Meyer had to suspend his prized defensive end Carlos Dunlap after he was charged with driving under the influence. That further darkened Meyer's mood. "His reaction was all about 'woe is me, the sky is falling,' rather than what our response would be," Marotti says. "It was almost like because we didn't have Carlos Dunlap, we couldn't win. That's when I was like, *This ain't good.*"

On the morning of the Alabama game, Florida's sports information director for football, Steve McClain, reached out to Shelley and said he wanted to talk to her. When she got to the stadium, McClain told her that he was very concerned about her husband. She was taken aback but figured they would deal with the problem once the season was over. Marotti had the same sense of foreboding as he stood next to Meyer on the sideline during the game. "I could see it on his face. Like, *Man, he don't look right,*" Marotti recalls. "It just looked like he wasn't even there. Then the game got worse, it just snowballed. He was fighting, but the tank had run out."

Florida lost that day, 32–13. That ended both the Gators' undefeated dream and their chance to play for a national championship. Later that night, as Meyer was lying in his bed at home in Gainesville, he experienced a chest pain more severe than any he had known. He let out a yelp and fell out of bed. Shelley dialed 911. As she knelt beside Urban listening to his breathing and checking his pulse, she felt confident he was not having a heart attack. She tried to pry him up—"Urban, honey, wake up," she said on the 911 call that later become public—but he would not stir. The ambulance soon arrived and transported him to a local hospital.

Meyer does not remember much about that night, which is a blessing. He does, however, recall waking up in the ambulance and thinking that he might be dying. "I remember asking them, 'Did my son see it?'" he told me. "When they told me he didn't, I was like, 'Okay, I'm fine now.' That's all I really remember."

When he was examined in the hospital, the doctors told Meyer he definitely had not suffered a heart attack. Instead of bringing relief, that loosed a set of deeper fears. "That's when your mind really starts playing games with you. It's not a heart attack. What is it, then?" he says. He was referred to a gastroenterologist, who suggested that his symptoms indicated a severe case of reflux. The doctor prescribed Nexium. Within two days, the pains subsided.

Meyer was relieved that he finally had a diagnosis, but clearly his problems went deeper. After a few weeks of thinking things over and talking with his family, he announced to a stunned public that he intended to resign following Florida's game in the Sugar Bowl on New Year's Day.

The next day, however, he backtracked, calling his separation from the team a "leave of absence" and saying he believed he would be on the sidelines the following season. Bud, in an interview with *New York Times* reporter Pete Thamel, voiced skepticism about the effects of taking a leave. "Of course he can't change," Bud said. "You can't change your essence. You can change if you drink orange or grapefruit juice for breakfast. You can't change the nature of your being."

Meyer coached the Gators to a 51–24 Sugar Bowl victory over Cincinnati, his alma mater. Though he ostensibly took a few months off to rest and recover, he stayed in touch with recruits, helping Florida to land the consensus No. 1 class yet again. By mid-March, he was back on the sideline for the spring game. His leave of absence was officially over.

With his chest pains under control, Meyer thought continuing to coach was what he wanted. His certitude was punctured later that fall, when his daughter Gigi signed a letter of intent to play volleyball for Florida Gulf Coast University. Gigi signed the letter at a public ceremony at her high school. Urban thought about skipping it—he had lots of work to do that day—but his assistant guilted him into attending. As Gigi spoke, she thanked Shelley for driving her to all her practices and matches. Then she said, "Dad, you were never there, but thank you, too." Gigi didn't mean it to come off as harsh as it sounded, but the pain that Urban felt was as bad as any reflux. He realized at that moment that even though he loved his daughter very much, he had not given her much of his T-I-M-E. And now it was too late.

The 2010 season was a disaster from the start. In mid-September, a wide receiver named Chris Rainey was charged with felony aggravated stalking. He had been arguing with a former girlfriend and sent her a text that read "Time to Die Bitch." The story became a major problem because Rainey was the twenty-fifth player to be arrested or face charges since Meyer had become head coach. The run-ins with the law had become so frequent that the year before, the *Orlando Sentinel* set up an online database to keep track of them all. Many of the charges were misdemeanors such as underage drinking and disorderly conduct, but there were some more serious offenses as well, such as domestic violence by strangulation, aggravated assault, aggravated stalking, and larceny. Meyer had taken action against the players, ranging from extra running to suspensions to dismissals, but the accumulation of incidents was a bad look, to say the least. "After a while, enough's enough," Meyer conceded following Rainey's arrest. "It's not a dirty program. We follow the rules and some guys make some mistakes and we've got to correct those mistakes."

(In September 2010, Rainey pled guilty to a lesser charge of misdemeanor stalking. After he underwent anger-management counseling and performed ten hours of community service, the charges were dropped.)

The litany of arrests was especially problematic because everyone knew Meyer had his fingers in every aspect of the program. He bragged about the discipline instilled by his culture, and he exalted the concept of "no gray areas" preached by his father and Earle Bruce. Those proclamations rang hollow as his team's rap sheet lengthened. It was more than fair to ask whether winning had become so important that Meyer was willing to abide bad behavior.

Not surprisingly, Meyer does not agree with that narrative. He acknowledges that the arrests were problematic, but he also defends his decisions to stand by his players and help them learn from their mistakes. "It used to really kind of eat me alive when someone would say 'This program lacks character' or 'Just get rid of a kid. Make an example of that player,'" he told me. "Think about that for a minute. I have three children. If someone ever makes an example of my kid, that person will lose that fight. So we're never going to do that. It's our job to set a road map for the kid to be successful and have a productive life. At all costs."

The Gators experienced a predictable post-Tebow hangover and limped to a 7–5 record, the worst in Meyer's six seasons there. Between losing Tebow, the press scrutiny, and his withering physical condition, Meyer found himself unable to get the Gators to *Us*. The losing crushed him, and many of the same old problems with sleep and eating returned. "That year was ridiculous," Shelley says. "I kept thinking, *Life doesn't have to be this way. I know it doesn't. So why is it?*"

Two weeks after the regular season ended, Meyer announced yet again that he was retiring from coaching, citing health and family concerns. This time there would be no walking back. He hung around long enough to coach Florida to a win over Penn State in the Outback Bowl on New Year's Day, and then he walked away at the age of forty-six with five years and $20 million remaining on his contract. Speculation immediately centered on whether he would return to the sidelines—and if so, when—but though Urban didn't know what he was going to do, there was no question what Shelley's preference was. "I really thought he was done. I was really hoping he was done, too," she says. "Because I was done."

When I discuss the "knowledge" dimension of the PEAK profile throughout this book, I'm usually referring to the sport-specific kind. But in Meyer's case, the time he spent away from coaching enabled him to accrue different kinds of knowledge: intellectual, emotional, psychological, spiritual. His sabbatical taught him the importance of living a balanced life and conserving energy, which replenished his persistence. Having to face his own weaknesses and limitations deepened his empathy. The time off gave him a chance to reevaluate what was important to him, which reset his authenticity. And he learned so much from books, travel, and conversations that he could apply down the road. The sabbatical made Meyer a better husband and dad, and certainly a better coach, one who possessed an even greater ability to get his teams to *Us*.

The first thing leaving coaching allowed him to do was sit still. This was never his forte. Shelley long suspected he had at least a mild form of attention deficit disorder. He has never been the kind to relax on a beach during a vacation. When he watched his son's baseball games, he had to walk around the ballpark and do push-ups and sit-ups between innings to keep his mind busy.

The best part about not coaching was the time it allowed for Urban to spend with his kids. He took Nate on a three-week trip to

Cooperstown and helped coach his middle school football team. He drove to Atlanta several times to visit Nicki, who played volleyball for Georgia Tech, and he also went to see Gigi at Florida Gulf Coast. They were no quick in-and-outers, either. He would stay for three or four days, trying to make up for lost time.

Meyer also rediscovered his faith. He had grown up Catholic, and he treated himself to extensive Bible reading, went to church (Shelley made him turn off his cell phone so he wouldn't be tempted to send text messages), and spoke with clergymen. He took his daughters to Rome and Israel and loaded up their itinerary. They went to the Vatican and saw the pope. They went to Jerusalem and retraced the steps of Jesus.

Perhaps the most valuable knowledge he acquired was through conversations with other coaches. These men are so locked in to their own world that they rarely get the chance to really spend time and share experiences. Urban met with Oklahoma football coach Bob Stoops, who has been one of the better coaches at balancing life and work. He sat with Chip Kelly at Oregon, Mack Brown at Texas, Brian Kelly at Notre Dame. He heard from countless peers who could relate to what he was going through. When he first announced he was stepping away, he got a call from Duke basketball coach Mike Krzyzewski, who took a leave of absence himself in 1995 because he returned from back surgery too soon. The two had never spoken before. After Meyer retired for good, he visited Krzyzewski in Durham so they could continue the conversation. "I realized through all of this that I'm not the lone wolf out there," Meyer says. "And it's not just coaches. There's CEOs and doctors and teachers. Everybody deals with this at some point in your life. It's work/life balance, health issues, the regret of neglecting your family."

Meyer was about two months into his sabbatical when he confessed to Shelley that he was feeling the desire to coach again.

She tried to shut down the conversation, but then their world was rocked on May 30, 2011, when Ohio State coach Jim Tressel resigned following a long-running scandal that involved dozens of players receiving illicit benefits, primarily from a local tattoo parlor, that Tressel failed to report to the NCAA. The school said it would appoint one of Tressel's assistants to serve as interim head coach for the coming season and then look for a permanent replacement once the season was over. That bought everyone some time, but media speculation that Meyer would be a candidate immediately ran rampant.

When the season got under way, Meyer traveled to campuses in his work as a game analyst for ESPN. This allowed him to continue visiting coaches, see how other programs did things, stay connected to the game—and still be home for Saturday night dinner. During one of those assignments, his broadcast partner, Todd Blackledge, gave him a book called *Lead . . . For God's Sake!* It's a novel about a coach who loses his perspective and becomes depressed. With the help of a spiritual janitor, he manages to rediscover why he coached in the first place. Meyer identified with the protagonist on a primal level. It made him reflect on what he loved so much about the job when he was making $6,000 a year and working his tail off at Illinois State. "I really felt this was our ministry opportunity. We weren't here just to win games but make impacts," he says.

Meyer found the author's email and wrote to say how moved he was. The author, Todd G. Gongwer, wrote him back, and his cell phone number was in the signature of the email. Meyer called him right away, and the two struck up a friendship. He has since given the book to dozens of colleagues and friends, and he wrote the foreword for the most recent edition. Today *Lead . . . for God's Sake!* sits prominently on the coffee table in his office.

As October turned to November, everyone knew that a major

decision loomed. Urban, however, had other things on his mind. His father was in failing health. Bud had lived a joyful, energetic life in the years after Gisela died. Both of his daughters were living in Cincinnati—Gigi had taken a job as a vice provost at the University of Cincinnati, and Erika was working at a data analytics firm— so he was able to spend lots of time with his kids and grandkids. Without a team to coach, Urban could fly home pretty much at a moment's notice. For the first time in forever, he and his dad were able to have long, lazy talks, with no distractions to occupy his mind.

Bud died in a hospital on November 11, 2011. In the end, it was his lungs that gave out. Urban held him as he passed. His two sisters were also there. "It was the only November of my brother's life when that could have happened," Gigi says. "God works in mysterious ways."

Meyer did not see a professional therapist during his time away from coaching, but he did develop a support system of friends, family, and pastors who were able to provide the counsel he needed. The whole experience altered his perception of the work his wife had been doing all those years. "He definitely realized that anxiety is real," Shelley says. "It can cause depression. It can cause stress that you can't manage."

A few days after Bud died, Ohio State athletic director Gene Smith called to see if Urban was interested in the job. He definitely was, but first he had to clear it with his family. As the children and Shelley discussed their concerns, Nicki proposed they draw up a contract. If Urban were to go back into coaching, he would have to follow its eleven provisions, which Nicki wrote out on a pink sheet of paper. They included: *My family will always come first. I will go on a trip once a year with Nicki—MINIMUM. I will sleep with my cell phone on silent. I will not go more than nine hours a day at the office.*

I will trust God's plan and not be overanxious. I will continue to communicate with my kids.

Urban signed, and on November 28, 2011, he signed again to become the new head football coach at the Ohio State University. Today, the pink contract hangs framed on a wall in his office, where it serves as a daily warning against the dangers of running too hard, too far, too fast.

When Meyer took over at Ohio State, he was more equipped than ever to get his teams to *Us*. He returned to the sidelines with a better understanding of the need to stop wasting energy on things that were out of his control. Shortly after taking the job, he was attending a fund-raiser and met a local man named Tim Kight, a former pastor who had founded a leadership consulting firm. They struck up a conversation, and Meyer later invited Kight to his home to talk some more. Kight conducted seminars for dozens of sports teams, including some in the NFL, that centered on the formula $E + R = O$. That is, Event plus Response equals Outcome. Kight's message is that while we cannot control outside events, we do have a choice in how we respond to them. That response will help determine the final outcome. The message resonated with Meyer so much that he hired Kight to work with his assistants and his players multiple times throughout each season.

Besides hiring many of his former assistants, such as Marotti, Meyer brought in Tom Herman to be his offensive coordinator. Herman had done wonders running a spread offense as the offensive coordinator at Rice and at Iowa State. It didn't take long for him to realize that his boss would not brook any slippage. Early in his tenure, Meyer had eaten dinner in the summer with several of the team's wide receivers and quarterbacks, and as he started quizzing them on various situations in the team's offense, he was disappointed to hear how little they knew. He called Herman and the receivers coach into his office to let them know in no uncertain terms that they needed to pick up the pace.

"The message never deviates with him," Herman says. "Everybody from the strength staff to the video staff to the equipment staff to academics and nutrition—everybody who touches the players there at Ohio State gets the same message and the same expectations and the same goals. I think that's very rare."

Meyer's favorite word in those early days was *juice*. He said he wanted energy givers, not energy takers, and nobody gave more energy than him. He managed every detail of the program, right down to having "Hang On Sloopy" playing in the offices. (That song has been played at the start of the fourth quarter at Ohio State's home games for nearly fifty years.) The Buckeyes would need every bit of Meyer's motivational spirit, because the program was ineligible to play in a bowl game as a result of the violations committed under Tressel. Yet they pulled off the remarkable feat of going undefeated anyway. It was a stunning accomplishment, and Meyer earned lots of hosannas not only for being a winning coach (again), but for doing so in a way that did not jeopardize his health.

Shelley, however, was skeptical. The real test, she knew, would come after a loss. It would take twelve more games, but the Buckeyes finally dropped one to Michigan State in the 2013 Big Ten championship game in Indianapolis. Besides snapping the team's 24-game winning streak, the loss also knocked the Buckeyes out of the hunt for a national championship. After it was over, Meyer was photographed in the tunnel underneath Lucas Oil Stadium, sitting forlornly on a golf cart and eating a piece of pizza. When that image pinballed around the Internet, many observers saw the same old Urban—lonely, depressed, brought to his knees by a loss. Shelley was standing just a few feet away, and she saw something very different, something she liked, a sign of genuine progress.

She saw he was eating.

The team's persistence would be tested to the extreme during the 2014 season. The Buckeyes entered the fall with a quarterback named Braxton Miller who possessed the perfect skill set to run the spread option. Two weeks before the season began, however, Miller suffered a season-ending shoulder injury. With Miller's backup, J. T. Barrett, under center, Ohio State lost at home to Virginia Tech in its second game. Meyer held steady. From there, Barrett led the Buckeyes to nine straight wins, but then he broke his ankle in the fourth quarter of the regular season finale against Michigan, which Ohio State won, 42–28. Cardale Jones, a redshirt sophomore who had entered the season as the third-string quarterback, was promoted to starter with the Buckeyes' championship hopes hanging in the balance.

The carnage at quarterback was not the only concern. Three days before the game against Michigan, a defensive lineman named Kosta Karageorge went missing. The following Sunday, he was found in a dumpster, dead from a self-inflicted gunshot wound.

With Karageorge's number adorning their helmets, the Buckeyes rallied behind Jones and walloped Wisconsin 59–0 in the Big Ten championship game. The win was overwhelming enough to persuade the committee of men and women who seeded a first-ever four-team playoff to give the Buckeyes the last slot. They took advantage, knocking off Alabama in the national semifinal game, and then defeating Oregon in the championship. It was Meyer's third and most unlikely championship.

There are plenty of explanations for why a third-string quarterback was able to win a title in an offense that was so heavily predicated on that quarterback's decision making. Certainly Jones deserves a large share of the credit, as does Herman, who worked closely with Jones all season to make sure he was ready if his moment ever came. In the end, though, the championship happened because the Buckeyes had gotten to *Us* like no other team Meyer had coached. That included how they held it together in the wake of Karageorge's suicide. "Things happened that just challenged our team, and they answered every test with flying colors," Meyer says. "It didn't matter who would've come out on that other sideline. That team wasn't going to lose. It wasn't because of the spread offense. It was because we were nine strong. Every unit was playing at maximum capacity. The human spirit is so much more important than the style of play and who's doing it."

There was one period the following season when Meyer started reverting to bad habits. It came after the team lost to Michigan State at home in the season's eleventh game. Meyer was so despondent that several players came to Marotti to ask him to get the coach out of his funk. He did, just in time to oversee a 42–13 shellacking of Michigan. That wasn't enough to get the Buckeyes back in the playoff, but they did get invited again in 2016. Urban watched the selection show from the maternity ward at Riverside Hospital, where Nicki was giving birth to his first grandchild.

Ohio State lost to eventual champion Clemson in the semifinal. Losses are never fun—and there have been scant few of them—but Meyer has learned how to process them in a way that allows him to function. For the most part, he has followed the terms of the pink contract, although everyone knew the clause about working nine-hour days was not going to be followed. He has been a stickler about staying in touch with his daughters, and he has managed to get to most of Nate's baseball games. Nate committed to play for the University of Cincinnati, so he won't be moving far away anytime soon.

Which is not to say Meyer has drastically changed the way he operates. Once in a while, his mood will darken or he'll seem dis-tracted, and his assistant will send Shelley a text asking if every-thing is okay. He remains both a delegator and a micromanager, fueled by his inability to leave well enough alone. The oft-said quip among his staff is, "If it ain't broke, Urban will fix it." It's as if he has to live in chaos and turmoil to be happy.

He has, however, adapted in the way he deals with his players. He knows they are not equipped to take nearly the same abuse he and his buddies did back when they played high school football in Ohio under the shadow of Woody Hayes. He is a much more wise and empathetic coach than he was even just a few years ago. "I un-derstand the player's journey much more now, and the player's jour-ney now is more complicated," he told me. "You know, when I first started coaching you dealt with the high school coach and the fam-ily. Now you've got social media and all kinds of pressures. If you'd have told me ten years ago I would need a sports psychologist, I would have said no, but you certainly need that now. My staff and I have nonstop conversations not just about the physical well-being but also the mental well-being of our players."

It also helps that his house is in Dublin, a suburb located eigh-teen miles from Columbus. Meyer has a semblance of a normal life there, plus a neighbor with whom he plays golf when he can. He still works long hours, but he knows better when it's time to go home. "I see him a lot more than I ever did at Florida," Shelley says. "He made lots of changes, and guess what? We still win football games. Who would have known?"

He remains carefully guarded, which is why he looks so uneasy at times sharing the intimate details of the past few years. Yet he has done so on multiple occasions, including with me in his office, tell-ing his story in hopes that someone new who hears it will glean some meaning. "It's not something I look forward to doing, but I also made a deal between myself and my Creator that if I got back into coaching, I would do the very best I can to help others," he says. "So talking about it is my way of giving back, and it has been tenfold the replies that I'm getting from people."

During our conversation in his office, Meyer recounted a recent visit he had with his good friend Bill Belichick, the coach of the New England Patriots, who had come to Columbus to speak at Meyer's coaching clinic. "He said to me, 'I'm at the point in my life where I just want to coach people I like.' I shared that comment with my team." At one point, Meyer and Belichick were sitting alone in the bleachers huddling with their cell phones. "People probably thought we were talking about how to beat the 3-4 defense," Meyer said. "What we were really doing was sharing pictures of our grandchildren for twenty minutes."

It makes for a nice tableau, two championship coaches taking a moment to step away from their shared obsession to share the joy of being granddads. Turns out Bud Meyer was wrong about one thing: Life *is* full of gray areas. Urban learned that the hard way, but he has finally figured out that it's not always the best strategy to use the entire field. Sometimes a coach is better off allowing a little pressure.

Tom Izzo

Guilt is his constant companion. When he's working, he feels like he should be at home with the kids. When he's home, he wonders if he should be back in the office, grinding. When someone he has known for a long time asks for an appearance, he knows he should decline, but that would *really* make him feel guilty. So he says yes. "I spoke at a Rotary Club last week. I'm still speaking at Rotary Clubs," Tom Izzo says with a laugh. "You know why? Cause the friend that was helping me out thirty years ago when I had no money, no food, and no job asked me to do it. All those people that helped me, I'm obligated to 'em."

Guilt rode shotgun on that sad, soulful car ride in late December 2015, when Izzo traveled back to his hometown of Iron Mountain, Michigan, to bury his dad. Carl Izzo lived until he was ninety, but he had suffered from dementia during his final year. When Tom visited him for a few hours on Christmas morning, his dad barely knew he was there. Tom was a doting son if ever there was one. He bought his parents a home in Wisconsin. He flew them in for games and tournaments. He called them often. Yet as he went to bid his dad a final farewell, Tom was nettled by the belief that he hadn't done enough.

"I only saw my parents four or five times a year," he tells me. "You justify it with the good things you were able to do. I got to buy them a house. I was able to take them to Hawaii and California for games. They came to the Big Ten tournaments. They came to Puerto Rico. They stayed at my house a lot. But I didn't see them as much because I was working during those times. So that part of it was hard to think about."

Carl Izzo's passing came in the midst of a basketball season unlike any that Tom had experienced during his two-plus decades as Michigan State's basketball coach. Two months earlier, Izzo lost one of his best friends, Flip Saunders, the president of the Minnesota Timberwolves, who had succumbed to cancer at the age of sixty. The two were so close that on several occasions Saunders had tried to hire Izzo to be the team's head coach. Izzo was one of the few people outside of Saunders's family who knew how sick he really was. He knew the end was coming, but it was jarring all the same. "I had just gone to see their new practice facility. He had all these plans," Izzo says softly. "Flip and I shared a lot of things, and then all of a sudden he was gone. It was surreal."

From there, Izzo watched his Spartans fight through injuries to become one of the finest teams he had ever coached—only to see them go down to defeat in the most shocking upset of his career, a 90–81 loss to 15th-seeded Middle Tennessee in the first round of the 2016 NCAA Tournament. The atmosphere in the locker room afterward was funereal, with Izzo shedding tears for one of the few times in his career. The team had seemed too good to be true. They were great players, great students, great leaders, great kids. Never gave him a moment's trouble. He wished he could feel angry with them, but instead he was overcome with empathy. And guilt. "We're going to have another chance at this," he said to his assistants. "Those seniors won't."

Izzo's lowest professional moment was followed three weeks later by his highest, when he was voted into the Naismith Memorial Basketball Hall of Fame in Springfield, Massachusetts. "I didn't think I'd get it on the first try. I really didn't," he says. "I didn't even know *how* you got in." When he called his mom, Dorothy, to tell her the news, she said how proud his dad would have been. Tom knew that was true. "My dad deserves a lot of credit," he says. "He taught me how to work."

Most coaches are trying to get to *Us*. Izzo was born there. He grew up in a big family, and at the age of twelve he started working in his grandfather's shoe store. Everything he ever needed to know about coaching, he learned while working in that store. When he achieved a level of success and fortune that exceeded his wildest dreams, he knew full well that he did not get there alone. It was his job—his obligation—to bring his family with him, in person and in spirit.

The same goes for his other family, his players. So even as he reached the pinnacle of making the Hall of Fame, Izzo could not totally enjoy it because the official announcement took place at the Final Four in Houston, and he knew his team should have been there with him. Izzo's former boss and mentor, former Michigan State head coach Jud Heathcote, who passed away in the summer of 2017, liked to say that Izzo was "the most unhappy successful person I know," but that is not really true. Izzo is content in his soul and comfortable in his skin. He is funny and upbeat and as well liked as any man in his profession. Most every coach has his detractors, but you literally never hear a bad word about Izzo. He is a coach's coach and a guy's guy, and underneath all that angst he knows goddamn well he belongs in the Hall of Fame.

The persistent guilt tortures Izzo, but it also drives him to get to

Us. There is a fine line between empathy and guilt, between gratitude and humility. Izzo embraces all of those things in a downcast yet chipper sort of way. For example, every year he complains that the schedule he put together is way too difficult for his team, but in the next breath he explains that his annual slug fests in November and December lay the foundation for his teams to succeed in March. There is no pleasure without pain, and there is no winning without work.

For Izzo, the only thing worse than losing a first-round game is knowing that he has disappointed someone who helped him, or that he failed to live up to the principles he learned in that family store. Show up. Work hard. Give back. Stay humble. He is a multimillionaire celebrity approaching the sunset of a brilliant career, and yet he will never, ever forget where he came from. That's pretty much impossible anyway, because he never really left.

When Michigan State was building a new office and practice facility for its basketball teams in 2002, Izzo had a novel idea: He wanted his office to have no door. "I thought it would set a tone," he says. "But I couldn't do it because of fire codes." Maybe he had to accept the door, but he doesn't have to close it, and even when he does, his players know they can pretty much walk in anytime they want. It isn't just a nice metaphor. It is Izzo's daily reality.

Denzel Valentine, who played guard for Michigan State from 2012 to 2016, jokes that Izzo is like a 24/7 concierge service, albeit one that regularly called him a dumbass for four straight years. "There were multiple times after a game when I would text him at one or two in the morning. He would always text me right back," Valentine says. "From day one, he creates a family atmosphere and makes it known that he cares about you as an individual." Izzo offers this service because he genuinely cares about his players, but he also believes that it helps the team win. "When people ask me what I do best, everyone thinks it's rebounding or whatever," he says. "The answer is I spend time with my players. That's how I get to know them and can determine which way I need to go with them."

This is the ethos he developed in Tony Izzo's Shoe Hospital, and it laid the foundation for his PEAK profile at an early age. One of the first things he learned was the proper way to give customers their change. First, look 'em in the eye. Second, count the dollars and cents deliberately and out loud. Not only did this establish trust with the customer, but it also ensured that he didn't accidentally give them too much change. Honesty was good for business.

Tony Izzo, Tom's grandfather, lived until he was ninety and never stopped working. Tom was one of seventeen cousins who worked at the shop after school, on weekends, and during the summers. Eventually the store expanded to be called Tony Izzo and Sons. Then it was Tony Izzo and Grandsons. "I made very little money, but I was brought up to work. It made me who I am," Izzo says. "I don't think I'm the best coach, but I do think I work as hard as anybody." He didn't just think of his coworkers as family. They *were* family. Same with his teams.

Tom was not a great student in school, but he was good enough. He figured out that if he just showed up and fulfilled his obligations, he could pull in a solid B average. The pressure to do well in school came more from his mother, who had a nursing degree, than his father, who dropped out of high school to join the Army. Yet when his father learned he couldn't run for a position on the board of education without a high school diploma, he finished up his work at Iron Mountain High School, sitting right there in the classroom alongside the pimply-faced teenyboppers. He later became president of the board.

Izzo's hometown was an extension of the store. Iron Mountain is a hardscrabble blue-collar community of fewer than 10,000 located on Michigan's Upper Peninsula. It's the type of town where families keep an eye on the neighbors' kids. Those bonds sustained the citizenry through the long, harsh winters. "You grow up having a certain work ethic and feeling a certain responsibility," says Steve Mariucci, the former NFL head coach who grew up with Izzo in Iron Mountain and remains his best friend. "If you don't get up early and shovel your driveway, you ain't going anywhere. It's that simple."

As in many such towns, particularly in the industrial Midwest, sports filled the cultural center. Izzo and Mariucci played on four different teams together and got to be real tight. Izzo was the best player on the basketball team, and Mariucci was the quarterback of the football team. They wanted to keep playing sports in college, but they weren't recruited by any big-time programs, plus they didn't want to go far away from home. So they enrolled in Northern Michigan, a Division II school just eighty miles away, and hoped to keep playing as walk-ons.

Tom wanted to buy an old automobile for school, but his dad talked him into saving up a little more money to buy a sleek new Monte Carlo. "That was a cool thing. All my buddies had clunker cars, and I had a nice car," he says. "Of course, all my other buddies were out riding in their cars while I was working all the time. So I had a nice car that sat in the parking lot."

It wasn't long before Izzo and Mariucci moved up to the varsity. As a guard, Izzo was short on talent—he was short, period—but he was indefatigable, eventually setting a school record his senior year for minutes played in a season. He was voted third team Division II All-American. Mariucci, meanwhile, was named a Division II football All-American three times. They got good grades, too.

Once college was over, Izzo and Mariucci remained in school as graduate assistant coaches in their respective sports. Izzo also took a job that season coaching basketball at a local high school. As if that wasn't enough work, the two of them still found time to try their hands at business, buying a trailer with their meager scholarship

money, fixing it up, and then renting it out. They made enough
dough to buy a couple of ramshackle houses in town, which they
also renovated themselves. "We bought a house that was the biggest
piece of shit you ever saw. My mother and his mother came in, they
almost started crying," Izzo says. "We were both GAs [graduate as-
sistants], so we were making about $3,500 each. We had to go to
grad school four nights a week and teach during the day. So we'd go
to this house, work until three, four in the morning, and we'd fall
asleep. We had these sleeping bags on the living room floor. No
beds. We'd wake up in the morning with all this sawdust in our
noses and our hair. I swear to God, I think back on that, and I laugh
so hard."

They were later hired as full-time assistants, but after a year
Mariucci left to become the quarterbacks coach at Cal State Ful-
lerton, putting him on a path that kept him on the West Coast for
most of his coaching career. Izzo stayed home. For him, Northern
Michigan was as comfortable as an old shoe—or an old shoe hospital. The coaches from the various sports at the school shared the
same office building, ate at the same restaurants (there weren't
many), went to each other's games, and drank beers together late at
night. "They were just a really good group of people," Izzo says. "It's
not like at the bigger schools where basketball is mad because football gets more, or the women's program is mad because the men get
more. There was no fighting, because nobody had anything."

Still, Izzo had his ambitions, so when an opportunity opened in
1983 to work part-time for Michigan State basketball coach Jud
Heathcote, he jumped at the chance. He was one of six coaches who
came to Michigan State from Northern. The others were four football coaches and a hockey coach. When another football coach lost
his wife to leukemia, Izzo moved in with him and helped take care
of his young son. Later he moved in with a student manager for the
basketball team named Mark Hollis. They lived together for two

years. Today, Hollis is Izzo's athletic director, charged with running the family store, only this time on a $127 million budget.

By the time Izzo joined Heathcote's staff at Michigan State, his PEAK profile was well established. He had learned from an early age the importance of persistence, which was as simple as being where you were obligated to be, on time, every day, ready to work. He was taught that empathizing with the people around him—literally, his family—was more important than whatever goals he had for himself. He carried a deep and abiding sense of who he was and where he came from, which strengthened his authenticity. And he gained a lot of knowledge about how to work, how to run a business, and how to deal with people.

There was, however, one area in which he did not have much knowledge. Michigan's Upper Peninsula is cleaved from the rest of the state by a stretch of water that encompasses parts of three Great Lakes (Superior, Michigan, Huron) as well as the St. Mary's River. It is not technically an island (the UP, as it is often called, shares a land border with Wisconsin), but culturally it might as well be on its own planet. For all the games Izzo played growing up, he recalls just a single instance in which he went up against an African American. This did not exactly give him a veneer of worldly sophistication.

In many respects, Izzo's naïveté worked to his advantage. He was taught to connect with people on the simplest of terms. They were either honest or they weren't. They either worked hard or they didn't. So while he didn't have much interaction with people of different races, he also didn't grow up in a place where it mattered.

One of the first really close friends Izzo made at Northern Michigan was Mike Garland, an African American basketball player from Ypsilanti, Michigan. When Garland first learned that Izzo was from the UP, he assumed correctly Izzo had not spent much time around black people, but he never picked up on any awkwardness. "I realized it was because he didn't have any preconceived notions," Garland says. "Nobody ever told him, 'Stay away from those guys.' There were no 'guys.'"

Garland was a year ahead of Izzo on the basketball team, and after Izzo joined the varsity, they found themselves battling for minutes at the same position. This should have been a source of tension, but if anything, it fortified their friendship. They both loved to compete, and they ended up starting alongside each other. Izzo already had designs on a career in coaching. He promised that if he ever got a head job, Garland would be his first hire.

"I can't work for you," Garland chided.

"Fine," Izzo said. "You get a job, and I'll come work for you."

After he got to Michigan State, Izzo was introduced to a young lady named Lupe Marinez, whose sister-in-law worked in the basketball office. He didn't know any Hispanics while growing up in Iron Mountain either, yet he quickly discovered they had a lot of shared experiences. Lupe grew up working for her family's water treatment company. She was an East Lansing native, a Michigan State grad, and a daughter of Mexican immigrants. She also had eleven brothers and sisters. It was not a complicated courtship. Tom and Lupe worked during the days, spent a few hours together in the evenings, and got married after only nine months.

Heathcote was an exacting mentor. He was hardworking, crusty, honest to a fault. Izzo endeared himself by agreeing to be a part-time assistant and then diving into the menial tasks of cutting video and overseeing academics. He acquired some important knowledge in those early days, but Heathcote, knowing what a hard, lonely grind the coaching profession can be, often encouraged Izzo to consider a different line of work. "It was really tough to hear because I was down about myself," Izzo says. "I had moved down there lock, stock, and barrel. I didn't know anybody. I was pretty disillusioned about what I was doing."

Midway through that first season, a member of Heathcote's staff took another job, so Heathcote installed Izzo as a full-time assistant. Three years later, in the spring of 1986, Izzo accepted a job at Tulsa University, where he would have been the top assistant and recruiting coordinator, but he came back to East Lansing two months later when Heathcote unexpectedly had another opening. For the next nine years, he was Heathcote's lead recruiter. The task suited his makeup. Recruiting required a lot of persistence. It rewarded hard, lonely work.

According to Heathcote, there was no breakthrough moment when he realized Izzo could be special. It happened because Izzo slowly accumulated a little bit more knowledge every time he showed up for work. "Each year, Tom got smarter and smarter and took on more and more," Heathcote said. When Heathcote realized that the time was approaching for him to step down, he knew he wanted Izzo to succeed him. However, the school's athletic director was cool to the idea of promoting an unknown assistant. So Heathcote went over the AD's head, made his appeal directly to the chancellor, and won the argument. The first person Izzo hired was his old buddy Mike Garland.

The early years would test Izzo's persistence. After the Spartans lost to Central Michigan at home early in his first season, he drove with his then-assistant, Tom Crean, to grab some lunch at Burger King. Along the way, they made the mistake of listening to local sports radio. "They weren't talking about if I was going to get fired, it was *when* I was going to get fired," he says. Izzo was so incensed that when he got back to the office, he immediately called a meeting of his entire staff, including trainers and secretaries, to buck everyone up.

Izzo's empathy powered him through. His most important early recruit was Antonio Smith, a rugged, hardworking 6′8″ power forward from Flint, Michigan. Flint was a more urban version of Iron Mountain, rife with economic hardship and gang violence. Smith played hard for Izzo, but he had difficulty dealing with his coach's daily withering criticism. Izzo sensed the strain. "It was like anything I said to him got him upset," he says.

After Smith played poorly in a loss at Iowa his freshman year, the team flew home to East Lansing. As Izzo was watching video of the game later that night, he was perplexed at Smith's desultory body language. So he picked up the phone, called Smith in his room, and asked if he wanted to get a burger. "It was like twenty below zero outside. We ended up riding around in my car for two hours, and he started telling me all these stories," Izzo says. "He talked about how his dad left him when he was young, and how it made him hate men. That was the problem. He didn't trust men. That really helped me in my career because I realized some of these kids have deep-rooted things. There are reasons for why they act the way they do sometimes. So if I didn't communicate with them, I wouldn't be able to have that empathy you need to be able to motivate them."

Smith's decision to go to Michigan State set the table for another Flint native to sign up the following year. He was Mateen Cleaves, an intense, bull-rushing, alpha male point guard who was also an All-American high school football player. Cleaves had grown up amid awful violence. "I went to a lot of funerals as a kid growing up," he says. He was a great athlete, so that helped him stay on a healthy path, but what really saved him was that his house was led by two strong, loving parents.

Izzo won Cleaves over by recruiting his parents as hard as him. "From the time he recruited me, my mother fell in love with him," Cleaves says. "All the other coaches came in like used car salesmen. He was so genuine. You could tell he had a vision."

Cleaves committed to Michigan State in the fall of his senior year of high school. He suffered a serious back injury during a car accident that winter, and when he got on campus in East Lansing he was still wearing a brace and badly out of shape. Izzo was empathetic but also demanding, and the two clashed often. Cleaves understood that when Izzo yelled at him it was "like a father getting on a son," but he had reason to wonder whether this man truly understood him. "I knew they didn't have any black people in the UP," he says. Adds Izzo, "He always thought of me as the white guy from the place where it snows a lot. I'd tell him, 'You know, where I'm from, we fought a lot, too. The only difference is we used fists, and you guys used knives.'"

Their first come-to-Jesus moment happened during Cleaves's freshman season. He had exchanged words with the team's strength coach and stormed out of the weight room. Cleaves didn't think it was that big of a deal until later that evening when he was hanging at a friend's apartment and there was a knock at the door. His friend opened it, and in walked the coaching staff, beginning with the assistants. Izzo walked in last—"like the Godfather," Cleaves says. He proceeded to let Cleaves know in no uncertain terms that that kind of disrespect to a member of his staff would not be tolerated. For someone like Cleaves, who had been given the star treatment all of his life, it was a reality check. "Whatever I did in the past meant nothing to him," Cleaves says. "He checked that at the door."

Later that same season, Izzo intervened to keep his point guard from making a potentially life-altering mistake. Izzo had gotten word that Cleaves had skipped class, and when he chased him down to find out what was happening, Cleaves told him that his cousin had gotten beat up by a bunch of kids back in Flint, and he was trying to find a ride home so he could confront them. Izzo talked him out of it by reminding him of how hard he had worked to get to that point. Was he really willing to throw all of that away?

Despite the conflicts—or perhaps because of them—it was a beautiful and authentic relationship. On the surface, they had come from starkly different backgrounds, but Izzo always had time for Cleaves. Whenever they sat down to share memories, they found common ground. "I loved hearing his stories," Cleaves says. "I learned that nothing was handed to him, and he had to work for everything. Coming from Flint, we always had a thing about not being a big city like Detroit. Plus, I was a younger brother, so I had a big-time chip on my shoulder. He felt the same way. So that was another thing that brought us together."

As for the team, things reached a nadir in February of Cleaves's freshman year, when the Spartans endured a stretch in which they lost seven out of ten Big Ten games. A local newspaper published a poll asking fans to rate Izzo's prospects as a coach. "That was one of the more demeaning things I went through because my parents were so down about it," he says. "I had to tell them not to worry. It's a tough profession in that respect. People can say stuff that is really bone-chilling."

What the public did not realize was that Izzo was building a culture that was authentically aligned with his own worldview, and it was just taking some time. He wanted his Spartans essentially to be a football team without the pads. He even had his guys work out in the football team's weight room, so they could lift and grunt alongside the players. Everything would be centered on defense and rebounding, basketball's version of blocking and tackling.

A coach normally puts his culture in place incrementally, but there are times when he must take dramatic measures. In the midst of that losing skid, Izzo took his team to an upstairs practice gym thirty minutes before a home game against Penn State and put his guys through his "War" drill. That's the exercise where an assistant tosses up an errant shot and all ten players try to get the rebound. While this is putatively a rebounding drill, the real purpose behind

War is to instill a pugnacious attitude. The guys got after it that night. At one point, 6′9″ freshman forward A. J. Granger got popped in the face and had his nose bloodied. The Spartans left the practice gym, went right into their layup lines, and defeated Penn State. They finished the regular season winning four of their last five games.

With Cleaves finally healthy and strong, Michigan State broke through in the 1997–98 season, reaching the Sweet Sixteen of the NCAA Tournament. The following year, they got to the Final Four, where they lost in the semifinal to Duke. The 1999–2000 season started off in difficult fashion, with Cleaves missing the first two months because of a broken foot. After he returned in early January, the Spartans won the Big Ten regular season title and looked like a good bet to return to the Final Four.

That prospect was in jeopardy during their Sweet Sixteen game against Syracuse. The Spartans started off nervous and tentative and trailed by 10 at halftime. When they got into the locker room, Cleaves exploded on his teammates. He was especially pissed at Granger, who had passed off a couple of open shots early on. Cleaves was so irate that Izzo had to step in and calm him down. It was a good lesson that it takes more than a coach to get to *Us*. "I've always said, a player-coached team is much better than a coach-coached team," Izzo says.

Michigan State blitzed Syracuse in the second half to win and then defeated Iowa State in the Elite Eight to return to the Final Four, in Indianapolis. After beating Wisconsin in the semifinal, the Spartans faced Florida in the final. They got a scare a few minutes into the second half, when Cleaves was fouled hard on a breakaway and came down awkwardly on his foot. As Cleaves was helped to the locker room to get X-rayed, Izzo reminded his guys that they had played without him early in the season, so they were prepared for this moment. It turned out Cleaves's X-rays were negative. He returned to the game and despite a severe limp helped the Spartans to an 89–76 victory.

It was a triumphant and emotional moment, made all the more so when Cleaves leaned on his crutches and wept openly as CBS's "One Shining Moment" anthem played on the large screen above. When the song was over, the Spartans conducted the traditional net-cutting ritual. They were almost through when Izzo invited Antonio Smith to climb the ladder. Smith had graduated the year before, but he had done as much as anyone to jump-start the program. Izzo wanted him to know how much he appreciated that. Smith grabbed those scissors and snipped himself a part of the historic net. He might not have been technically on the roster that night, but he was still a part of the family.

I first got to know Izzo before the start of that championship season. *Sports Illustrated* was going to make the Spartans our preseason No. 1–ranked team, and the magazine flew me to East Lansing to spend the day with him and his team. While sitting across from Izzo in a conference room, I asked whether he might grant me some exclusive access if the Spartans made the Final Four. Izzo pounded the table and said, "You can ride our bus." When I asked if he really meant it, he nodded and said, "I like how you operate."

Looking back, it's clear that he was referring to my willingness not just to interview him, but to take time to come to East Lansing, watch his practice, meet his coaches and players, and make my request face-to-face. When I would talk to him on the phone during that season, he repeatedly brought up our deal, relishing the opportunity to keep a promise.

I was in Auburn Hills, Michigan, when the Spartans clinched their place in the Final Four in the Midwest Regional final. The day before that win over Iowa State in the Elite Eight, I had interviewed Izzo again in his hotel suite. I distinctly remember riding the elevator down to the lobby afterward. A family of Michigan State fans got on the elevator, and the dad introduced Izzo to his young son. Izzo flashed the kid a faux growl, balled his fist, and tapped him in the gut—as if to say, *Whatcha got in there?*

That, in a nutshell, is how Izzo coaches his guys. He's constantly asking, "Whatcha got in there?" And they better have an authentic answer. Valentine will never forget the time he missed a few shots in the first few minutes of a Big Ten game and Izzo called time out so he could shred him. With his eyes bulging and his nose a few inches away from Valentine's, Izzo taunted him. "You're scared, aren't ya?" he said. "You're all talk. You don't even want to be here, do you? Should I just sit you down the rest of the game?" The words infuriated Valentine—which was exactly the point. He played aggressively the rest of the way.

Izzo can be harsh, but he is also fair. If he is going to give his guys shit, he understands that sometimes they will want to give it back to him. "My attitude is, I'm hard on them, so if they want to challenge me, they better bring the goods," he says.

Cleaves tells me about a time when Izzo was screaming at him in a huddle for playing so shitty, until Cleaves finally blurted, "Yeah, well, you ain't called a good play all day!" Izzo never blinked. That kind of clash occurred on a near-daily basis with Draymond Green, who played forward from 2008 to 2012 and has gone on to great success with the Golden State Warriors despite being a second-round draft pick. Green was a ticking time bomb, but Izzo tolerated his outbursts because most of the time Green was angry at himself. He did, however, have a bad habit of kicking balls into the upper deck of the Breslin Center when he got frustrated in practice. Says Izzo, "I had to tell him one day, 'Hey man, we're gonna have five-hour practices if we gotta fetch the ball every time you kick it.'"

A coach who allows that kind of candid dialogue might be taking on certain risks, but he also builds trust. That was evident late on Saturday night at the 2000 Final Four, after Michigan State had defeated Wisconsin in the semifinal. Izzo was bunkered in the team's hotel with his coaching staff studying video of Florida. At one point, Cleaves walked in with his co-captain, 6'7" senior forward Morris Peterson. They pulled Izzo aside and told him they didn't think the team should "tape" for the Sunday walk-through— meaning they shouldn't tape their ankles and have a full-contact practice, but rather a light one. Izzo trusted that these guys wanted to win as badly as he did, and he believed they had better knowledge of what the players needed at that point than he did. He granted their request.

On the flip side, Izzo tried to give his guys the morning off during the 2009 NCAA Tournament regional in Indianapolis, but his senior guard, Travis Walton, objected. Walton was one of the toughest, most vocal leaders Izzo ever had. Izzo would even let him run drills sometimes in practice. Izzo agreed to have a walk-through the next day, but he told Walton he better make sure that everyone came in on time and ready to work. "When they came in, it was almost like the Bataan Death March," he says, chuckling. "We went through about three things and I said, 'That's it. We're done.'" Later that day, they beat No. 1 Louisville, 64–62, to return to the Final Four.

For someone who admits he was just an okay student, Izzo is quite stringent when it comes to his players' academics. He doesn't ask his guys to get a 4.0 grade point average. He just wants them to fulfill their obligations. In his early days, he would get so worked up when his players disappointed him in this area that his then-assistant, Brian Gregory, had to tell him to chill because he was going to practice in a bad mood. When a player inevitably complains that he doesn't like school, Izzo will stand up, give him a hug, and say, "I hated it, too." Then he'll tell him to get his ass to class. "I always say, if we can get a kid to do something he doesn't like, just think what we can do when it's something he does like, which is basketball," he says.

As the Final Fours have piled up—seven as of this writing— Izzo has ensured that he remains most available to the people who matter most: his family and his players. He had children relatively late in life, at the age of forty-one. Lupe gave birth to a girl, Racquel, in 1996. Six years later, they adopted a boy and named him Steven Mateen. (Yes, those names were chosen in honor of Mariucci and Cleaves. Cleaves returned the gesture when he named his own son Izzy.) Izzo has resisted getting overly involved with USA Basketball because it would have taken too much time away from the family store. Though his office is always available to his players, he does not like to have too many personal discussions there. He doesn't want them to feel like they're in the principal's office. He'd rather go to their dorms, drive them around, invite them to his house, take a long walk on campus, or go get a burger. "I think sometimes they see me as a rich guy driving a nice car and owning a beautiful home," he says. "They didn't see me at twenty-nine trying to get my next meal."

To watch Izzo conduct practice is to see a man in a constant state of wretched agony. His dyspeptic facial expressions on the sidelines are the stuff of legend. Even Mariucci, who comes from the tough-guy world of pro football, is taken aback at times. "Do you ever see him talk to his players? He gets eyeball to eyeball. He looks right through their head," Mariucci says. "I don't know if it's intimate or barbaric."

The more Izzo has won, the more he craves that connection— and the more hostile he has grown to artifice. He knows that many of the people now showering him with hosannas would ditch him the moment he started losing big. That's because he remembers what it was like when the Spartans finished seventh and sixth in the Big Ten, respectively, in his first two seasons.

Having persisted through those early struggles, Izzo has a deep respect for coaches who handle adversity with authenticity and class. "Jud Heathcote always said that only a coach understands a coach. He'd call Izzo's worst enemy if the guy was going through a tough time," he says. Michigan State has had six different football coaches during Izzo's time there. Each time one of them was fired, Izzo went to the press conference. He went largely to support the fired coach, but also to see how the guy handled being in a roomful of media that included many who had been advocating for him to get the axe. In those situations, there is no hiding behind a camera or a laptop. Everyone is eyeball to eyeball.

Izzo will spend hours studying how other coaches, especially football coaches, conduct press conferences. If he sees something that impresses him, he will cold call a guy and commend him. "I enjoy that about my job. People who I've never met will take my call," he says. "Football guys are so intriguing to me because they have to be so organized. It's fun to talk to people who are in the same profession but a different venue. Plus, they're not trying to cover up anything because you're not recruiting against them."

Izzo has fielded numerous NBA offers over the years. The closest he came to accepting was in 2010, when the Cleveland Cavaliers pursued him. Izzo really likes the team's owner, Dan Gilbert, and if LeBron James hadn't left to sign with the Miami Heat, there's a very good chance Izzo would have said yes. He is intrigued by the idea of coaching pros, but the NBA does not fit him authentically the way college does. The league is too corporate. He prefers the family store.

Meanwhile, he recruits all the messengers he can get. Lots of coaches invite their former players to come back and work out with their current ones, but Izzo may be the only one who built a separate locker room for them. The room contains fourteen lockers plus a steam room, sauna, and shower, not to mention a flat-screen and lounge area. And lest anyone think that he gives preferential treatment to the guys who made the NBA, Izzo also has a big wall in the facility dedicated to the program's former managers.

Lupe and their two children are mainstays at games and tournaments, but from the time he and Lupe started dating, Tom has been reluctant to share details about his work when he walks through the door. She learns much about what is going on with the team by reading the newspaper. "Being home is his release," she says. "When he's home, he's connected with the kids. He wants to know what's going on in the house."

For years, Izzo's home phone number was listed. He is so generous in granting access to the media that the United States Basketball Writers Association gave him an award. He went to the USBWA's banquet to accept it on a Sunday morning at the Final Four, even though his team was playing for the national championship the next night. When he is on vacation at his lake house in Grand Haven, he likes to mix it up with the locals. "A lot of people come there and say, 'Why don't you put some trees up? Why don't you go there and have privacy?'" he says. "Man, I don't like privacy. I like smelling my neighbor's cookout, y'know?"

It's remarkable enough that Izzo would take his team to the Final Four seven times in his first twenty-one years. What's even more remarkable is that during an era when the top programs are dependent on the so-called one-and-done guys—players who are good enough to become first-round draft picks after their freshman season—Izzo only had three such players during that span. Instead, he has won with guys like Cleaves, who played four years in college and was unable to stick as an NBA player after being chosen 15th in the draft by the Pistons, and Green, a lightly recruited forward who also stayed four years before being selected by the Warriors in the second round of the 2012 NBA draft.

Oftentimes, when a coach gets to that many Final Fours and comes up empty-handed, he is tagged with the "underachiever" label. That hasn't happened to Izzo because fans recognize that many of his Final Four teams had no business getting that far. If anything, he has been seen as an overachiever. But that is its own form of insult, because it reinforces Izzo's suspicions that his program has yet to achieve truly elite status.

The notion that Izzo is winning the "right way" while men like Kentucky's John Calipari, Kansas's Bill Self, and Duke's Mike Krzyzewski are doing it the "wrong way" with one-and-dones is a false narrative, and Izzo knows it. He goes after one-and-dones with just as much zeal as they do. The difference is, he keeps losing out. Izzo does not hide his disdain for what he sees as the instant-gratification culture that has overtaken his sport, not to mention the world in general. He believes that building relationships and developing players takes time. In his view, there is no such thing as a quick fix. Work isn't authentic unless you can smell the sawdust.

That craving for contact has led Izzo in recent years to launch a one-man crusade against what he perceives as the evils of social media. He is far from alone in holding this view, but unlike most coaches, his primary concern isn't that one of his players will post something embarrassing. He's far more worried about what they are reading, good and bad. It drives him to distraction knowing that so many people are spending so much time engaging in something that is so artificial.

"I worry about all the time spent on Twitter. I told my wife, 'I'd rather my kid have a drinking problem. At least when he wakes up in the morning, he's hungover,'" he says. "If a doctor is going to tell you that you have cancer, you want him to email it to you? That's why there are no leaders on teams anymore. Kids can't communicate. I tell my staff that I'd like to invent a uniform so I can send my guys a text during a game that says, 'Will you please guard somebody?'"

Izzo's assistants cringe when he goes on these rants. They fear it will hurt recruiting. They've already heard the chatter from some of Izzo's younger rivals that he is from the old school, that he might not understand the proclivities of today's players. His recruiting has yet to fall off, but even if it did, it's doubtful he would dial back. Izzo is not opposed to progress. He's opposed to bullshit. "We're teaching kids that they should have your own 'brand.' Be your own guy. So now at fifteen, fourteen, thirteen, it's *me me me me me*. That's the society they're growing up in. I don't like that," he says. "So don't tell me it's because I'm old school. Fuck that old-school shit. This is not about old school/new school. It's about right school/wrong school."

On the day the Spartans closed out the 1999–2000 regular season with a home game against archrival Michigan, Izzo told his best friend and assistant coach, Mike Garland, that all he wanted was to be winning by enough so he could just enjoy the last minute of the game. He was only half serious, but when the Spartans built a 50-point lead with four minutes to play, Garland walked up to his boss and told him to go sit with his guys and savor what was happening. So Izzo walked down the bench, sat between Cleaves and Peterson, and turned himself over to the moment. "I got to enjoy four minutes, just watching," he says with a gleam in his eye. "It was awesome."

It was also unusual. The reason Izzo remembers those four minutes so well is that there haven't been many of them. This is the curse he carries inside his PEAK profile. Getting to *Us* is something he does for other people. He has a much harder time getting to *Me*.

This is human nature, of course. Our best qualities and our worst ones come from the same place. If Izzo experienced all of his successful moments like he did those four minutes, he might lose the authenticity he first acquired in his family's shoe store. When I mention this observation to him during a phone conversation, he laughs. "I feel like I'm in therapy here because you're right on the money," he says. "I think what you're talking about is true for 99.999 percent of successful people. I don't know how you can enjoy your success without losing your edge. I wish I could learn to enjoy life a little bit more, but I still think I'm doing it the right way for me."

Izzo is inarguably one of the finest college basketball coaches in the game's history, yet he still sees his program as residing on a tier below the likes of Duke, North Carolina, Kansas, and Kentucky. "That club still selects more than it recruits," he says. "I'm not being humble here. You know what I have to do every summer. If those guys are gonna watch someone play two or three times, that means I've gotta be there ten times. That's just the way it is."

Perhaps, but in many ways, Izzo is much more suited to a second-tier program, or at least a second-tier mentality. It has always been difficult for him to relax. Even when he is sitting in a basement lounge chair in his house and eating french fries out of a Styrofoam box, his legs are crossed tight at the ankles, his feet vibrating rigidly back and forth. He has a lovely vacation house on Lake Michigan in Grand Haven, Michigan, but he is not the type to take a nap on the beach with a novel in his lap. He'd rather get up early in the morning, climb aboard his utility vehicle, and grate the sand into neat, even lines. He does his neighbor's beach, too. "I just think he likes to see the finished product," Lupe says. "He's always thinking and moving."

"I worry about him," Mariucci says. "I worry about his health. I worry about burnout. He's full speed ahead all the time. I know he enjoys it, but it doesn't always show. I'm like, 'Show me a smile once in a while.'"

He would if he had the time. His office is, as he puts it, "a recruiting mecca." Every coach at Michigan State brings their recruits to meet him—football, basketball, hockey, softball, women's golf, track, you name it. The kids don't get a quick meet-and-greet, either. Izzo sits with them, chats for a while, joshes with their families. When a good friend offered a few years ago to make a big donation to the basketball program, Izzo persuaded him to give it to women's softball instead so they could build a practice facility.

That's a big reason why Izzo takes losses so personally. He's constantly afraid of letting other people down. "It's a big burden, but it's also pretty awesome that I get to be in this position," he says. "For someone like me to stay in one place this long is pretty unusual. Everybody is more transient now."

Like every great coach, he has learned to adapt. "It used to be that players used to trust you because of your position. They had to earn your trust, not so much the other way around," he says. "I don't feel that I'm owed that just because of my position. I guess that's one of the biggest adjustments I've made. And you know what? I don't blame them. Why would you trust anybody in this day and age with everybody screwing everybody?"

Two months after the loss to Middle Tennessee, Izzo traveled to the Bay Area to visit Mariucci and his family. Mariucci hasn't coached since he was fired by the Detroit Lions in 2005. He has a cushy TV gig with NFL Network (which is based in Los Angeles) and spends much of his down time at a vacation home near San Diego. During the visit, Izzo and Mariucci went to see Green play for the Warriors. They visited the locker room beforehand and had a grand old time. The trip gave Izzo a tantalizing hint of what life could be like for him, someday, when the grinding is done.

He has long insisted that he won't be one of those lifers who are still coaching into their seventies. When he got his 400th career win in January 2012, Mariucci told him he wanted to be there for his

500th. "If I'm still coaching that long, shoot me," Izzo said, half joking. He picked up No. 500 in November 2015. He may laugh off the idea of going a long while, but he is still as good as he has ever been. "He may coach till he's ninety," Garland says. "Trust me, he knows what he's doing. It's controlled chaos. If anything, he's adamant about what we can do to take this thing to another level. He wants to make it even greater."

Izzo hasn't given much thought as to how or when he will step away, but he knows what he doesn't want. He doesn't want a long drawn-out goodbye like Heathcote had. He doesn't want a court named after him, because he saw how Purdue named its court after longtime coach Gene Keady and then the fans turned on him when he won only seven games during his final season. Most of all, he doesn't want to stay longer than he should. "You'll never see me do a half-ass job," he says. "The university is not going to get ripped off."

What he really means is that he would never rip himself off. So he grinds and he grinds, searching for contact, meeting every obligation, eyeball to eyeball, always doing what is best for the family business. He'll go as long as he can smell the sawdust. He'll go as long as he can feel the guilt.

Mike Krzyzewski

"I BELIEVE IN ETHNIC PRESSURE."

What's my name?

Even at the age of five, the boy believed in being prepared. He and his family were about to ride the bus across town to see relatives. The boy knew that as soon as he walked in the door, his uncle Joe, the cop, would ask him to say his own name. The answer was not so obvious, because the boy's name was different from his father's. For some reason, so was Uncle Joe's, although Joe's children—the boy's cousins—used the same name his dad did. Looking back, it all seems rather confusing, but at the time it was just normal life in the 1950s as a Polish kid on the South Side of Chicago.

It's not that the boy's dad was ashamed of his heritage. William Kross was nothing if not proud. He bowled in a league with his buddies, and whenever he won a tournament, he would bring home that trophy and display it alongside the others in his living room. His decision to use a different surname was purely practical. He worried that if he used his real one, the one with all the consonants, it would be harder to support his family.

And it worked. For many years, William was employed as an elevator operator in Willoughby Tower downtown, nodding hello and goodbye dozens of times each day to all those well-heeled professionals with their plush offices and easy-to-spell last names. He later owned a tavern, which he would open at five o'clock each morning so the truckers and blue-collar guys could down a few shots before heading to work. When he came home, his wife, Emily, would leave for her job as a cleaning lady at the Chicago Athletic Club. They weren't struggling, exactly, but it wasn't an easy life, either. Using an anglicized surname just made things a little less hard.

His two sons used their real name, but it was hard to spell and weird to pronounce, especially for a five-year-old boy. So knowing his uncle's question was coming, the boy would ask his parents exactly how to say it.

"Mike . . . *Sha-SHEF-ski*," they told him. He practiced it out loud.

Mike's grandparents had emigrated from Poland and Austria and entered America through Ellis Island. His family lived in a mostly Polish neighborhood on the top floor of a two-level flat on Cortez Street. More family members lived in the apartment below. Mike didn't deal with a whole lot of discrimination in those days; consonants were plentiful in the world he knew. If anything, he was a beacon in the neighborhood, an excellent student, a terrific athlete, a natural-born leader. His parents understood, however, that consonants could be a problem in the world beyond. They didn't teach their sons how to speak Polish and didn't want them learning it at school. Mike didn't discover until many years later that it was because his parents didn't want him to develop an accent. He left that neighborhood with a distinct Chicago twang, but there was nothing Polish about it.

Mike, of course, would go on to become a highly successful basketball coach, famous and wealthy beyond his parents' wildest dreams. He would face plenty of adversity in his career, but it was never due to his name. If anything, he used it as comedic foil. On the day that he was announced as the head basketball coach at Duke University—a move that shocked the public, for he had never been mentioned as a candidate—the first thing he did was crack a joke about it. "First of all, it's pronounced *Sha-SHEF-ski*. K-R-Z-Y-Z-E-W-S-K-I," he said. "And if you think that's bad, you should have seen it before I changed it."

Unlike his father, Mike never changed his name, although many people simply call him Coach K. Yet the experience of growing up in an immigrant family imbued him with a healthy mix of pride and defiance. It set in motion the dynamics that enabled him to become one of the greatest coaches of his generation in any sport. It is at the core of how he gets his teams to *Us*. Krzyzewski's ethnic roots straightened his back, the better to carry his family's legacy on his shoulders, not to mention a very healthy chip. He is grateful and humble and always just a little bit pissed off. The lingering image of Krzyzewski, now past his seventieth birthday, is not of him celebrating big moments, or the sheepish grin he wears when he snips yet another championship net. It is the petulant pose he strikes on the sideline, hands on his hips, lips tight, an angry, disapproving scowl etched on his chiseled face.

What's my name? His PEAK profile emerged from his search for that answer. The persistence required to overcome stereotypes. The empathy born out of the risk his grandparents took to immigrate to America, following "the courage of their convictions," as he often says. The authenticity that comes from taking on all those consonants, regardless of the barriers they might erect. The knowledge of who he was and where he came from, and learning from his parents' example that the only way to improve your lot in life is to work hard and do your best, never complaining, never apologizing for who you are.

Many years after leaving that neighborhood, Mike received the ultimate honor in his profession by being inducted into the Naismith Memorial Basketball Hall of Fame. His father, William, was not alive to see it, but he probably would not have been all that surprised. He knew his son was intelligent and hardworking, and that there was no limit to what he could accomplish in the United States of America.

But Mike . . . *Sha-SHEF-ski*? Getting into the Hall of Fame? That would have blown him away.

To understand how Mike Krzyzewski leads, we have to begin with the night he earned his most important victory.

It was March 30, 1991, when the Duke Blue Devils pulled off what was considered one of the greatest upsets in NCAA Tournament history by knocking off unbeaten and top-ranked UNLV in the Final Four, 79–77. When the game ended, the Duke players celebrated deliriously. But when CBS showed Krzyzewski on the sideline, he was standing there with that trademark pissed-off look on his face. His arms were extended, his hands were out, his palms were down. He motioned up and down as if to tell his guys to knock it off.

It came across as a spontaneous gesture, but Krzyzewski told me it was actually premeditated. That was the fifth time he had taken his team to the Final Four, and in each of the previous trips the Blue Devils had fallen short of the championship—including the year before, when that same UNLV team had embarrassed Duke by 30 points in the final. While that didn't eat away at him the way many assumed, he did puzzle on why his teams hadn't won. He arrived at a single word: *rationalization*. "I thought maybe, not consciously, I was rationalizing that getting there was enough," he said. So before the game began, Krzyzewski decided that if Duke pulled off the win, he would not show any signs of celebration and insist his players do the same.

It is hard to imagine almost any other coach reacting to that moment in that way. It resulted from some hard-earned knowledge, and it revealed Krzyzewski's persistence and authenticity. As for his empathy, well, let's go back a little further to an off-camera moment I witnessed up close. It occurred during my freshman year at Duke. I was standing in the student section of Cameron Indoor Stadium a few rows behind the home team's bench. It was early in the season, and Krzyzewski saw something he didn't like from his prized 6′10″ freshman forward, Christian Laettner. So he yanked Laettner from the game, knelt in front of him on the Duke bench, and delivered a blistering, profane message just inches from his face.

I was taken aback by the force of Krzyzewski's anger. I sure was glad it wasn't being directed at me. Though we've since come to know Laettner as a supremely arrogant athlete, at the time he was just a callow freshman. As Krzyzewski took his own seat at the head of the bench, Laettner dropped his head.

"Christian!" Krzyzewski yelled. "Keep your head up! Learn from your mistakes!"

That is how Krzyzewski coaches his guys—from the inside out.

Like a lot of great basketball coaches, Krzyzewski was naturally gifted at math when he was a boy. Words, however, did not come easy. His first language was the argot of the inner city, with a lot of yo's and head nods and a healthy dose of curse words. But really it came down to how his mind worked—or rather, how it didn't work. He strongly suspects that if he had been tested as a child, he would have been diagnosed with attention deficit disorder. "I had ants in my pants all the time. Still do," he says. When he did his homework, he needed distractions around him—the radio, for example, or a television tuned to a Cubs game. To this day, Krzyzewski is not much of a reader. "For me, reading is not a joy," he says. "I'd rather listen to a book on tape."

His parents were not helpful in this department. His dad didn't say much to begin with. He worked, he came home, he smoked his cigarettes, he fell asleep in his chair . . . and that was pretty much it. When I asked Krzyzewski to tell me what his father was like, he replied, "I wish I could tell you about him. I didn't really know my dad, not because he was bad to me or anything. He just worked all the time. He was very supportive of me, but he wasn't like, 'Let's sit down and have father-son talks.'"

It fell to his mother, Emily, to give him his empathetic foundation. She was an avatar of feminine strength. He remembers how meticulously she took care of their home, how even though she had only two dresses in her closet, they were always clean and ironed and hung with care. When she baked cookies, she put exactly three chips in each one. If they didn't turn out right, she threw away the entire batch. "I'm like a lot of kids in the inner city growing up in ethnic families," Krzyzewski says. "You got to know your mother better because she was home."

His older brother, Bill, was bigger and stronger, but Mike was the superior athlete, especially at basketball. He attended two all-boys Catholic schools, St. Helen for elementary and Weber for high school. During his junior and senior years at Weber, he led Chicago's Catholic League in scoring and drew interest from a few Division I colleges. Creighton and Wisconsin offered him scholarships, and Mike figured they were good options. But his exploits as a student and a player caught the attention of an assistant coach at Army named Bob Knight. When Knight visited Mike's home in December of 1965, the coach was twenty-five years old and just four years removed from being a reserve on the 1960 NCAA champs at Ohio State.

As far as Mike was concerned, Knight was wasting his time. If he went to West Point, he would have to serve in the U.S. Army for five full years after he was through playing. Mike had no interest in that. Besides, in his mind there was something traitorous about going that far from home to attend such an elite school. He worried his buddies in the neighborhood would think he was putting on airs.

His parents were flabbergasted. They had two years of high school between them. His father had changed his name just to get some menial jobs and provide a living for his family. He had even served in the Army under his anglicized name. What little money they made was spent to send their boys to private schools. Now here was Uncle Sam himself, in their living room, offering their son a first-class education and a place in the American tapestry . . . and Mike was turning it down? It was inconceivable.

William and Emily were not the type to express their disapproval to Mike, so they chose to express it *near* him. They sat in their kitchen and talked about how dumb he was to pass this up. They talked and talked until they finally wore him down. It was a lesson in persuasion that he would carry into his career as a coach. "I believe in ethnic pressure," Mike says. "They believed in me, and they believed in opportunity. They invested in my education. I trusted them because I loved them. Turning down West Point was the best decision I never made."

Sitting in Krzyzewski's office at Duke more than fifty years later, I asked him if there was ever a point during his time at Army when he wanted to quit. He sat up and looked at me incredulously. "Point?" he said. "There were *hundreds* of points. But I couldn't quit, because I couldn't let my parents down."

Playing for the tyrannical Knight was the least of Mike's problems. His days as a first-year plebe started early, ended late, and were filled with orders to do things he couldn't. Each time he failed, he was berated by an upperclass cadet. One of the first things they made him do was jump into a swimming pool. He was a city kid who had no idea how to swim. Krzyzewski struggled, but he didn't drown. It wasn't fun, and it wasn't fair.

"I was a golden boy in my neighborhood. I only did things I was good at," he told me. "Then all of a sudden I'm at West Point and there are a lot of really good people and you have to do new things. And you look like crap. I found out two things. These are rock solid in my foundation. Failure is not a destination, and you're never going to do it alone."

As challenging as the environment was, it also served as a cocoon that sealed Krzyzewski off from the tumult that was engulfing the country in the late 1960s. The Vietnam War was raging, and though Krzyzewski knew a few older students who were killed, he had little inkling of the extent to which the war was tearing the country apart. "We were kind of isolated," he recalls. "We didn't think we were doing anything wrong. It would be pretty hard to be in that environment if you did." His only window into what was happening occurred during weekend visits to New York City. He and his fellow cadets felt out of place but not necessarily uncomfortable. "Here we had skin heads, and everyone else has long hair and they're smoking pot and burning incense. It was two extremes," he says. "I didn't feel like we hated those people, but it was like, *Man, they're weird.*"

Krzyzewski knew he had to give the Army five years after he graduated, but he didn't put much thought into what that would entail. He was too focused on basketball. He worked hard to please his coach, mostly by heeding his instructions to shoot the ball only when he absolutely had to. He and Knight had their battles, but Krzyzewski's hard-nosed defense, resilience, and natural leadership skills made him the ideal Bob Knight point guard. Knight named him captain at the start of his senior year, but when the team lost five consecutive games in December and January, Krzyzewski could sense everything coming apart. Yet he persisted, leading the team to a 14–8 record and a berth in the postseason National Invitation Tournament, where he led Army to the semifinals in Madison Square Garden. The Black Knights lost to Boston College that night, but Krzyzewski never forgot how intoxicating it was to play a basketball game on such a grand stage.

His most searing memory of that season, however, came on March 1, 1969. Shortly after leading his team to a win at Navy, Krzyzewski got a phone call from home reporting that his father had suffered a cerebral hemorrhage. He and Knight rushed to the airport and flew to Chicago, but by the time they landed, William was dead. Knight stayed in Chicago for a few days, holding Emily's hand and consoling her as they sat at their kitchen table. Knight stood by his point guard as his father was lowered into the ground. Since William was a veteran, his tombstone was paid for by the Army. It displayed the name *Kross* because that's what William used when he served. A few years later, Emily purchased a new tombstone and put *Krzyzewski* on it. It was his name, after all.

June 4, 1969, was not just Krzyzewski's graduation day. It was also his wedding day. Just a few hours after receiving his diploma, he and Mickie Marsh were married in the Catholic chapel at West Point. She was a Baptist from Virginia who was living in Chicago while working as a stewardess for United Airlines when she and Mike met at a mutual friend's apartment in the summer of 1967. She was, as she puts it, "one hundred percent WASP, plain old nothing," who never new about ethnic pressure until she met her new boyfriend's family. "I was a complete outsider," she says. "His dad was the only one that openly accepted me. He liked that I could talk sports. I had to win my way with everyone else. His mom was the last one to come around."

There were two things that attracted her to Mike: his muscular legs and his authenticity. Shortly after Mike returned to West Point, he wrote Mickie a letter inviting her to go to a Chicago Bears game with him during his next visit home. She accepted, and when she expressed her pleasure at being invited, he confessed that he had asked another girl first.

"So I was your second choice?" Mickie asked.

"Actually," Mike replied, "you were my third."

A year later, she was transferred to New York City, which gave her the opportunity to spend time with Mike on his weekend visits. One day, he took her to the airport so she could work a Detroit turnaround. She invited him to sneak onto the plane, which would be easy since there were plenty of seats and she was the one taking boarding passes. He declined her offer, saying it wasn't honorable. Just before the plane took off, Mike walked on board and handed her a ticket he had just purchased.

Following graduation, Mike trained to be a field artillery officer, first at Fort Sill in Oklahoma for six months, and later at Fort Carson in Colorado for another two years. His name was on a list of potential candidates to be deployed to Vietnam, but his basketball skills, which were good enough that he was considered a possible candidate to play for the U.S. Olympic team, kept him from being sent into combat. Instead, he was deployed to Korea, where he worked in the field liaison office at Camp Pelham and played for the All-Army team, which played against American and international military teams all over the world, from San Francisco to Lebanon to Iraq. "I guess there are people who love being in combat. I would have done it out of duty, but I'm glad I didn't have to," he says. "Look, I didn't want to go to Vietnam—especially then. There's five minutes to go in the game and you're not gonna win. We're getting the hell out of there. I didn't want to go in the game."

Krzyzewski's stint in Korea was supposed to be a hardship tour, meaning no family was allowed, but Mickie came anyway for the last three months. She stayed a few miles away at a recreation center, where she and their eighteen-month-old daughter, Debbie, slept in a supply room. After his tour was up, Krzyzewski was transferred to work as a basketball coach at a prep school in Fort Belvoir, Virginia. He had done a little bit of coaching in the past, but this was the first time he had tried doing it full-time, and he loved it. When his Army commission ended in 1974, Mickie assumed they would live the life of a career officer and his family, which promised long-term financial stability. Her husband, however, surprised her by saying he wanted to take a job as an unpaid graduate assistant at Indiana University, where his former college coach, Bob Knight, had just been hired. Mickie tried to talk him out of it, but when Mike told her it was something he had to do, she knew the battle was lost.

After just one year in Bloomington, Mike interviewed for the head coaching position at Army, which had fired its coach following a 3–22 season. Mickie was not thrilled that her husband wanted to pursue this profession, but she was especially concerned about returning to the then-all-male world of West Point. Her only request was that he wouldn't tell her she couldn't go somewhere (aside from the players' locker room) because women weren't allowed. He promised her he never would, and he never did.

There are moments when even the most persistent of men feel broken. For Mike Krzyzewski, that moment came after a game on December 12, 1981, when he cried alone in a shower.

It was early in his second season at Duke. His team had just lost,

72–55, at Princeton. Its record was now 1–4, with an unforgiving
ACC schedule on tap. Krzyzewski swears he never doubted his
ability, never believed he was in real danger of losing his job, but on
that night he was truly daunted by just how far his team had to
climb. "Losing to Princeton isn't good, but you can't lose like that,"
he told me. "You have to have your moments of weakness, but not in
front of a group, and not in front of your family. Those building
years are very lonely, but out of it, I think, comes toughness."

Duke had a respectable program, but it had long been relegated to
second-tier status in the Atlantic Coast Conference. The school's previous coach, Bill Foster, had resigned to accept the head job at South
Carolina, even though he was two years from having taken the Blue
Devils to the NCAA championship game. Duke's athletic director,
Tom Butters, interviewed Krzyzewski largely on Knight's recommendation, but given that Krzyzewski was an unknown commodity whose
team had just gone 9–17, Butters had a hard time pulling the trigger.
After weeks of hemming and hawing, he finally introduced Krzyzewski to the press, which was taken completely off guard.

In Krzyzewski's first season at the helm, the Blue Devils went
17–13, but that was with Foster's players. His real test would come
in how he recruited—and he failed spectacularly. Krzyzewski and
his staff had scoured the country and come up with a long list of
prospects. By the time they got to the end of the recruiting season,
they had narrowed it down to five players, including Chris Mullin,
a 6'6" sharpshooter from Brooklyn. Mullin chose St. John's, which
was not a huge surprise, but one by one, the other recruits spurned
Krzyzewski as well. One prospect, Rodney Williams, was supposed
to announce his commitment to Duke at his high school team's
postseason banquet. Krzyzewski flew to Florida to speak at the
banquet, but when he pulled up to the school, Williams's coach
apologized and informed him that Williams had just signed with

Florida—and he wouldn't even be at the banquet. Krzyzewski spoke anyway. He had promised he would.

As a result, Krzyzewski altered his recruiting philosophy. Instead of beginning with a long list of candidates, he would narrow it down right away to just a few choices, and then recruit those players with intensity. It was the professional equivalent of jumping into a pool without knowing how to swim, but Krzyzewski trusted he would make it out alive. That has been his modus operandi ever since. "I think that's kept us on the cutting edge," he says. "You kind of back yourself into a corner and say, 'We gotta get this guy.'"

By the fall of 1981, Krzyzewski had his targets. The most talented among them was Johnny Dawkins, a wispy 6´2˝ point guard from Washington, D.C. Dawkins had no idea who Krzyzewski was, but he was taken with the coach's vision. He eventually gave Krzyzewski his commitment.

Dave Henderson also had no idea who Mike Krzyzewski was— and he lived in North Carolina. Curious as to what this new coach was all about, Henderson attended a game in Cameron Indoor Stadium to watch Duke play Wake Forest. During one exchange, a Duke player was bumped by the Wake Forest coach. It was probably accidental, but Krzyzewski went ballistic on the referees. "I saw that and I thought that this is a guy I could play for," Henderson says. "I liked how he defended his player."

Not only did Jay Bilas not know who Krzyzewski was, he barely knew what Duke was. But he realized how badly Krzyzewski wanted him the day the coach flew across the country just to watch Bilas play in a light practice on a blacktop outside his school in Rolling Hills, California. Bilas soon committed, as did Mark Alarie, a 6´7˝ forward from Phoenix who chose Duke over Stanford. "He was just different from any other coach that was recruiting me," Alarie says. "While he was talking to me, he would literally have goosebumps on his arms and legs. He was so much more passionate than any other coach who came into my living room and made a pitch."

The new arrivals might have been prized freshmen, but they were still freshmen, and as they set out for the 1982–83 season, they often looked like boys playing against grown men. The Blue Devils lost four straight games in early December, and they were later humiliated at home when they lost to Wagner, 84–77, to fall to 5–5. As the players walked off the court, they could hear fans lean over the railings and shout obscenities at their coach.

As the losses piled up, so too did the talk that Krzyzewski was on his way out. Bilas was friendly with a female student whose father was a prominent member of the program's booster club, the Iron Dukes. One day she showed him a petition of signatures calling for both Krzyzewski and the football coach to be fired. "I don't know what was going on in the administration building at the time, but we definitely talked about how worried we were," Bilas says. "It was like, 'What are we going to do?' The only reason I came to Duke was because of the coach."

If the treatment from Duke's own fans was this bad, imagine what opposing fans were saying. Duke is a small private school (the enrollment is under 5,000) that draws much of its student population from outside the state. It sits between two large state institutions that play in the ACC, the University of North Carolina at Chapel Hill and North Carolina State. Krzyzewski and his family learned early on that they had alighted behind enemy lines. "Our girls took a beating at school," Mickie says. "It was pretty brutal."

The season ended in ignominious fashion, with a 109–66 annihilation by a Ralph Sampson–led Virginia team in the first round of the 1982 ACC Tournament. After the game, Mickie walked into the Duke hospitality room at the team hotel and stumbled upon a group of Iron Dukes—at that point they were calling themselves the Concerned Iron Dukes—talking about how they could persuade

Butters to fire her husband. Later that night, Krzyzewski went to dinner with a couple of Duke staffers as well as a young *Washington Post* reporter named John Feinstein. When one of the staffers raised a glass of water and toasted to "forgetting about tonight," Krzyzewski raised his own and said, "Here's to *never* forgetting about tonight."

The comment sounded like a reference to the game, but Krzyzewski was really talking about the larger forces that were conspiring against him, challenging his ethnic pride. "It was just, 'Excuse me, fuck you, man. We're gonna do this,'" he says. "I got angry at the people who wanted to get rid of me. I used that anger properly. There are still people that I have nothing to do with, who now want to cuddle up and say, 'We believed in you.' No you didn't."

He was wounded, but he would persist. When Alarie, Bilas, Dawkins, and Henderson took the floor for the first day of practice the following October, they looked up at the scoreboard. The numbers 109–66 were on display, just in case they had forgotten.

B y the time the 1983–84 season got under way, Mike and Mickie had added two more girls to their home roster. Lindy came along in April 1977; Jamie was born four years later. Krzyzewski's home environment provided quite the contrast with his work one. Raising three girls broadened his empathy. "He had to learn to communicate in a softer way," Mickie says. "He was constantly surprised when he said the wrong thing. It made him think, *Why was that wrong? Why did she accept that in that way?*"

Unlike many coaches in high-pressure situations, Krzyzewski did not rigidly separate his work and family lives. Mickie had roles in the program that played to her creativity, such as producing the official team poster and season-ending video tributes to the seniors. Staff meetings and film sessions were held at his house. His wife and girls hung around the offices and rode the team bus. The players came to refer to Jamie as "Mo Minutes" because they deduced that if they let her sit on their lap, they would get more playing time. "We never felt that basketball was taking him away from us," Jamie said. "This wasn't his thing. It was our thing."

Unfortunately, growing up Krzyzewski meant being subjected to a lot of cruel taunts. This was especially difficult after North Carolina won the NCAA championship in 1982, delivering a first title for its longtime legendary coach, Dean Smith. The specter of Smith and North Carolina presented Krzyzewski with an enormous challenge. The campuses were just eight miles apart. He didn't want his players to make their games against UNC more important than any others, yet denying that was literally like asking them not to notice the color of the sky. His frustrations boiled over in January 1984, when, with four minutes to play during a taut game in Cameron Indoor Stadium, Smith tried to get the referees' attention so he could make a substitution. When that failed, he walked to the scorer's table and attempted to sound the horn. Instead, he accidentally added 20 points to North Carolina's tally on the scoreboard. It took a few minutes to fix the score, and play resumed. Amazingly, Smith was never assessed a technical foul. After the game, which Duke lost, 78–73, Krzyzewski went into his postgame press conference and complained about what he called the "double standard" in the ACC that unfairly benefited Smith.

Five days later, Duke lost at home to N.C. State. It was the Blue Devils' fourth consecutive defeat and dropped them to 1–4 in the conference. The howls from the Concerned Iron Dukes had never been louder. The next morning, Krzyzewski arrived at work and learned that his boss, Tom Butters, wanted to see him. Krzyzewski had every reason to worry he might be getting fired, but Butters instead presented him with a five-year contract extension. As the players boarded the bus to play at Clemson the next day, Krzyzewski let them know about his new deal. His job status was never spoken of again.

Krzyzewski immediately validated Butters's move by leading his team on an eight-game win streak. To outsiders, it appeared that the team had made a sudden turnaround, but in fact the streak resulted from all the small but important ways Krzyzewski had applied his PEAK profile over time. Even in the worst moments, the players had faith in their leader's knowledge. "I always felt we were the most prepared team," Henderson says. Practice plans were scheduled down to the minute, but they also included notes explaining how each drill would prepare the team for its next opponent. That allowed his players to visualize the big picture. "It was like getting a West Point battle plan every day," Alarie says. "I played a lot of basketball, including five years in the NBA, and I never had a coach that put one-tenth the elbow grease that Coach K put into every one of those practices."

Krzyzewski's empathy also enabled him to help his players maintain their confidence even as they were losing. He wanted them constantly diving into pools, trusting he would never let them drown. Dawkins, for example, would get easily discouraged if he missed a few shots, but Krzyzewski insisted that he keep shooting. "A miss is not a mistake," he would say.

When the breakthrough came, however, Krzyzewski did not handle it authentically. It happened later that March, when he scored his first victory against North Carolina with a two-point win in the ACC Tournament semifinal. Krzyzewski had warned his players beforehand that if they won, they should not celebrate excessively. Yet as soon as the buzzer sounded, he ran onto the court and embraced Dawkins. When Dawkins reminded him of his pregame warning, Krzyzewski screamed "Fuck it!" and continued to hug him. Krzyzewski would regret it the next day when his team, emotionally spent, lost to Maryland in the final.

After winning 23 games in 1984–85, the Blue Devils embarked on a historic season the following year. With Dawkins and his classmates now seniors, the Blue Devils started the season ranked No. 6 in the country. They won their first 16 contests, claimed the ACC championship, and entered the NCAA Tournament ranked No. 1 with a 32–2 record. *Sports Illustrated* put them on its cover under the headline DUKE'S THE TEAM TO BEAT. The Blue Devils fulfilled that billing by advancing to the NCAA championship game, where they lost to Louisville, 72–69. It was a painful way to end the season, but it represented a major triumph for the players, the program, and the up-and-coming coach with the hard-to-spell last name.

Plenty of college basketball programs have ridden the wave of a single recruiting class, only to sink back into oblivion when those players leave. So in many respects, the real validation came the following year, when Duke won 24 games and reached the NCAA Tournament's Sweet Sixteen. In 1987–88, the Blue Devils returned to the Final Four thanks largely to junior forward Danny Ferry, who was Krzyzewski's most heralded recruit to that point. That was the first of three straight Final Four appearances, but each time the Blue Devils reached the big stage, they found ways to come up short.

The many near misses elevated Krzyzewski to a rare and short-lived tenure as a lovable loser. He was humble, bright, well-spoken, and very funny. His players were good students as well as excellent athletes. They charmed the national press, which was all too eager to contrast them with teams like UNLV, whose players were mostly African American and were coached by Jerry Tarkanian, an avowed renegade who was always in hot water with the NCAA. Krzyzewski bristled at the blatant racial stereotyping, but it continued nonetheless.

Looking back on those years, Krzyzewski laughs at the notion that all those trips to the Final Four without a title were weighing on him. "I used to say to my family and staff, 'You gotta be shitting me,'" he says. "We won thirty eight games in three years. Now we get to the Final Four and because we don't win it, someone says I'm a failure? I've got a monkey on my back? If I was a zookeeper, I'd want about eight more of those monkeys on my back."

All the near misses provided Krzyzewski with the knowledge he would need to coach his players through their upset over UNLV in the 1991 Final Four. He continued to fight off rationalization the next day, when he got all over his guys at practice for acting cocky, even though they really weren't. His anger forced the players to maintain their edge, which propelled them to a win over Kansas on Monday night, delivering Krzyzewski his first NCAA championship.

Almost every top player returned the following season. The Blue Devils started off as the consensus No. 1 team in America and never relinquished that ranking, even though they lost two games by a combined six points. That team was a juggernaut, and Christian Laettner was its face. With his movie-star good looks and pissy attitude, Laettner engendered all kinds of vitriol, not only from opposing crowds but also from his own teammates. Many coaches might have tried to smooth out Laettner's rough edges, but Krzyzewski never did. Friction may be unpleasant, but it is authentic. And it warded off complacency in the locker room.

The 1991–92 Duke Blue Devils were a team of traveling rock stars, but it looked like the party was going to end on March 28, when they were taken to overtime by a plucky Kentucky squad in the NCAA Tournament's East Regional final in Philadelphia. After the Wildcats took a one-point lead with 2.1 seconds remaining, Duke called time out. As the players came to the huddle, their coach faced the ultimate PEAK moment. The first thing he said to them was, "We're going to win." That showed persistence. He took out his clipboard and designed a play calling for the team's sophomore forward, Grant Hill, to launch a three-quarters-court pass to Laettner. "Can you throw it?" Krzyzewski asked Hill.

"Yes," Hill replied. This demonstrated empathy. Krzyzewski understood that Hill might be nervous, so he redirected his focus. By asking that question, he forced Hill to picture himself making that pass.

Then Krzyzewski asked Laettner, "Can you make the shot?"

Laettner replied, "Coach, if Grant gets me the ball, I'll make the damn shot."

Laettner's confidence was rooted in his certainty that Krzyzewski would not change who he was and what he believed because of the circumstances. It also reflected his trust in Krzyzewski's knowledge. He knew his coach was drawing up a good play. Sure enough, Hill made a perfect pass, Laettner made the damn shot, and the following weekend the Blue Devils became the first school in nineteen years to win back-to-back NCAA championships. For all the friction in that locker room, for all expectations and the growing sense that the outside world wanted to see them come up short, the Blue Devils tapped into their ethnic pride and staked their claim in America. Krzyzewski had gotten his players to *Us,* and they stayed there.

There would be no more sympathy for the Devils. As his teams continued to dominate the sport—two years later, Duke returned to the NCAA championship game, where it lost to Arkansas—Krzyzewski dealt with a level of celebrity and enmity that he could never have prepared for. That had implications nationally, where his team became the premier brand in college basketball, as well as locally, where he was increasingly devoting time and energy to areas that had nothing to do with basketball. He took on too much, too fast, always encumbered by the soldier's duty to fulfill his commitments.

His hard-charging nature took its toll in the fall of 1994, when Krzyzewski started experiencing intense pain in his lower back. For months, he refused to see a doctor, but Mickie finally talked him into going—and insisted she go with him. She was aghast when Mike downplayed the situation, saying only that his back felt "tight." She was not pleased. "He would use euphemisms for the word *pain*," Mickie says. "I finally stopped him and said, 'Wait a minute, that is not what is happening. Tell him the truth.'"

Krzyzewski's doctor ordered an MRI, which revealed that the coach was indeed suffering from a herniated disc. He had surgery on October 22, but instead of heeding his doctor's advice to take his time recovering, he was back in his office the following week. Practice had already begun, and there was no way he was going to desert his troops.

The pain got worse. It kept him from sleeping. As the weeks went on, Mickie could see her husband slowly deteriorate. The worst was a weeklong trip over Thanksgiving to a tournament in Hawaii. Krzyzewski didn't sleep all week, and the flights were ruinous. After he returned to Durham, things continued to worsen, but Krzyzewski would still not admit he was hurting. Grant Hill had graduated and the team was in a rebuilding season. He knew how badly his guys needed him.

As the Blue Devils stumbled, Krzyzewski became increasingly frustrated at his inability to stem the tide. One night after he returned home late from a road game, Mickie heard him chewing himself out as he stood in the bathroom. "You compromising son of a bitch," he barked at the man in the mirror.

When the Blue Devils started off the ACC season with a rare loss at home to Clemson, Mickie decided the situation was truly dire. As her husband was leaving for work the day before a road game at Georgia Tech, she informed him that she had made an appointment with his doctor, and she wanted him to meet her at his office. When he started to protest, she cut him off. "If you're not there when I show up," she said, "don't come home." It was not like her to issue such wifely ultimatums—"Our relationship is not one where I am particularly hysterical around him," she says—and she honestly didn't know what she would do if Mike refused her. "I drove to the doctor's office the whole time just praying he would be there," she says. "When I pulled into the parking lot, I saw his car."

That very afternoon, the doctor admitted Krzyzewski to a hospital, where he was treated for pain and exhaustion. At first, the school announced that he was taking a brief leave, but it was soon clear he could not return that season. Krzyzewski, in fact, wondered whether he would ever return. Besides the physical pain, he was racked with guilt at leaving his team, which went into a hellacious tailspin under his assistant, Pete Gaudet, winning just two ACC games and failing to reach the NCAA Tournament for the first time in twelve years. As the weeks went on, Krzyzewski fell into what sounds very much like depression. He underwent daily therapy at his house with Keith Brodie, the recently retired university president who had previously been the chair of the school's psychiatry department. Knowing that Krzyzewski wasn't much of a reader, Brodie showed him movies he hoped would deliver a healing message. He also showed Krzyzewski video of him coaching with joy and passion, which only underscored for Krzyzewski how far he had plummeted.

"It was more than back pain. I lost emotion. I lost feeling," he told me. "I would watch me coach and then wonder, 'How the hell would I do that? How the hell was I that passionate from all that?' That's why I offered my resignation to Butters. I didn't feel it. I couldn't feel anything, to be quite frank with you, and I was sick.

It was kind of like the perfect storm. But I didn't drown, and it wasn't because of me. It was because of the help I had."

The time away, combined with the therapy, allowed Krzyzewski to slowly climb out of the water. At the end of the season he held a press conference and declared himself fit to return. He changed the way he managed his time, made some adjustments to his staff so it would be younger, and dove back into recruiting with his usual energy. It took a few years, but the succession of classes produced yet another dominant season in 1998–99, when the Blue Devils, who featured two sophomore forwards, Elton Brand and Shane Battier, spent most of the season ranked No. 1. A disappointing 77–74 loss to No. 2 Connecticut in the title game did nothing to diminish Krzyzewski's ethnic pride. "I have a hard time being sad. Sorry," he said in his postgame press conference. "I don't coach for winning. I coach for relationships." Krzyzewski was widely ridiculed for the remark, but he didn't care. He would rather people mock him than see his pain.

When Bobby Hurley was a junior point guard during the 1991–92 season, Krzyzewski invited him into his office to watch some tape. Instead of seeing basketball plays, however, Hurley was treated to a spool of images showing him in various states of whinery—mouth agape, arms raised, eyes rolling, yelling at his teammates, complaining to referees. "Is this how you want your teammates to see you?" Krzyzewski asked. That meeting provided Hurley with a moment of clarity. It made him smarter and tougher, which enabled him to lead the Blue Devils to a second consecutive championship.

That type of exchange has been paused, freeze-framed, rewound, and replayed countless times during Krzyzewski's coaching career. It is a critical tactic in how he gets his teams to *Us*. He doesn't want his players just to think like winners. He wants them to *feel* like winners. That means they need to see what he sees.

Most every player who has come through Duke has at some point been on the business end of Krzyzewski's ethnic pressure. At the end of J. J. Redick's sophomore season, which ended with the Blue Devils losing to UConn in the 2004 Final Four, he came to the coach's office for what he thought was going to be a nice pep talk. Instead, Krzyzewski told Redick that it was his fault the team had lost, that his off-court conditioning, sleeping, eating, and partying habits made him unworthy of being a champion. Redick was pissed, but he knew Krzyzewski was right. Two years later, Redick was the national player of the year, largely on the basis of his superb conditioning.

Quinn Cook was a freshman reserve midway through the 2011–12 season when he got word that Krzyzewski and his top assistant, Jeff Capel, wanted to meet with him in the coach's office. Cook also assumed he was in for some praise, but instead the coaches showed him video of him sitting on the bench during games and not cheering for his teammates. Krzyzewski and Capel ripped Cook for his selfishness and suggested that he should turn in his uniform. Cook was devastated. He felt like he was letting the family down.

By the time he was a senior, Cook had become one of the best leaders Krzyzewski ever had, serving as a captain on Duke's 2015 NCAA championship team.

This ability to empathize with his players based on facial expression and body language is Krzyzewski's great coaching gift. When senior forward Kyle Singler had a subpar game in the 2010 South Regional final win over Baylor, Krzyzewski showed him video that focused not on Singler's shooting form or decisions with the ball, but on his posture. "You're being an upper-body player here. That means you were thinking about just yourself," Krzyzewski said. "If you're talking and giving instruction, you get outside of yourself, and you become a lower-body player. Your feet are wider. You're in a stronger stance. Your arms go out, your feet go out." Singler got the message. The next weekend, he was lower-body strong again, winning Most Outstanding Player as Duke won yet another crown.

Krzyzewski used the same approach while coaching the U.S. National Team at the Olympics. While preparing the Americans for the 2012 Olympics in London, Krzyzewski observed to Kevin Durant that every time he spoke, his eyes were on the floor.

"That's because I'm shy," Durant said.

"Kevin," Krzyzewski said, "you *can't* be shy. The guys need you *not* to be shy." Later, while watching video with the team, Krzyzewski saw Durant make a great play and run downcourt with a confident look on his face. He paused the video and asked each of Durant's teammates to tell him how empowered they felt when he looked like that.

He wants his players to be instinctive, not calculating—to follow the courage of their convictions, just as his grandparents did when they set sail for America. That's why he uses a motion offense, which he learned from Bob Knight. The system does not involve set plays. Rather, it puts players in position to read and react to what the defense is doing. That's why Krzyzewski tends to recruit versatile players, and while he rules his team with West Point discipline, he wants his guys to play with freedom. Thus his favorite metaphor: "If you put a plant in a jar, it will grow to the shape of the jar. But if you put a plant outside, there is no limit as to how much it can grow."

Instinctiveness begets adaptability. Krzyzewski is constantly on guard against being trapped by old habits. He makes decisions on playing time based on performance, not hierarchy. I remember interviewing him once at an early-season practice when he told me he was leaning toward starting freshman Elliot Williams at point guard over Greg Paulus, who was a senior. When I asked him if he was worried that Paulus would be upset by that, he shot me an annoyed look. "No," he said. "This isn't some inherited wealth."

The willingness to share blunt truths gives Krzyzewski his authenticity. If he is willing to tell a new girlfriend she was his third choice for a date, he damn sure isn't going to be shy about telling a player he isn't good enough to start. "They know they're going to get the truth from me all the time," he says. He insists his players do the same for each other. Krzyzewski often says that he works to instill three systems—an offensive system, a defensive system, and a communication system. His practices are a cacophony of conversation. If the players stop talking, he will halt the action and remind them he wants to hear their voices.

Krzyzewski's Blue Devils have been clipped a few times in the early rounds of the NCAA Tournament, but by and large they do not lose many games they are supposed to win. This is remarkable given that every time Duke plays a road game, it gets its opponent's best shot. He believes that by keeping players in attack mode, it renders them impervious to pressure. After his former assistant, Mike Brey, became the coach at Notre Dame, he found himself coaching an excellent team that had risen to the top of the rankings. When Brey asked his former boss for advice, Krzyzewski replied, "Coach like you're playing with house money."

Krzyzewski has been approached many times about coaching in the NBA, but he only seriously considered two offers: in 1990, when the Celtics offered him their head coaching position, and 2004, when the Lakers tried to hire him. He turned them down because he understood who he was and where his skills would be best applied. The one job he did take coaching pros was the only one that paid no salary. In 2006, he agreed to become Team USA's national coach. USA Basketball had suffered a string of humiliating losses, but Krzyzewski revived the organization by treating it like a college program, even though the players were now seasoned professionals. He coached the United States to three Olympic gold medals. Many people speculated that by taking on the added responsibilities, Krzyzewski was going to drain himself of precious energy, but if anything, it revitalized him. By working with NBA coaches like Nate McMillan, Mike D'Antoni, and Tom Thibodeau, not to mention his good friend Jim Boeheim of Syracuse, Krzyzewski added to his basketball knowledge, which infused him with newfound energy he could apply to his Duke teams. "When you learn another way of doing things, you're anxious to do it," he says. Being the USA coach also helped with recruiting, which has prompted much envious sniping from his peers.

It would be inauthentic for Krzyzewski to encourage his players to trust their instincts if he weren't willing to do the same, even in the most pressurized situations. Krzyzewski did just that in the final seconds of Duke's 2010 NCAA championship game against Butler. The Bulldogs were a No. 5 seed, and their romp to the final had echoes of the movie *Hoosiers,* whose final scene was filmed in Butler's home arena, Hinkle Fieldhouse. That the Final Four was being hosted just a few miles from Butler's campus in Indianapolis only added to the storyline. With 3.6 seconds on the clock and Duke clinging to a one-point lead, Duke's senior center, Brian Zoubek, went to the foul line. Krzyzewski's instincts told him that his team would be in trouble if the game went into overtime. So after Zoubek made the first free throw, he gave his player an unconventional order: Miss the second on purpose. That meant Butler, which did not have a time out, would have to find a way to advance the ball 94 feet without an in-bounds pass. On the other hand, it preserved the possibility that Duke could lose in regulation if Butler made a three-pointer.

Many coaches in that situation would consider such a risky maneuver, but very few would actually follow through on it.

Krzyzewski did, and it almost backfired, but a halfcourt heave by Butler forward Gordon Hayward rimmed out.

In 2015, Krzyzewski claimed his fifth NCAA championship, which left him in second place all-time behind UCLA's John Wooden. Three of Duke's five starters were one-and-done freshmen. Not only was that team young, but it relied heavily upon a lumbering 6′11″ freshman forward named Jahlil Okafor. Because of Okafor's size, he had difficulty defending the screen-and-roll, and his teammates were too inexperienced to understand the complicated maneuvers that could compensate for that. So midway through the season, Krzyzewski did something he had never done before: He played zone defense. He also dismissed an upperclassman guard named Rasheed Sulaimon for disciplinary reasons in late January, which left his team with just eight scholarship players. His belief never wavered. "Eight is enough" became his mantra, and sure enough it was. After the Blue Devils came back from nine points down in the second half of the final to defeat Wisconsin, his oldest daughter, Debbie, stood amazed in a hallway. "Nobody believed this could happen," she said, "except the kids in that locker room."

Unlike Tom Izzo and a lot of other coaches, Krzyzewski has no problem with his players using social media. He assumes they will post stupid things that get them in hot water, but that, he says, is part of getting an education. Though he has not set up an official Twitter account, Krzyzewski does have an alias so he can follow what is going on. He is a prolific texter and emoji enthusiast, and he has always made an effort to get to know his players' favorite music. "Part of that is you feel music," he says. "If I want to find out how to make them feel a certain way, I have to understand the things they do. If I use some words or a phrase from a song they like when I'm talking, their attention picks up. It's like saying I'm in their world. And I like it. It keeps me young."

If he didn't adapt, if he didn't maintain his persistence and grow his empathy while staying true to who he is, Krzyzewski would be unable to continue acquiring the knowledge he needs to stay relevant—and indeed, highly successful—for this long. Jay Bilas, in his role as an ESPN broadcaster, spends as much time around Krzyzewski as any of his former players. He is struck by how often his old coach says something insightful that Bilas has never heard before. "He's still the same great guy, still has the same core principles, but in the way he goes about his job, he's infinitely better," Bilas says. "The guys ten years after us played for a better coach than we did. The guys playing today are playing for a better coach than J. J. Redick or Grant Hill did. We probably feel the same way that guys who played for John Wooden felt, or guys who played for Dean Smith. We would all say we played for the best coach ever. It just happens that we're the ones who are right."

On December 22, 2016, I interviewed Krzyzewski in his office for my Campus Insiders show. My timing was not great. The night before, Duke had defeated Elon in a game that was marred by an ugly episode where Duke's volatile junior guard, Grayson Allen, had kicked an opposing player. It was the third and most blatant such incident involving Allen over the previous year, and the sports world was ablaze with hot takes and recriminations. Given the circumstances, I wondered if Krzyzewski would go through with our interview and, if so, whether he would be in a talkative mood. But despite getting almost no sleep he was sanguine when I arrived the next morning. When I asked how he was doing, he grinned and said, "Oh, you know. Life is a cabaret."

Krzyzewski did not handle the situation well in the immediate aftermath. He reflexively reverted to the defiant posture that is forever a part of his makeup—the ethnically proud soldier trapped behind enemy lines. He made clear that while he believed what Allen

did was wrong—and he had brought him into the Elon locker room
to apologize to the player he kicked—Krzyzewski did not think
there should be further punishment. "I don't need to satisfy what
other people think that I should do," he said. "Anyone else who wants
to take shots about anything else, about Duke and me or whatever,
go for it. Because that's territory that I'm comfortable with."

By the time I got to his office the following morning, Krzyzewski was thinking more clearly. He was also listening to the smart
advice being given to him by his communications staff and athletic
director. The school issued a statement that Allen would be sus-
pended indefinitely. (It turned out to be for one game.) I told
Krzyzewski that I thought it was good that Allen had faced the
cameras in the locker room to express his remorse, but I wished he
had sat up straight and looked everyone in the eye instead of slouch-
ing and keeping his head down.

Krzyzewski disagreed. He preferred the authenticity. "People
should see what he was really feeling," he said. "I mean, look at him.
He's just a fucking kid."

Krzyzewski's office has an ultra-high ceiling and is filled with
pictures—of his family, his players, his staff, his closest friends.
Krzyzewski likes to tell people that he is a big *picture guy*, not to
mention a *big-picture* guy. He likes being surrounded by images that
evoke feelings. They remind him to trust his instincts.

One of those special memories occurred in 2001, when Krzyzewski was inducted into the Naismith Memorial Basketball Hall
of Fame. The ceremony was emotional for many reasons. He and
Bob Knight had experienced a very public falling-out dating back to
the 1992 Final Four, when Duke defeated Indiana in the semifinal
en route to winning Krzyzewski's second title. In the run-up to that
meeting, there had been much conversation in the press about the
pupil-versus-teacher matchup, and though Krzyzewski offered
Knight much praise, he also tried to downplay the storyline by

emphasizing that he had other mentors as well. Unbeknownst to Krzyzewski, Knight took offense. When the game was over, he blew by Krzyzewski, refusing the postgame handshake. He also handed a letter to a mutual friend, who delivered it to Krzyzewski right before he took the dais for the postgame press conference. The letter informed Krzyzewski that if a divorce was what he wanted, then that's what he would get. Aside from a few brief stretches of civility, the two had not spoken until 2001 when Krzyzewski, in a move that shocked his wife, called Knight and asked if Knight would present him for induction into the Hall. When Knight gave his speech and summoned Krzyzewski to the stage, Krzyzewski fell into his arms with tears in his eyes.

Fittingly, Knight was also on hand as a game analyst for ESPN on November 16, 2011, when Krzyzewski passed him on the NCAA's all-time wins list with a victory over Michigan State in Madison Square Garden. The two shared an embrace that night as well and remained close thereafter, although with Knight in the mix, they are always one perceived slight from another rupture.

For a guy who wanted to quit hundreds of times while he was at West Point, in many respects Krzyzewski never left. To this day, before he goes to bed each night, he maps out his plan for the next day. "I think it comes from West Point, where you lay out your uniform the night before," Krzyzewski told me. "It helps you make effective use of your time. It gets me excited because I'm going to do something I've planned to do, what I love to do, and it's different every day."

His program is not on autopilot by any means, but it benefits from the culture instilled over three decades of working hard and winning big. Call it ethnic momentum. When players come to Duke, they are reminded every day that there is a great history they must honor and advance, just like Krzyzewski understood that he owed it to his grandparents to make the most of the opportunities America afforded him. If the freshmen fall short of those standards, the seniors apply the pressure. If the seniors fall short, there are plenty of former players hanging around to deliver the message. That includes the former players who are assistant coaches. "We give them a set of values that they need to take forward," Krzyzewski says. "Like, our culture has gone through so much. We fought for that, and we're passing that along to you. Take it, knucklehead."

Krzyzewski went through the most painful experience of his life the day after Christmas in 2013, when his brother, Bill, died of complications following cancer surgery. Just as was the case with his father, Krzyzewski tried to get back to Chicago before his brother passed, but he did not make it in time. It's one thing to see a parent die—Krzyzewski's mother succumbed to cancer in the fall of 1996—but this was a much deeper loss. "One of the reasons he's a good coach is he never believes it's over," Mickie says. "He's always saying, 'We're gonna fix it, we're gonna get better, we're gonna learn from our mistakes.' So something as final and painful as death just knocks him for a loop."

That stubbornness has gotten him into trouble before, but he is older now, more knowledgeable. Two weeks after our visit, Krzyzewski underwent back surgery to repair another herniated disc. There was no rushing back this time; he waited the full four weeks before returning to his team. Over the years, there have been a few times when Mickie had to remind him that he was overextending himself again, but for the most part he has kept things in balance. He looks a lot younger than he is, thanks to his remarkably persistent hair, which he insists remains mostly black with no outside help. "I do not color my hair," Krzyzewski once said in a postgame press conference. "That's a myth. My buddies would kill me."

Krzyzewski told me that when the time does come for him to retire, he does not want to choose his successor, although he hopes it will be one of his former players. Speculation as to when that day will come is a popular guessing game in the sport, but there is no

sign that Krzyzewski is slowing down. Besides, it's not like he needs
to stop coaching to spend more time with his family. Krzyzewski's
daughters have borne him ten grandchildren at last count, and they
all live in the Durham area. All three of his daughters have roles in
the program. Debbie is an assistant athletic director, special events
coordinator, and fund-raiser; Lindy owns a master's degree in clini-
cal psychology and works as a counselor for the athletes; and Jamie
is a writer who has coauthored three books with her father. And of
course, Mickie can still come and go as she pleases.

The family also helps Mike oversee his many philanthropic projects, from the Emily K. Center in Durham, which provides college
information and support for low-income residents, to the Coach K
Center on Leadership and Ethics at Duke's Fuqua School of Business. Along with his position as an executive in residence for the
Center on Leadership and Ethics, Krzyzewski is on the board of
several charities, including the Duke Children's Hospital and the V
Foundation, which raises money to fight cancer in honor of his late
friend Jim Valvano, who coached N.C. State to the 1983 NCAA
championship.

Nor does he have a lot of hobbies. He is a basketball coach, plain
and simple, full stop. He does a little gardening at home, but that's
about it. He doesn't play golf. The one outside passion Krzyzewski
has adopted is wine. It started with a fund-raiser he hosted for the V
Foundation at a winery in Napa Valley, California. Though he does
not consider himself a true expert, he keeps an extensive collection
in a temperature-controlled wine cellar at home, and he has developed considerable knowledge about how wine is made and where it
comes from. "Wine is the best drink of all because usually it's shared.
It's a lovely drink," he said during our phone conversation. I prodded
him to tell me more about his tastes. He reported that he's "basically
a Cab guy." When he drinks white, it's usually a Sauvignon Blanc or
Pinot Grigio. He's not into Chardonnay. He also informed me that

"rosé is coming back a lot," which I did not know. "And you know what?" he added. "I like the people who do it. They have the highest standards and they want you to love their product. If there's something wrong, they don't want you to have it at all."

I didn't want to offend him, but I couldn't help but laugh. It was hard to imagine him sipping Sauvignon Blanc with his parents in that second-floor flat on Cortez Street, or discussing whether rosé was coming back when he was running the streets with his buddies at night. "I grew up where we had highballs, y'know?" he said. "Whiskey and ginger ale. I was never a beer guy. My brother drank mostly Crown Royal." When I pointed out the contrast, I got the feeling that it had never occurred to him before. Then he laughed, too. "No, you're right. Polish family. Inner city. Wine was not our thing," he said. "It's kind of an upset, really."

Jim Harbaugh

"PEOPLE CAN WORK WITH THE TRUTH."

He couldn't take not competing. It killed him to stand still. So what if he was a rookie quarterback with a bright future? He needed to get into the game—now. So Jim Harbaugh went to his head coach with a strange request: Put me in on special teams so I can cover punts and kickoffs. "My first reaction was, 'Are you crazy?'" Mike Ditka told me. "But he was serious. He just wanted to contribute."

It was early in the 1987 NFL season. Harbaugh was a first-round draft pick of the Chicago Bears. He started out as the third-string quarterback, which meant he might warm up a little before kickoff, but then he'd spend the rest of the game holding a clipboard. "I'd leave the stadium and it was like I wasn't even in a game. Just shower and go home," he said. Harbaugh wasn't trying to be a hero when he made the request. Lord knows, his presence covering kicks was not going to determine the outcome. But for as long as he could remember, Harbaugh had a deep and abiding need for competition. It was literally in his blood. "I wanted to sweat," he told me. "I wanted to be sore. It feels good to get out there and be sore and feel like a man. Football's a great game for that."

Ditka was open to the idea. So during practice the following week, Harbaugh got some reps with the special teams unit. When Sunday came, Ditka put him in the game. "He had no fear," Ditka recalled. "He went down and hit the wedge as hard as he could." This continued for several weeks. Harbaugh recalls one particular play when he was running down the sideline and fending off a blocker. A second blocker came out of nowhere, knocked him clear off his feet, and sent him flying out of bounds. It hurt like hell, but not nearly as much as standing on the sideline did.

Eventually, Ditka thought better of the idea and pulled Harbaugh off the field. The Bears' starting quarterback, Jim McMahon, had gotten hurt, and besides, Ditka said, "I'm not sure my owner was too crazy about it." But the episode gave Ditka a window into the brash young quarterback's competitive soul. That need for contact, that disdain for standing idle, drove Harbaugh to play for fourteen years as an NFL quarterback far more than his physical talents did. And it now lies at the heart of his ability to get to *Us* as a coach who has won big and fast wherever he has been—one NFL job plus three in college, including his current one at the University of Michigan, his alma mater.

No one knows Jim's manic competitiveness better than his father, Jack, who coached football for four decades at ten different colleges. But even he was taken aback by a phone conversation he had with Jim during his redshirt sophomore season at Michigan. After sitting out as a freshman, thereby preserving four years of eligibility, Jim was trying to work his way up the team's depth chart. Wolverines coach Bo Schembechler was putting the players through grueling two-a-day practices in the summer heat. Jim told his dad during that call that he went on a two-mile run during the breaks between workouts. Jack had always exhorted his children to attack the day with "an enthusiasm unknown to mankind," but this seemed extreme even to him. What he realized was that his son didn't go running just to help his endurance. Jim needed to know he was working hard while his competition was resting.

The athlete's code has always taught the mantra of "no pain, no progress," but Harbaugh bristled at my suggestion that he is not comfortable unless he's uncomfortable. "*Comfortable* is not a word I have ever associated with sports and football. It's a confusing word for me," he said. "It's just about building a callus. The human body is an amazing organism. It craves contact. Like on your foot, if you've got the wrong shoes and you get a blister. It's soft and pussing and then eventually it pops and calluses over. So the body repairs itself, and then it's tougher and stronger."

Harbaugh has a studious mind, with a train of thought that vacillates between fixation and distraction. Mike Ditka was not the first person to ask him if he was crazy, and he certainly wasn't the last. Harbaugh has often described himself as forever being the kid in school who liked to throw rocks at beehives. He doesn't want to get stung, necessarily, but he needs to know that he might.

Discomfort, pain, soreness—it doesn't matter what Harbaugh calls it. What matters is that he feels it. That's the great thing about this sport. It hurts like hell, but it never lies. "Nothing tells the truth like football," Harbaugh told me. "You cannot email or bullshit your way into being good. Throw the balls out there and compete. Maybe the other guy's stronger, but there's still a way to beat him. You can outlast him, you can outthink him, you can outrun him. Maybe get yourself stronger. I don't always know what it is, but I always know there's a way."

The office is unimpressive for a coach of his stature. It's not very big, and the walls are white and spare. He has a few pictures and memorabilia in a bookcase, but mostly the walls are uncovered save for a greaseboard affixed to a closet. As a rule, Harbaugh prefers to have very few things on display. Soon after he took the job here in December 2014, he stripped a bunch of sayings and quotes off the team's meeting and weight rooms. "I would ask guys who were in the weight room every single day, 'What's the best saying you've seen in here?' And they couldn't come up with one," he said. "It just struck me that that's a lot of white noise, so you can't remember any of it. If you can't remember, then it's going to be hard to execute."

His desk, on the other hand, is a bit of a mess. Harbaugh is constantly jotting ideas on random sheets of paper as well as in his ever-present spiral notebooks, which he keeps in cabinets in his office and other areas of the facility. Harbaugh is excellent in spontaneous moments, but he would rather his actions be meticulously planned. He often writes down ideas he wants to impart at the start of a day's practice. The way he figures it, he only spends ten minutes talking to his team each day. He wants to make every second count.

Amid the spartan walls and the cluttered desk sits the center-piece of the whole operation: a desktop computer with dual monitors. This is where Harbaugh organizes his entire life into an endless row of Excel spreadsheets. He is an avowed Excelholic. He uses it for all kinds of tasks. "I can paint pictures with Excel. I'm very proud," he told me. He wrote a 9,000-word introduction for a photography book about Michigan football entirely on Excel. He reached for his mouse and started clicking through the different tabs, dating back to his days as the head coach of the San Francisco 49ers. He could use premade templates, but he prefers to create them himself. He'll spend hours working on a calendar just so he can save ten minutes when things get rolling. As his father, Jack, put it, "Nobody likes busywork more than Jim."

As Harbaugh clicked through his spreadsheets, he landed on the schedule he put together for his team's recent weeklong trip to Rome. Most coaches would be happy to delegate such tasks to an underling so they can spend time recruiting or studying video. Not Jim Harbaugh. "I like to do the itineraries," he said. "Then I'm not out there going, 'Why aren't we doing it this way? We could save five minutes.' Can't have that. Have to cut down drag."

If we follow this workflow, from the unadorned walls to the disorderly desk to the precision of his spreadsheets, we can glean an understanding of how Harbaugh gets to *Us*. If his players can remember what he tells them, then they can execute it. "A good coach or teacher can make the hard subject matter seem easy," he said. "Like, I'm really good at teaching kids how to ride bikes. I've got a simple plan. It's A, B, C. A, accelerate. Get going. B, balance. Find your balance. C, confidence. Now you're riding a bike. It's a metaphor for life in some ways."

When Harbaugh was eleven years old and living in Iowa, he entered a Punt, Pass and Kick competition. Having won the local competition first, he advanced to a regional competition that was a couple hours' drive away. His parents couldn't take him, so he hitched a ride with two other boys. He worked hard to prepare, but he came up short. Even worse, he lost to one of the other kids in the car. So he had to travel all the way home alongside the trophy and the boy who won it. It hurt like hell.

"I remember I didn't say a word. I just sat there," he told me. "Nobody talked to me. My vivid memory was just staring out the window and I was crying. But I didn't want them to *see* that I was crying. It was just that gut-wrenching, nasty feeling of losing. I was seven, but I was like, 'Okay, for the rest of the year, I'm gonna work on my punt and my kick and my pass.'"

The tears stung, but they watered his seeds of persistence. Fortunately, he would have many more chances to compete. He had a built-in teammate, opponent, and tormenter in his brother, John, who is fifteen months older. They were exposed to sports since liter-ally before they could walk. Their mother, Jackie, used to put them into strollers and take them to her husband's football practices. When the Harbaugh boys were young, the family moved three times in five years. That forced the boys and, eventually, their younger sister, Joani, who is five years younger than Jim, to learn how to adapt to unfamiliar environments. "I always liked the new adventure," Jim said. "It taught me a lot of things. When you go in a new environment, you can't just sit around the house and expect good people to knock at your door and want to be your friend. You've got to get out there and engage."

Jim and John did their fair share of battling, but they also loved being on the same team. When they were young, they set up pretend basketball games in the basement, creating a makeshift hoop out of a wire hanger. As they grew, they competed at everything, from sports to school to mowing the lawn to seeing who was quicker at racing upstairs to fetch their dad a beer.

Besides their parents, John and Jim had another important role model in their grandfather, Joe Cipiti. Grandpa Joe, as he was called, came over from Sicily when he was four years old. He was loving and stern, but he was empathetic to his core. Jackie recalls the early days of their marriage when the hours were long and the money was tight. Every few weeks, her parents would show up at their doorstep with a bag of groceries. "My dad always said, in the end, the only people you really have is your family," Jackie says.

Joe was an auto mechanic in those days. Jim fondly remembers working at Grandpa Joe's filling station, where he and John pumped gas, squeegeed windshields, and kept the change. In many ways, Grandpa Joe was Jim's first coach. "If you were going to cut the grass, he'd teach you, he'd show you, and then he'd let you do it," Jim said. "That's how it works in coaching. You give them a tool, give them a teaching point, but at some point the player has to learn to do it himself."

Both Harbaugh sons played hard, but Jim had a hot streak that could be problematic. As a close high school buddy, Rob Pollock, once put it, "Neither one liked to lose, but Jim had a screw loose about it." As a baseball pitcher, he once beaned a girl because she was crowding the plate. When he was in the fifth grade, his mother was called into school to discuss some problems he was having on the playground. She was initially told that several boys were involved, but when she got to school, she discovered she was the only parent who had been called in. When they told Jackie that the real problem was that her son was too competitive, she set them straight, Harbaugh style. "Being competitive is not a bad thing," she lectured. "People compete every day of their lives."

The episode hinted at a dynamic that follows Jim to this day: He plays hard, plays to win, but it puts people off. Jack guesses Jim was about nine years old and living in Iowa when he asked if Jack was going to take another job and make the family move again. Jack said he didn't think so. "Well, I hope you get one," Jim replied, "because I just lost my last friend."

As it turned out, Jack did take a job the following year as a defensive backs coach at the University of Michigan. Ultimately, this would give the family the stability of living in one place for six years. Jim and John were regulars at practices and games. They would hang with the players in the locker room, play catch on the sidelines of the practice field, and work during the games as ball boys.

The move to Ann Arbor brought the Harbaughs under the sway of Bo Schembechler, who in his fourth season was already building a powerhouse. During Jack's time on Schembechler's staff, the Wolverines won four Big Ten titles, finished ranked in the top 10 every year, and at one point went to three straight Rose Bowls.

Schembechler was austere and imposing, but he also felt like part of the family. One time Schembechler walked into the Harbaughs' house and found Jim lying on the couch watching television. "Why don't you do something productive!" he barked. Jim grabbed a book and pretended to read it. Then there was the day Schembechler walked into his office and found Jim sitting in his chair with his feet on the desk. Bo teased him about it, but not so badly that Jim felt the need to put his feet on the floor.

Jim and John shared a third-floor bedroom of their house in Ann Arbor that had been converted from an attic. When they wrestled, their parents could swear they were going to fall through the living room ceiling. One particularly fierce argument prompted them to lay down a piece of duct tape to divide the room properly, which led to an even fiercer argument about where exactly the tape should go. John has told a story about the time they were wrestling in a pool and Jim tried to drown him. Their feelings might get hurt, but the wounds never cut deep. "We had our set-tos here and there, but we could just laugh them right off," Jim said.

When Jim became a sophomore at Pioneer High School, he moved up to the varsity football team and won the job as starting quarterback. John, who was two years ahead of him, was a decent player, but there was no question as to who was the better athlete. John and Jim both insist there was no jealousy. "We were always competing, but we had each other's back and we always rooted for each other," John told me.

The six years the family spent in Ann Arbor were some of the happiest of their lives. Schembechler made everyone feel a part of the program. Jack worked long days, but he would try to come home for an hour for dinner every night before heading back to the office. He would take his kids on one or two recruiting trips per season. Even Joani learned how to splice game film. Alas, it didn't last long, as Jack took a job in 1980 as the running backs coach at Stanford.

John was heading to Miami University in Oxford, Ohio, where he would play defensive back, but it was a pivotal year for Jim, who was entering his junior year of high school. While Jackie stayed behind with Joani to sell the house, Jack took Jim to California during the summer to get a head start.

After working out in camps, Jim became the starting quarterback at Palo Alto High School. Jack didn't think of Jim as a big-time prospect until one day when he was at practice throwing the ball with Stanford's star quarterback, a cocky young flamethrower named John Elway. After the workout, Elway walked by Jack and said, "Your boy's very impressive." By the time his senior season ended, Jim had received just two scholarship offers from Division I-A schools, Arizona and Wisconsin. But he wasn't getting the offer he really wanted.

Little did he know that that school's coach knew full well he wanted to recruit Jim, and knew full well Jim wanted to come. So Bo Schembechler waited until the end of the spring to invite Jim to campus for an official visit and offer him a scholarship. A few days later, Jim called to accept. He did have one question, though. "Uh, Coach, this is a full scholarship, right?" he asked. Schembechler laughed and assured him it was. After all that moving around, Jim Harbaugh was headed back to the only place he really thought of as home.

I n Harbaugh's mind, Bo Schembechler could do no wrong. "It was like playing for a living legend," he said. "I hung on every word he said, because I knew he was right." That could make things difficult when Schembechler got salty—such as the first time Harbaugh showed up late to a meeting and Schembechler bellowed, "You'll never play a down for Michigan in your life!" It wasn't the last time Bo made that threat.

The barbs would continue throughout Harbaugh's tenure in Ann Arbor. The words stung, but they never cut deep. "It didn't bother me because I knew he was being honest," Harbaugh says. "If the truth hurts, then so be it. It might hurt your feelings for a couple of days, but he never lied to me. People can work with the truth. At least they know where they stand."

It didn't take long for Harbaugh's work ethic to differentiate him from the other quarterbacks. He first became the starter as a redshirt sophomore, but his season ended in the fifth game, when he broke his left arm during a loss to Michigan State. He took over again the following season, leading the Wolverines to a 10–1–1 record and the nation's No. 2 ranking. He was tough, smart, and highly competitive, and he developed a remarkable ability to ad lib his way out of trouble.

As a senior, Harbaugh led the Wolverines to victory in nine of their first ten games. Once again, the season came down to the annual showdown with rival Ohio State. Harbaugh had yet to play in the Rose Bowl, and he simply couldn't imagine his career ending without it. A few days before the game, he was speaking to reporters when he blurted out, "We're going to play in the Rose Bowl this year. I guarantee it. We'll beat Ohio State. We'll be in Pasadena on January first."

Those comments caused quite a stir, but Schembechler was not angered in the least. "I might have said the same thing if I had any guts," he quipped. Looking back, Harbaugh says his remark was uncalculated, that he was just saying what he felt. People can work with the truth, right? It also taught him the importance of backing up one's words, which he did by throwing for 261 yards in a 26–24 win. After the game, Schembechler shared a quiet moment with his quarterback in his office and said, "I can't imagine how proud your dad must be."

Harbaugh finished third in the Heisman Trophy voting, and

even though Michigan lost to Arizona State in the Rose Bowl, he ended his career as the school's all-time record holder in passing yards. The Bears selected him with the 26th pick in the first round of the 1987 NFL draft. (One of the things that impressed the team was the way Harbaugh showed up for his pre-draft interview suffering from a bad case of chickenpox, yet he still played five games of racquetball against one of the assistants.) Harbaugh became the Bears' starter early in his second year. It was an awesome responsibility. He was the face of one of the league's marquee franchises, which was just three years removed from having won the Super Bowl with arguably the best team the NFL had ever seen.

Quarterbacking the Bears put Harbaugh under the auspices of yet another hot-tempered coach. He loved playing for Mike Ditka, respected that he was a Hall of Fame tight end who played with great toughness, but it was not easy functioning under Ditka's methods of truth telling. Things boiled over in humiliating fashion in October 1992, during a Monday Night Football game against the Vikings. With the Bears leading 20–0 early in the fourth quarter, Ditka signaled a running play for Walter Payton. Harbaugh got a little too careless with his ad libbing; he audibled at the line of scrimmage and threw an interception that was returned for a touchdown. Ditka erupted on the sidelines, screaming mercilessly at his quarterback before a national television audience. After the Bears lost 21–20, Ditka continued his diatribe in the postgame locker room, telling reporters, "I'm not going to put forty-seven players' futures in the hands of one player who thinks he knows more than I do."

Ditka told me that in retrospect, he regrets losing his cool the way he did that night. Nevertheless, he admired his quarterback's persistence. "Jim never got caught up in mistakes," Ditka said. "He always pushed forward. You don't see that much in a quarterback."

Things unraveled rather quickly for Harbaugh in Chicago. The team waived him in 1993 following back-to-back losing seasons. His career was resurrected in Indianapolis, where he took the Colts to the 1995 AFC Championship Game and finished second in the league's MVP voting. Harbaugh led the team to so many come-from-behind wins that season that he earned the nickname "Captain Comeback." His coach with the Colts, Ted Marchibroda, said of him, "I don't think I ever saw a guy who enjoyed football as much as he did. He enjoyed everything."

The one hiccup during his time in Indianapolis came in 1997, when Harbaugh had to take an unpaid one-month hiatus because he broke his hand during a fistfight with former Buffalo Bills quarterback Jim Kelly, who in his role as an ESPN broadcaster had suggested that Harbaugh "overdramatized" his injuries. Asked later whether he regretted the incident, Harbaugh replied, "I regret that I have a crack in one of my bones in my hand." It wasn't the most diplomatic answer, but at least it was the truth.

As Jim was grinding his way through the NFL, John was grinding his way through their father's profession. After finishing a nondescript playing career in college, John took a job as a running backs and linebacker coach at Western Michigan, where Jack was working as a college head coach for the first time. After Jack got fired in 1987 following a 3–8 season, he and John both went to the University of Pittsburgh to work as assistants. A year later, John moved on to Morehead State before landing at the University of Cincinnati in 1989 as a special teams coordinator. Jack, meanwhile, got another shot as a college head coach that same year, when he was hired by Western Kentucky.

Jack put together a decent record during his first five seasons at Western Kentucky, but when the spring of 1994 came around, the university president informed him that the school was going to drop the football program. Even though that turned out not to be the case, the anticipated move drove away recruits and depleted the team's schedule. The president made it clear that he intended to deprive the program of the resources it needed to succeed, thereby ensuring a slow, painful demise.

Jack was distraught. He was convinced he was on the verge of losing another job. As it happened, Jim was driving through the area on his way to vacation in Florida and he stopped by to visit. When Jack told him that he was resigned to losing his program, Jim said, "That doesn't sound like you. How can I help?" Jack said he doubted he could. "Well," Jim said, "you just got rid of some coaches. How about if I come on as an unpaid assistant to help you recruit? Would I be allowed to do that?"

They checked with the school, and it turns out he was. So that very day Jim signed a contract to be an unpaid assistant coach at Western Kentucky. Since he was on his way to Florida, Jack checked a recruiting newsletter for a list of prospects in the state. The first name on the list was a quarterback from Bradenton named Willie Taggart. Jim called him right away. He also contacted several other players in Florida with help from John, who from his perch at Cincinnati had a deep familiarity with the recruiting landscape. Jack thought the entire enterprise was a fool's errand, but he didn't have the heart to tell his boys. "I didn't think we had a chance, but I saw them so engaged," he told me. "I couldn't tell them what I really felt."

Taggart ended up being the cornerstone for a recruiting class that would go on to win the Division I-AA national championship in 2002. All told, Jim spent seven years working as an unpaid assistant while extending his own NFL career. After playing for four years with the Colts, he suited up for four different teams in four years. He retired in 2001 at the age of thirty-eight and did what he always knew he was going to do—get into coaching. He latched on with the Oakland Raiders, spending one season as a quality control coach and a second as a quarterbacks coach.

Those two years gave him the chance to build his knowledge, particularly during the long hours he spent with the team's owner, Al Davis, another intense competitor who tended to alienate people. Harbaugh peppered Davis with questions about how to evaluate players, develop talent, run an organization. Every day was an opportunity to learn—on the field, in the film room, and in the office, where he went from not knowing how to turn on a computer to mastering Excel spreadsheets.

Still, Harbaugh couldn't stand being a low-level assistant. It was just like being the third-string quarterback again. His limited experience gave him limited options, but he did secure an opportunity to be head coach at the University of San Diego. It was a Division I-AA program, but that didn't matter. Harbaugh had won a chance to get in the game.

There's a large hill behind the football practice field at the University of San Diego that is the perfect spot for a long, hard conditioning run. Imagine the reaction of the USD players when the new head coach told them to sprint up the hill in the hot sun, then joined them, then ran by them, then puked in a trash can. It was an authentic moment if ever there was one.

Harbaugh never saw the USD job as beneath his "level." From the start, he wanted to confer a big vision, and he thirsted for ways to enhance his knowledge of what he had inherited. "He really wanted to know all the information, everything that was going on within the program," says Tim Drevno, who was Harbaugh's first offensive coordinator at USD. "He dug in on recruiting. He wanted to know about the budget, about how the secretary did her job. He really set the tone that we were all in this thing together and we're going to collaborate on this. Everybody's got strengths, everybody's got weaknesses, we need each other to make this thing great. So it doesn't matter whose idea it is, as long as it works."

Harbaugh knew it was important to have a great staff. He hired as his defensive coordinator an NFL journeyman named Dave Adolph, who would follow Harbaugh to his later coaching stops and become one his most important mentors. Adolph had a deep well of knowledge about the game, and he had a way of doing things that Harbaugh wanted to emulate. For example, Adolph wore khaki pants every day, no matter where he was or what he was doing. From that point on, Harbaugh has worn khakis almost every day. "I just saw the genius in it," he said. "You had pockets. You had a place to put your script, your pens, your gum. Then the amount of time saved where you don't have to spend fifteen minutes thinking, *Wow, what am I going to wear today? Should I go shorts? Should I go sweats?* I probably save forty-five minutes a day not standing in a closet."

At San Diego, Harbaugh was as far from the NFL as a man could get. His office was in a double-wide trailer. The school did not even offer full scholarships. So he called upon his PEAK profile to ignite the program. His pedigree as a fourteen-year NFL quarterback was the foundation of his empathy. The players knew that he understood where they were coming from, and that he had the knowledge to help them get better. He was only a few years removed from playing in the NFL, so he was able to join their drills and compete with them, whether it was throwing the football or dropping to see who could do the most push-ups. He enlarged the roster with recruits from all over the country (the longer depth chart fostered competition at every practice) and assembled a far more ambitious schedule featuring more games and tougher opponents, such as nearby San Diego State, a Division I-A school. Sure, there were moments when Harbaugh felt like he was in over his head, but that's when his persistence kicked in. "When I'm fearful of something, then as fast as I can I just turn that into aggression," he said.

Harbaugh was coaching a Division II All-Star Game in Las Vegas when he met the woman who would become his second wife. He and his first wife, Miah, had recently divorced after ten years of marriage. (They had two sons and a daughter together.) Jim approached Sarah Feuerborn at a P.F. Chang's restaurant. She was a real estate agent and not much of a football fan. She didn't even realize until their third date that he had played in the NFL, and that was only because she mentioned his name to her brother. During a night out with some of his assistants and their wives, one of the other women pulled her aside and sternly warned, "Whatever you do, do *not* marry a coach." It was good advice, but Sarah would ignore it.

With Jack on board as the team's running backs coach, the Toreros went 7–4 in Jim's first season. They went on to put together back-to-back 11–1 seasons and claim consecutive conference championships. One of the few blemishes on Harbaugh's record was an arrest for driving under the influence in the fall of 2005. He pled guilty to a charge of reckless driving. That did not dissuade plenty of high-powered colleges from reaching out in hopes of hiring him. Harbaugh accepted an offer from Stanford. He was going back to Palo Alto.

The Cardinal had gone 1–11 the previous season, which meant the program was a long way from challenging USC for dominance in what was then the Pac-10. The USC program, coached by Pete Carroll, was the league's biggest and baddest beehive, and Harbaugh couldn't resist throwing rocks at it. A few months after he took the Stanford job, he claimed to have heard from a member of the USC staff that Carroll, who had previously coached in the NFL for the New York Jets and New England Patriots, would be the coach at

USC for one more year. Carroll did not appreciate the not-so-subtle effort to undermine his recruiting. "If he's going to make statements like that, he ought to get his information right. And if he has any questions about it, he should call me," Carroll said. (It should be noted that Harbaugh was wrong. Carroll ended up coaching at USC for three more years before leaving to take over the Seattle Seahawks. And it was Harbaugh, not Carroll, who two years later interviewed unsuccessfully for the vacant New York Jets job.)

Stanford went 4–8 in Harbaugh's first season, but in week five the Cardinals pulled off one of the biggest upsets in the history of the sport when they knocked off undefeated, top-ranked USC, 24–23. Stanford came into the game as a whopping 41-point underdog. As Harbaugh continued to improve Stanford's lot, no element of the program was too small for him to tinker with. He even decreed that the team's bench should move to the opposite side of the field so his players could be in the shade on hot days. Stanford won just five games in 2008, but the improvement started to take hold the following year when he mentored a quarterback prodigy named Andrew Luck. Together they helped the Cardinal to a second-place finish in the conference and a victory in the Sun Bowl.

The program was on a remarkable trajectory, and it looked bound to continue as Stanford returned most of its starters, including Luck, for the 2010 season. Harbaugh, however, felt compelled to shake things up. He fired members of his defensive staff and stripped some of offensive coordinator David Shaw's responsibilities. Many of the jettisoned coaches were angry and hurt, and they took shots at Harbaugh in the media. But he saw the moves as necessary. He was not in the friendship business. He was in the winning business.

Thus stirred the beginnings of a narrative that Harbaugh's high-wattage personality, insatiable competitiveness, and cutting bluntness grates on people after a while—that he can be successful coaching a group in the short term, but eventually he frays relationships, just as he did as a kid on the playground. Harbaugh has said he does not quite understand this impression, but given how entrenched it has become, he acknowledges there must be some validity to it. Even those who are close to him sometimes have a hard time explaining his behavior. "Jim has a tendency to wear people out at times," Shaw told NFL Network broadcaster Rich Eisen. "He drives people, he pushes people, he is the most competitive person on the planet. It's just who he is. He's going to rub some people the wrong way. He's going to find a way to win football games, because that's what he does."

There is also a quirky, odd aspect to Harbaugh's interactions that comes off by various turns as endearing, mystifying, and offputting. Former Virginia Tech coach Frank Beamer recounted a conversation he had with Harbaugh for Lars Anderson of Bleacher Report. The two were chatting at a dinner function a few days before their teams met in the 2010 Orange Bowl. He noticed that Harbaugh kept referring to Beamer's team as Georgia Tech. At first Beamer thought he was kidding, but then he realized Harbaugh was honestly mistaken. So he pointed out the error to Harbaugh and told him he couldn't wait to tell his players that the opposing team's coach didn't even know the name of their university.

According to Beamer, after a long, uncomfortable silence, Harbaugh finally blurted, "Well, I can't wait to tell my players that you said we were going to play Samford, not Stanford!" And he stalked away.

Stanford won the game, 40–12, and finished the season with a 12–1 record, ranked No. 4 in the country. This time, Harbaugh got the NFL offer he had been denied two years before. He was scooped up by the hometown San Francisco 49ers, who were coming off a 6–10 season. In his first season, Harbaugh engineered the most stunning turnaround of his career, leading the team to a 13–3 record and a berth in the NFC Championship Game, where it lost to the New York Giants in overtime.

Along the way he rankled yet another opposing coach. This time it was Jim Schwartz of the Detroit Lions. After the 49ers beat the Lions on October 16, 2011, the two coaches went to shake hands on the field. Harbaugh was so amped by the win that he jammed his hand into Schwartz's and let out a primal scream. Schwartz did not take kindly to the breach of etiquette, and he literally chased Harbaugh off the field. Harbaugh was clearly in the wrong and he acknowledged as much the following week, both in a phone conversation with Schwartz and to the public. But he stopped short of apologizing. He considered that to be an inauthentic gesture.

While one Harbaugh brother was rising in the west, the other was doing the same in the east. John had been hired as head coach of the Baltimore Ravens in 2008. Imagine the pride felt by Jack, who now had two sons working as head coaches in the NFL. Every week, Jim and John both overnighted their coaches' game videos to their dad so he could study them at his home in Wisconsin. When the 49ers and Ravens played each other on Thanksgiving Day 2011, it marked the first time in NFL history that teams coached by brothers faced off. The Ravens won, 16–6. The many stories written in advance of that game highlighted the difference in the brothers' personalities—John's steely determination versus Jim's spicy volatility.

In 2012, Jim guided the 49ers back to the NFC Championship Game, where they beat the Atlanta Falcons to advance to Super Bowl XLVII in New Orleans. Their opponent? The Baltimore Ravens, naturally. It was a truly historic occasion—two brothers facing off in the biggest sporting event on the planet. Jim and John did their best to downplay the obvious storyline, but it didn't work. As the relatives started pouring into Louisiana, John found himself try-ing to figure out which cousins or uncles were rooting for whom. "It was kind of interesting to see where everyone was lining up," he says.

During pregame warm-ups in the Superdome, John tried to ap-proach Jim on the field as he would do with any other opposing coach, but Jim kept avoiding him. Eventually, John started chatting with 49ers kicker David Akers, whom he had coached in Philadel-phia. That got Jim's attention. He walked over to John and said, "Why are you distracting my kicker?"

"I'm going to talk to you or your kicker," John replied. "Let me know which one."

So Jim stayed and exchanged a few words, and the two shook hands. When Jim tried to turn away, John pulled him back and said, "Gimme a hug, man." Jim obliged him, briefly.

Super Bowl XLVII was memorable for many reasons. The Ra-vens took a 28–6 lead early in the third quarter, and it appeared the game was going to become a laugher. But the action was interrupted by a power outage in the Louisiana Superdome. That led to an un-comfortable 34-minute delay. The hiatus seemed to stall the Ra-vens' momentum, and when play resumed, the 49ers went on a tear and cut the lead to five points. They had a chance to take the lead with under two minutes to play, but on fourth and goal from the five-yard line, Ravens cornerback Jimmy Smith appeared to hold Niners receiver Michael Crabtree, preventing him from making an attempt at a catch. That ended San Francisco's drive and enabled the Ravens to escape with a 34–31 win.

Inside a swarm of clicking cameras, the Harbaugh brothers shook hands and barely embraced. Jim took off. Their parents had been invited to come down to the field with a few minutes to go, but they didn't want to miss the final moments, so it took them a while to reach John and his family. When they climbed onto the podium for the trophy presentation, they took a place next to Grandpa Joe, a ninety-six-year-old immigrant from Italy who had never graduated from high school, and who was now standing amid falling confetti as one of his grandsons received the Vince Lombardi Trophy from NFL commissioner Roger Goodell.

Once the celebration ended, Jack and Jackie went back to the 49ers' locker room. Jim was sitting in an office by himself not wanting to see anyone, but when he heard his father was around, he asked him to be brought in. Jack walked into the room to find his younger son sitting behind a desk, his lip quivering. Jim's wound was still very fresh, the callus yet to be formed.

"You saw it, didn't you?" Jim said.

"Saw what?" Jack asked.

"The last play. He held him. You saw it."

There was no good answer. "If I say he held him, I've demeaned my oldest son who just won the Super Bowl, and I can't do that," Jack told me. "If I tell Jim that he didn't hold him, that they aren't going to call that on a fourth down at the end of the Super Bowl, that's not good with what we're discussing right here. So I thought to myself, *You can't say anything.*"

Eventually the players and coaches packed up their stuff and headed for the buses. Jack and Jackie climbed aboard and took a seat toward the front. So did Joani and her husband, Tom Crean, who was then the basketball coach at Indiana. Finally, Jim came on board with Sarah and their kids. His son Jimmy took the seat next to him. As the bus pulled away, Jim put his arm around his son's shoulder, and Jimmy rested his head on his dad's chest.

Jackie had said as little as possible to her son in the aftermath of the game. She had been around football coaches long enough to know that the less said after a painful loss, the better. But she was moved by the empathy her grandson showed his dad. When they climbed off the bus, she finally spoke up. "The best moment of the game for me was seeing your son show you that he understands how you feel," Jackie said to Jim. "Win or lose, it still comes back to family."

Losing hurts Jim Harbaugh, but it doesn't crush him. He's way too persistent for that. He put it to me this way: "There's a quote from one of my favorite books, *The Old Man and the Sea*. 'A man can be destroyed but he can't be defeated.' That resonates with me."

He proved that to be true in the 2013 season, when Harbaugh took the 49ers back to the NFC Championship Game, where they lost to a Seattle Seahawks team that was coached by his old nemesis, Pete Carroll. Despite the loss, Harbaugh's record in San Francisco was truly amazing. He had come to a franchise that had missed the playoffs for eight straight seasons, and during his first three years on the job he took the 49ers to three NFC Championship Games and a Super Bowl. Under normal circumstances, that would earn a coach a lifetime contract. But one year later, the team forced Harbaugh out.

How could something that was going so well turn sour so quickly? First and foremost there was Harbaugh's tetchy relationships with Jed York, the team owner, and general manager Trent Baalke. Harbaugh was never the type to work well with heavy-handed bosses. Sure, in a university setting he had to answer to an athletic director, chancellor, and president, but they rarely meddled in the program. In San Francisco, Harbaugh had no compunction about walking into Baalke's office early in the morning and demanding that something be changed immediately. Diplomacy has never been his forte. Things eventually got so bad between them that he and Baalke would reportedly ride the elevator together without being able to make eye contact. York later said there was a "rawness" between Harbaugh and Baalke that infected the entire franchise.

In such a poisonous environment, small slights become big problems. When the team held a ribbon-cutting ceremony to commemorate the opening of Levi's Stadium, Harbaugh arrived in his practice attire (read: khakis and sneakers) and then left after a short stay. That became a "thing" in the press. So did Harbaugh's repeated refusals to sign a contract extension, which led the 49ers to try to engineer a trade that would have ended with him coaching the Cleveland Browns. When the team suffered a few losses to start the 2014 season—including one in the preseason to John's Ravens—Harbaugh noticed that the media coverage, which had been so glowing in the past, turned sharply negative, with quotes attributed to anonymous sources casting him in a bad light.

It's also apparent that some of Harbaugh's players grew tired of his act. It was one thing when he was in college and dealing with young players who were less inclined to challenge the head coach's authority. In San Francisco, the players were grown professionals who didn't always take kindly to things like Harbaugh's decision to ban music and card games on flights because he wanted them to focus on the game. Alex Boone, a 49ers offensive lineman (and Ohio State graduate) who had praised Harbaugh's enthusiasm while he was the coach there, had a far less flattering take during an interview for HBO's *Real Sports* after Harbaugh got the boot. "I think he just pushed guys too far," Boone said. "He wanted too much, demanded too much, expected too much. You know, 'We gotta go out and do this. We gotta go out and do this. We gotta go out and do this.' And you'd be like, 'This guy might be clinically insane. He's crazy.' . . . He kind of wore out his welcome."

If being too demanding is a crime, then Harbaugh will happily plead guilty. "I take full responsibility and I apologize for none of it," he told me. "When you're a coach or a leader of an organization, you really want to build a ball team, as simple as that sounds. We had a great ball team. Tiny things came up that [management] disagreed with that were irrelevant. If I told you the little things they got upset about—like who got the credit. Who cares? It doesn't matter. That's not relevant. It's about being a ball team."

The speculation surrounding Harbaugh's status engulfed the team during the 2014 season. After the 49ers slogged their way to an 8–8 finish, the team issued a press release claiming they had reached a "mutual" decision to part ways. Harbaugh refused to toe the inauthentic party line. "I was told I wouldn't be the coach anymore," he said. "I didn't leave the 49ers. I felt like the 49er hierarchy left me."

He had no shortage of suitors, but one in particular stood out. Three weeks before, his alma mater, Michigan, had fired its head coach, Brady Hoke, following a 5–7 season. Some folks at the school were still annoyed with Harbaugh for making a typically candid comment eight years before suggesting that Michigan cut corners academically for its football players. Still, there was never a doubt whether the school wanted its favorite son to return. The only question was whether Harbaugh wanted to go back to coaching in college. As it turned out, the tug of the Big House, the legacy of Bo Schembechler (who had died in 2006), and the fond memories he had from spending six years of his childhood—not to mention a seven-year contract that paid him $5 million annually and included a $2 million signing bonus—tipped the balance. On December 30, 2015, Harbaugh was introduced as the head football coach at the University of Michigan. He was home again.

As usual, Harbaugh alighted with the subtlety of a tornado. It started with the very first spring practice. Normally a coach will put his players through meetings and video work before sending them on the field, but Harbaugh used the field for the entire four hours. It was a callback to the knowledge he got from Grandpa Joe: You can either teach 'em to do something, or you can show 'em what to do and then let 'em do it.

Michigan opened the 2015 season with a loss at Utah, but from there the Wolverines won nine out of ten games, returned to the national rankings for the first time in two years, and walloped No. 19 Florida in the Citrus Bowl, 41–7. The winning continued in 2016, when Michigan entered the top five of the Associated Press's national rankings for the first time in nine years and opened with nine straight wins, including a 78–0 thumping of Rutgers. After stubbing their toe at Iowa, they entered their annual showdown with Ohio State ranked No. 3 with a chance to play their way into the four-team College Football Playoff. The game was decided in the second overtime, when the Buckeyes benefited from a controversial spot by the referees that gave them a late first down. That set up the winning score. Speaking to reporters afterward, Harbaugh didn't mince words. "I'm bitterly disappointed with the officiating," he said. The Big Ten fined him $10,000 for those comments. He paid but never apologized.

In many respects, Harbaugh has been a breath of fresh air for college football. While a handful of coaches have taken to Twitter to promote their programs, Harbaugh has been borderline Trumpian in his use of the social media platform. From his @CoachJim4UM account, he has thrown rocks at beehives like Ohio State athletic director Gene Smith, Alabama coach Nick Saban, Ohio State coach Urban Meyer, Tennessee coach Butch Jones, and Georgia coach Kirby Smart, among others. "For every tweet that makes it out there, there are a hundred that don't because of me," Sarah says. "I'm the type that tries to avoid conflict. I want people to like me, but he doesn't care. He doesn't want to ever sit back and let people speak an untruth."

Unlike most football coaches, Harbaugh has shown a willingness—an eagerness, even—to apply his talents to subjects beyond the football field. For example, he has recently become a staunch advocate for the Legal Services Corporation, a publicly funded nonprofit that provides civic legal aid to poor people. Harbaugh is not one to speak on things he doesn't know about. He has attended several LSC meetings and acquired a deep well of knowledge about what it does and why its work is so important. His celebrity platform was especially useful in early 2017 when it was revealed that President Trump planned to eliminate funding for the LSC from his budget. I was warned by a media colleague that if I brought this topic up to Harbaugh, it would be hard to get him to stop talking about it. I did, and it was, but it was fascinating to hear him delve into detail about the challenges that the working poor face in the American legal system. "People try to stop you from talking about this stuff," he told me. "They'll say, 'Hey, it's complicated.' It's not complicated. It's simple and there's a better way to do it. All of this would work better if you ran it like a football team, instead of half the team trying to undermine the other half all the time."

This is what it is like to spend a couple of hours inside Jim Harbaugh's mind. His thoughts race every which way, but when they land, they land. It's like the time he was driving to work as the coach at Stanford and pulled over for thirty minutes because he was so fascinated with the way a traffic cop was doing her job. That process of letting his mind go where it wants, focusing only on the things that truly matter, and casting off everything else as drag—that's the way he brings his teams together. Harbaugh disdains the notion that there is some big secret to coaching, a neat little list of tricks that can be inputted into a spreadsheet. "People try to ask you, 'Tell me the key thing.' There is no one *thing*," he told me. "It's a thousand little things that are going to add up and make all the difference. Should this outroute be running nine yards? Should we roll it to twelve? It's so many things. And you've got to be right about 95 percent of the time. No one is going to be 100 percent on their decision making, but you should strive to get an A. If you're not in the mid-high 90s, then people aren't going to follow you."

Jack Harbaugh has his own little office inside Bo Schembechler Hall. It's located just a few feet from the head coach's work space. Jack is free to attend just about any practice or meeting, which he has done often since he and his wife moved to Ann Arbor permanently in the summer of 2016. Jim frequently asks his father for suggestions, but just as often Jack will be enlightened by something Jim has said and jot it down on a notepad. He doesn't have a team to coach anymore, but old habits die hard. "I had a very average career," Jack said. "I would have been a better coach if I had been able to know Jim and John and study them back then."

Besides giving Jack proximity to practices, living in Ann Arbor allows them to spend time with Jim's seven children, four of whom he has had with Sarah, whom he married in 2008. The latest addition came in January 2017, his son John. Life as Jim Harbaugh's wife is every bit the whirlwind as one might imagine. He may have a brilliant football mind, but he has no idea how to hang a picture on a wall. He often leaves his car with the motor running and the door open. He misplaces his cell phone and wallet with regularity. Cooking for himself is out of the question. He also suffers from sleep apnea, which he tries to make up for by downing Diet Cokes and chewing tobacco all day long. And let's just say he is not exactly meticulous when it comes to washing his underwear. It's a little gross, but then again, it makes it easier to pack for trips. Jim can be gone from home for days at a time and bring only a toothbrush that he stashes in the pocket of his sweatshirt.

"He's distracted all the time," Sarah told me. "He goes into what

I call 'Football World,' and there's really no breaking through it. He has a brilliant football mind, but he just doesn't have room in his head for the easy stuff. I treat him now like he's my child."

Still, there is no question he is a doting dad, just like Jack was. When Jim was still playing in the NFL and started having children, he made the mistake of listening to people who cautioned against pushing his kids into sports. "People said, 'You don't want them to be in your shadow all the time,'" he said. "I backed off for a little bit, but then I noticed it's easier for kids to quit or not be good. You've got to demand that they don't quit and that they are practicing."

He went on to tell me of a recent experience he had with his daughter Addy, who is seven years old. One day she came home from basketball practice, and Jim asked her who was the best player on her team. "Our coach says it doesn't matter who's the best," Addy replied. "Everybody's the same."

"Well, Addy, I don't think everybody's the same," Jim said. "And it matters to *me* that you're the best player on the team."

So Jim took his daughter to a court and started teaching her the fundamentals of basketball. He showed her how to dribble, how to shoot, how to box out for rebounds. She may have gotten a few blisters on her feet, but she got better. Whereas she used to turn her back when a missed shot came her way, Addy learned to beat her opponents into position and aggressively pursue the ball. Instead of getting rid of the ball as soon as it came to her, she learned to make plays for herself and her teammates. She may not have become the very best on her team, but she was close. All it took was a little coaching and a lot of determination. Acceleration, balance, confidence.

I asked Harbaugh if he was concerned that by pushing his daughter to practice like that, he might turn off her desire to play. "Well, we made it *fun*," he said. He further explained that when he is recruiting, he prefers players whose parents are hands-on when it comes to their development. "It just seems those players are better than the ones whose parents aren't involved," he told me.

I was reluctant to probe Jim on his relationship with his brother, figuring he has been asked so many questions on the topic that he would be turned off. But that was the one time when Jim was at his most disarming. "If I could wish anything for you or anybody else, it would be to have a friend like John in your life," he said. "Not just a friend you've had the last six months or the last year, but someone you grew up with. We shared the same room for sixteen years. Anytime we ever got into a kerfuffle, within minutes or hours we were laughing again. I couldn't wish anything better for somebody than to have that."

They still talk trash about all the battles they had while growing up, but even though John holds the ultimate trump card, he told me he has never once teased his brother that his Ravens beat Jim's 49ers in the Super Bowl. "I would never say that," John said. "I feel like I don't have to bring that up. I have too much respect for him. We played them three times, and we were very fortunate to win all three. I'm very proud of that, not because he's my brother, but because I know how good he is. You beat Jim Harbaugh, to me that's an accomplishment."

At the age of fifty-three, Harbaugh can still make a football whistle through the air, and though he is no longer able to run alongside his players until he pukes, he still embraces every opportunity to feed his competitive jones. Over Memorial Day weekend in 2016, he and John got together with their families at John's cottage on Lake Huron in Michigan. One afternoon, the moms, dads, and kids were enjoying what they thought was a friendly little basketball game on the driveway. That is, until Jim's family fell behind 5–1. Suddenly, Jim was seven years old again, and he was in a car driving back from a Punt, Pass and Kick contest, and he was *pissed*. He started boxing out John's thirteen-year-old daughter and bullying his way past John's wife to the basket. John playfully suggested that maybe Jim should let his kids touch the ball once in a while, but Jim wasn't having it. So John had no choice but to guard him closely and throw a few elbows into his gut. At one point, he sent Jim into a nearby bush. In the end, though, Jim's intensity carried the day, as his family came back to win 7–6. He let out a whoop of excitement, picked up his toddler son, and screamed, "Doesn't it feel great to win?" He was still floating when he crossed paths with his brother an hour later in the backyard. "Hey John," he crowed. "Have you won anything yet?"

Jim Boeheim

He saw dead people.

They were right there in his house, lying in caskets one floor underneath the bed where he slept. They were young and old, big and small, grandparents and parents and townsfolk, sometimes people he knew. There was a viewing room and an embalming room, and if it was a particularly busy time, a third casket would rest in the living room. That's the good thing about the funeral business. Good times may come and go, but death is the one true constant.

It was all so . . . *normal.* That was life for Jim Boeheim while he was growing up in the small central New York town of Lyons in the 1950s. The Boeheim Funeral Home had been founded by his great-grandfather in the mid-nineteenth century. It got passed down to Jim's grandfather, and eventually to his father, Jim Sr. When Jim Jr. was twelve years old, his parents moved with him and his sister to the funeral home, in downtown Lyons. The family slept upstairs, the corpses downstairs. Sometimes, if the viewing room was empty, Jim's sister, Barbara, would have slumber parties there with her girlfriends.

Jim first remembers seeing a dead person when he was about five years old. When he became a teenager, his father put him to work. Jim would ride with his dad around town and help him pick up the bodies. The hearse served as a backup ambulance for the town, and Jim would go on those outings as well. "One time, I saw a woman give birth," Boeheim says. "Now *that* was gross."

For anyone who has watched Jim Boeheim during his four-plus decades as the curmudgeonly head basketball coach at Syracuse University, it should come as no surprise that he grew up the son of a mortician, surrounded by dead people lying in wooden boxes inside his own house. Makes sense, doesn't it? The loping gait, the pallid aspect, the haughty disdain, the won't-suffer-fools-gladly attitude, the eye rolls, the shrugs, the condescending snickers, and, yes, the whiny, nasal voice—it all conspires to deliver the message of, *What's the point? We're all gonna die anyway.* Boeheim tends to be shy and thoughtful, but he is not one for introspection. Ask him how growing up surrounded by death formed his character, and he will shrug and roll his eyes. "I don't think that it did. It was just a part of my life," he says. "Maybe I can accept death a little bit easier than most people, because I lived it. I'm not sure that's such a great attribute."

We are sitting in a hotel conference room in Colorado Springs during the summer of 2016. It is late at night, and Boeheim, seventy-one, has spent a full day overseeing a tryout at the Olympic Training Center. He doesn't seem to understand my fascination with this line of questioning, so I tell him a story about the night my wife and I showed the movie *Stand by Me* to our three young sons. The movie tells the story of a group of teenage boys who go on a search for another boy who has gone missing and is presumed dead. At the end of the movie, they find the body. When that young dead boy appeared on our flat-screen, my boys freaked out. They had never seen an image of a corpse before, much less that of a boy their age. My wife and I tried to explain that the boy on the screen was just an actor, that as soon as the scene was over he got up and played with his friends again, but it didn't matter. They had seen a dead boy and that was all there was to it. They had nightmares for days.

Boeheim is nonplussed. Don't read too much into it, he cautions. It was no big deal. As I reflect on our exchange, it occurs to me that maybe I was asking him the wrong questions. It wasn't the dead people in Boeheim's home that impacted him so much as the living ones who came to pay their respects. His childhood home was routinely filled with sad people speaking in hushed tones. That is the dynamic that became the foundation for his PEAK profile.

Think about what it feels like to be at the funeral for someone you don't know well. You look at those who loved the dearly departed, and you know that, sad as they may be, they must persist. As you watch them weep and grieve, you empathize with their sorrow. You ruminate on your own mortality, which makes you come to an understanding of what really matters—who you are authentically and what it is you really want out of life, brief as it is. Most of all, you're grateful that you're sitting in a chair instead of lying in that box. That is quite a piece of knowledge for a young boy to inherit.

It all makes perfect sense to Jason Hart, who played for Boeheim at Syracuse from 1996 to 2000. He has given this matter much thought. "He grew up real spooky," Hart tells me. "Think about it. The sun was never out. It was gloomy in that funeral home. The house was always quiet, with dead bodies around. That's the kind of thing that would make someone real reserved. When I found out about all that, it tripped me out. But it made sense given what I know about Coach's personality."

We think of great coaches as being naturally extroverted, but Boeheim does not fall into that category. He does not get to *Us* by firing up his players with inspiring speeches or sitting them down for long conversations. Rather, he gets to *Us* by earning their confidence in the knowledge he has accrued during his lifetime spent playing, learning, and thinking about basketball. Not just thinking—brooding. And as one of the very few coaches who have won so much for so long at the same place—his alma mater, no less—Boeheim is nothing if not persistent. His teams reflect that in the way they play.

If the constant specter of death robbed Boeheim of a childlike effervescence, it also imbued him with an innate even keel. True, he never seems all that happy, even in the best of times, yet he also possesses a steely resilience that has carried him through the worst of times. That equanimity has been his teammate through the elation of Final Fours and a national championship and a Hall of Fame induction to the countless painful losses, a pair of devastating NCAA investigations, a pedophilia scandal that engulfed his longtime assistant coach, a divorce, and the constant, withering public criticism that nips at his ultra-thin skin. Boeheim is the first to concede he is not likable at times, but through all the ups and downs of his career he has remained authentic, never straying too far, in person and in spirit, from that small town and modest funeral home.

In a profession where so many men suffer a nagging itch to seek out new challenges, Boeheim has been the one true constant. He has often quipped that each loss is like a temporary death, but he doesn't really mean it. If there's one thing Jim Boeheim knows, it's that there is nothing temporary about death.

Juli Boeheim knows the look. She sees it on her husband's face as he climbs into his car, pulls out of the driveway, and begins the brief trip to his office at the Carmelo K. Anthony Center on the Syracuse campus. "He's not even out of the driveway," she says, "but his mind is already a million miles away."

Mike Hopkins knows the look, too. He played for Boeheim for

four years and was his assistant coach for twenty-one years before becoming the head coach at Washington. Boeheim is an avid reader, but there were times when Hopkins saw him with his nose in a book (or, lately, in front of his iPad) and knew the words are flitting into Boeheim's head but not really staying there. "He finishes a novel every road trip, but then you see him put the book down so he can think," Hopkins says. "Everybody has some form of meditation. Some people go to church. Some people work out. He's a thinker."

He inherited this inclination from his parents. Jim and Janet Boeheim were master bridge players who traveled all over the East Coast competing in tournaments. Jim Sr.'s abilities at the card table were abetted by a dogged competitive streak and a prodigious memory. If he won a hand, he might turn to the other fellow and remind him that he made the same mistake in a hand many years before. It usually did not go over well.

So one of the first things young Jimmy learned was the importance of knowledge. He had to cultivate his mind because his body was unimpressive. He was skinny and awkward, all arms and legs and sharp elbows. He may have been born wearing glasses. Like many small towns, Lyons was mad for its high school football and basketball teams. Football was out of the question for Jim, but basketball suited him. He loved the game right from the start. As a little kid, he would toss wadded-up socks into the hoop that was hanging in his bedroom. When he was in grade school, he joined a program run by Richard Blackwell, the coach at Lyons Central High School. Blackwell put the kids through brutal four-hour workouts on Saturday mornings. Jim would grind through that practice and then remain at the gym for hours more. "I was the only third grader that went to all the varsity high school games," he says. "I wanted to play basketball from the beginning. There was never any doubt that was what I was going to be."

As Boeheim got older, he'd spend much of his spare time playing with friends on the driveway behind his house. The garage at the funeral home was in a separate structure, leaving a substantial space to serve as the court. His dad put up lights so Jim and his buddies could play at night. Jim may not have looked the part of a good basketball player, but he was tough, and his eye-hand coordination was off the charts.

Playing with his friends was a lot healthier than going up against his old man in anything. When Senior and Junior competed, it rarely ended well. Blackwell was also the golf pro at the town country club, and whenever he saw the Boeheims getting ready to tee off, he would ask how many holes they would play before one of them stormed off the course. He wasn't kidding.

Jim's descriptions of his old man are not flattering. "He had a good side, but he kept it well hidden," is how he likes to put it. Jim Sr. had a withdrawn, stoic manner that owed to his German heritage. He was also in chronic pain. When he was a young boy, his brother accidentally shot him in his back during a hunting trip. His doctors thought it would be too dangerous to try to remove the bullet, so Jim Sr. carried that bullet in his back the rest of his life. One of his legs was shorter than the other. A major reason why he gravitated toward playing cards was because it was something he could do while sitting.

Boeheim's best friend growing up, Tony Santelli, says Jim Sr. was "about as cold a person as you could imagine." Jim agrees. "He was like me in my bad Jim Boeheim mode," he says. "We were never close. He always wanted to win. He'd try to beat me as much as he could at everything we played. Eventually, I beat him at everything, so of course he quit playing me. I can be nice sometimes, but my father never really could be."

Their arguments weren't just limited to sports. At any moment, a battle could erupt. "Jim and Dad were alike in so many ways," his sister, Barbara, says. "Each one of them was *always* right. They butted heads constantly." Boeheim's father taught Jim how to fish and hunt pheasants, but there were many times when Jim would simply go fishing by himself past midnight, alone with his thoughts.

His mom, on the other hand, was pure sugar. Janet was an athlete herself, an excellent golfer who used to be a pretty good high school basketball player. Unlike Jim Sr., however, it didn't crush her to lose. Jim remembers one year when she failed to win the club golf championship but was still happy because her best friend claimed first place instead.

The twin strains of his parents' personalities gave Boeheim his authenticity, for better and worse. He loved basketball and he loved to compete. When his high school career was done, Boeheim had a chance to go to Colgate or Cornell on a partial academic scholarship, but he preferred Syracuse because it was a Division I program. He pitched his services to the head coach, Fred Lewis, who told him he didn't have any scholarships available. However, Lewis promised him that he could try to walk onto the team as a freshman, and if he was good enough, he might be able to earn a scholarship later on.

When Boeheim got to school, he became discouraged. That's because one of the scholarship freshmen was a smooth, 6'3" shooting guard from Washington, D.C., named Dave Bing. Boeheim had never lacked for confidence, but he knew he wasn't remotely in this guy's league. When he expressed his insecurities to his mom, she asked him about the other players. "They're good, but not nearly as good as Bing," Jim said.

"Well," Janet replied, "you'll just have to be better than those other guys."

In other words, persist. It didn't take Bing long to realize that the skinny nerd with the glasses was plenty tough. He remembers an occasion early in their freshman season when an older player tried to bully Boeheim in a game of one-on-one. "One time he ran into him, and Jim's glasses broke in half," Bing says. "I think the guy felt that

Jimmy was going to quit, but Jimmy just got some tape, put his glasses back on, and continued to play. I knew right then this was a guy who didn't back down."

Later that fall, Boeheim invited Bing and two other teammates to stay at his house for Thanksgiving. The three teammates walked through the front door, went into the back room . . . and saw an old white guy lying in an open casket. They weren't having it. "We knew his father was a mortician—he looked the part, quite frankly—but we didn't know the funeral parlor was connected to the house," Bing says. "I had never seen a dead person before. Right away, all three of us said, 'There's no way in hell we're spending the night here.' As soon as dinner was over, we went back to school."

Boeheim knew he would never be as good as Bing, so it was up to him to figure out how to be good while playing *with* him on the freshman squad. (Freshmen were not eligible to play varsity ball back then.) If there's one thing Boeheim could always do on a basketball court, it was shoot. He saw that every time Bing beat his man off the dribble, he drew extra defenders. So all Boeheim had to do was move into the open space, catch Bing's passes, and convert the shots. He did well enough that first year for Lewis to put him on scholarship over the summer.

The players at Syracuse and around the Eastern College Athletic Conference (ECAC) soon learned what the folks back in Lyons had already known. Looks aside, the Boeheim kid was not to be trifled with between the lines. Not surprisingly, Boeheim was also a smartass in practice, asking Lewis lots of questions and constantly challenging his decisions. Lewis could be a merciless scold, but Boeheim wasn't fazed. He was used to that kind of treatment from his father. "Lewis was hard on everybody. He cursed you out all the time," Boeheim says. "Nobody really liked him, but he rebuilt the Syracuse program and was a very good recruiter."

Boeheim's parents made the hourlong trip with Barbara to

Syracuse to attend every one of his home games. When the Orange-men were on the road, Jim Sr. would repeatedly ask Barbara to go into the kitchen to check the score on the radio. "Dad was always proud of Jim," Barbara says. "He just never said so."

By the time Boeheim was a senior, he was starting alongside Bing in the backcourt. The team went 22–6 and reached the 1966 NCAA Tournament, where it suffered a disappointing loss to Duke in the East Regional final. Boeheim was the third-leading scorer on that team with a 14.6 average. Over the years, Lewis often said Boeheim was "the worst leaper I ever had," but he also called him one of his smartest players. "It's amazing how you can be the smart-est player and then you can be a dumb coach later on," Boeheim says.

After he graduated in 1966, Boeheim pursued a playing career for a short while. When his former coach in Scranton became head coach of the Detroit Pistons of the NBA, Boeheim went for a brief tryout, but he quickly realized he wasn't good enough to make the team. He had known for a while that he wanted to coach, so he re-turned to Syracuse to take a job as a graduate assistant under its new head coach, Roy Danforth. In 1972, Danforth promoted Boeheim to full-time assistant. The grinding nature of recruiting, which re-quired long hours, a keen eye for talent, and persistent pursuit, fit his personality.

Over the next four years, Syracuse averaged 21.5 wins and reached the 1975 Final Four, where it lost to Kentucky in the semi-final. Things took a surprising turn the following year, when Dan-forth left to become the head coach at Tulane University in New Orleans. Syracuse put together a search committee to find his re-placement, partly because the school was hesitant to take a chance on someone who had never been a head coach.

Boeheim was irked by the delay. He had been recruiting a 6′11″ man-child from Rochester named Roosevelt Bouie, who was close to deciding between Syracuse and St. Bonaventure. Boeheim believed that if he wasn't named head coach soon, he would lose out on Bouie. Boeheim had also interviewed for the coaching vacancy at Rochester University, which was about ninety miles away. Finally, he informed Syracuse's search committee that he intended to accept that job.

Later that day, he received a phone call inviting him to be the head basketball coach at Syracuse. He was only thirty-two years old, but he knew who he was, what he wanted to do, and where he wanted to do it. You can see it in the options he created for himself. Boeheim was either going to coach at Syracuse, or he would coach at Rochester. Either way, he wasn't going far from home.

Having lived his entire life in central New York, Boeheim knew the type of player who would thrive at Syracuse. He didn't have the luxury of recruiting a ton of All-Americans, so he searched for guys who had raw potential and a combative attitude—like Louis Orr, a 6´8˝ forward from Cincinnati. Thanks to what became known as the Louie and Bouie Show, Boeheim's success as a head coach was immediate. During his first four years, the Orangemen went 100–18, won 54 out of 55 games on their home court in Manley Fieldhouse, and played in four straight NCAA Tournaments.

The program was galvanized by two major decisions made by the university. The first came in 1978, when the school broke ground on an indoor stadium that would host both football and basketball games. The Carrier Dome was going to have room for more than 30,000 fans for basketball. Boeheim thought the idea was preposterous—the entire town of Syracuse had only around 200,000 people, and his team almost never lost in Manley Fieldhouse—but the school proceeded over his objections. In the final game before the big move, Syracuse, which was ranked No. 2 in the country, lost a heartbreaker to Georgetown, 52–50. That led to one of the great shit-talking moments in the history of sports, when Hoyas coach John Thompson walked into his postgame press conference and bellowed, "Manley Fieldhouse is officially *closed*!"

The other big change occurred in 1979, when Syracuse left the ECAC to join the Big East, a brand-new conference that was comprised of schools in major media markets along the East Coast. The increased television exposure, coupled with the unveiling of the jampacked Carrier Dome, proved seductive for recruits, beginning most prominently with Dwayne "Pearl" Washington. The 6´2˝ dervish was a New York City playground legend before he put on a Syracuse uniform. He arrived in the fall of 1982, and the fans turned out to watch him whirl. Washington piloted the Orangemen to a 71–24 record during his three years there, but he was never able to get Syracuse past the Sweet Sixteen. In his final game, the Orangemen were knocked out in the second round of the 1986 NCAA Tournament by David Robinson–led Navy. Pearl left for the NBA that spring.

Boeheim was rightly hailed for his recruiting prowess, but when that failed to translate into postseason success, he was branded an underachiever. The criticism bothered him more than it should have. He devoured the local newspapers and filed every slight into his steel-trap mind. To this day, Boeheim winces as he recalls reading a poll that tabbed him as one of the worst coaches in the country, even though his team was winning 81 percent of its games.

The emerging negativity brought out the mortician in him. If the Orangemen went through a losing stretch, Jim would tell his wife, Elaine, whom he had married in the summer of 1976, to stop spending so much money because he was sure he was about to be out of a job. It didn't matter that he was winning the vast majority of his games. The losses cut deepest, and still do to this day. "It's all about losing," he says. "When we win, I'm pretty happy for about an hour, and then I'm thinking about the next game. When we lose, I'm thinking about that game until we get to the next one."

Two years after Pearl Washington left, Boeheim welcomed the most gifted recruit he had ever signed. His name was Derrick Coleman, an All-American power forward from Detroit. Coleman was a strong, sturdy 6´10˝, 225-pound lefty, with a nose for the ball and a soft touch around the rim. He thought Boeheim was aloof, even when he was recruiting him, but he loved the way Boeheim gave his big men free rein to showcase their ball skills away from the basket. "If anything, Coach would get on me for not shooting enough," Coleman says. "He was way ahead of his time with that."

Coleman joined a group that included Sherman Douglas, a lightly recruited point guard from Washington, D.C., and Rony Seikaly, a raw 6´10˝ center who was born in Lebanon and grew up in Greece. As a freshman, Seikaly averaged 11.9 points and 8.8 rebounds, helping Boeheim to reach his first-ever Final Four. After defeating Providence, Syracuse met Indiana in the final. The game was famously decided on a baseline jumper by Hoosiers guard Keith Smart with four seconds to play, delivering Indiana to a 74–73 victory. To this day Boeheim has never watched a video of the game in its entirety. It's not just that he doesn't want to relive a painful experience. It's also a waste of his time. He knows how the movie ends—with his own funeral.

A few years ago, Boeheim was shown an article that sought to divine which college basketball programs did the best job developing players for the NBA. Correlations were made between where players were ranked as high school seniors and how they performed as pros. Based on that metric, the writer concluded that Syracuse had done this better than any other school.

Boeheim was proud but hardly surprised. He is rarely able to convince the very best high school players to turn down blue-chip programs and play for him. So over the years he has had to nurture his skills as an evaluator, one who is able to spy potential as much as physical prowess. Since his players don't typically leave for the NBA after one season, he has time to impart his knowledge of the game. He and his players battle from time to time, but they usually end up trusting him because they understand he knows what he is talking about, and they believe he cares about them.

Boeheim is not much of a speechmaker. He doesn't have a lot of heart-to-heart talks in his office. He would rather take a few minutes before a practice to let his players know what he is thinking. Then he motivates them through the sheer force of his persistence. "The only way to get players to play hard is to push them every day," he says. "Not just day to day but minute to minute. It has to be a constant challenge. To me, that's really the key to coaching. There's motivational things, there's X's and O's, but the main thing is getting them to go after it every play."

"The biggest thing about Coach is the fact that he can motivate but still teach," says Gerry McNamara, who played guard for Syracuse from 2003 to 2006 and is currently an assistant coach. "There's no sugarcoating. You always know where you stand and what's expected of you. If you're seeking his approval, it's not going to necessarily come."

It can be rather unpleasant to be on the receiving end of his daily doses of acid. Seikaly in particular had a hard time with it. Growing up in Greece, he did not take up basketball until he came to the United States to go to high school, which meant he had been exposed to very little coaching, much less the kind that he heard every day from Boeheim. Seikaly wasn't sensitive so much as strong-willed. When Boeheim would correct him, he would argue.

One day in practice, Seikaly finally got frustrated and asked Boeheim why he never yelled at freshman Stephen Thompson. Fine, Boeheim said, and spun on Thompson. "Stevie, stop working so hard! Stop making so many good plays! Stop doing what I tell you to do! Stop doing all the things I want without me having to say anything!" Boeheim turned back to Seikaly and said, "Happy now?" Suffice to say, Seikaly was not happy.

"There was a love-hate relationship between us, and, yes, I did hate him at times," Seikaly told author Jack McCallum, who cowrote Boeheim's autobiography, *Bleeding Orange,* in 2015. "He was not a good communicator in the sense that, when gym time was over, you would get a hug or that tap on the shoulder that let you know everything was okay. And that was hard for some players, including me."

In the wake of that loss in the '87 final, Boeheim's teams continued to win consistently. Syracuse reached the Elite Eight of the NCAA Tournament in 1989 and the Sweet Sixteen the following year. And yet as he kept advancing in the tournament but failing to win it, the Boeheim-as-underachiever chatter took deeper root. Things got worse in late 1990, when the *Syracuse Post-Standard* published a two-part investigative series that detailed potential violations in Boeheim's program. When the NCAA followed up with its own investigation, it banned Syracuse from the 1993 postseason.

The scandal, the pressure to win, the public criticism, the long hours, the worrying, the brooding—all of it took a toll on the Boeheims' marriage. Jim and Elaine had been unable to conceive a child, but they adopted a baby girl in 1985 and named her Elizabeth. They divorced in 1993, but as separations go, this one was quite civil. Boeheim could come home after a long road trip and be able to see his daughter whenever he wanted. He is quick to give Elaine the credit. "My ex-wife, she never liked me much," he says. "It was largely my fault the marriage broke up. She was upset, but she wanted our daughter to have complete access to me. She really made it seamless."

Boeheim enjoyed a vindication of sorts during the 1995–96 season. Though Syracuse lost eight games and was given a No. 4 seed in the NCAA Tournament, it unexpectedly reached the Final Four, losing to a powerhouse Kentucky team in the final game. Besides forcing his critics into a grudging sense of appreciation for getting to *Us* with that team, Boeheim also evinced an uncharacteristically sunny persona that season. That was largely due to the presence of a new lady in his life. He first met Juli Greene during a trip to the Kentucky Derby in 1994. She was a native of Lexington, and they struck up a conversation at a party. Greene was beautiful, intelligent . . . and twenty-two years his junior. She had graduated from the University of Kentucky, but she didn't know who Boeheim was. They talked for a while and played some backgammon, which Juli won. They've never played since.

The romance budded quickly, first with phone conversations that lasted upwards of four hours, and later with visits by Juli to Syracuse. Juli came from a large family (she is the youngest of six brothers and sisters), and they were understandably skeptical. He was much older than she, and they were concerned that he was just trying to charm her the way he did recruits. It wasn't until Boeheim went with Juli to her sister's wedding that her family came around. "They all met him and fell in love with him," Juli says. "I said to them, 'See? He recruited you guys, too.'"

Boeheim had no desire to rush back into marriage, but he did ask Juli to come live with him in Syracuse beginning in 1995. Once again, Elaine was immediately welcoming to her ex-husband's new (and much younger) girlfriend. "I have to give Elaine all the credit. She was bigger than any circumstance," Juli says. The two women even developed a close friendship independent of Jim. Elaine shared recipes she used to make Jim's favorite dishes. Sometimes when Juli would head over to Elaine's house, Jim would ask her to take an alimony check.

Jim and Juli got married on October 10, 1997. Elizabeth was the maid of honor. Juli was well aware of the fertility problems that Jim had experienced during his previous marriage, but she kept faith that whatever happened would be for the best. They were both surprised when she got pregnant and had a son, Jimmy, in May 1998. Just eighteen months later, she got pregnant again with twins, even though Jim had been away for most of the summer and they had had very few "opportunities," as she puts it. "I want to go back to that doctor who said that I had a bad sperm count," Boeheim says. "Guess he was wrong about *that*."

It would be seven years before Boeheim would get another crack at the Final Four. He got there courtesy of a stellar freshman class that featured Carmelo Anthony, a supremely talented 6′9″ small forward from Maryland, and Gerry McNamara, a knockdown shooter and point guard from Scranton, Pennsylvania. Boeheim set his usual tone from the start of the season, not only with regard to the freshmen but also to Kueth Duany, the 6′6″ fifth-year senior who was looked upon as the team's leader. "We all knew how hard Kueth worked and how much it meant to him because it was his last year," McNamara says. "When we saw how hard Coach was on him, we all fell into line."

The team sailed through the early part of the season, when Boeheim typically loads up on home games against weaker teams, but even as the wins piled up Boeheim was concerned with the team's chemistry. He may not have been a sugar-with-the-medicine kind of guy, but he was plenty empathetic, and he had a knack for discerning what was happening between his players' ears. The Orange stubbed their toe a couple of times once Big East play started, most notably in a late January loss at Rutgers. Boeheim didn't like what was happening between McNamara and Anthony in that game. Before the start of the next practice, he sat the two of them down and told them in no uncertain terms that he would not tolerate players who were so pissed that they weren't getting enough shots that it threw them off their game. McNamara was surprised to hear Anthony say he was frustrated at not getting the ball enough, and he promised he would run the offense through Anthony from that point forward. "Coach Boeheim really read the situation perfectly," McNamara says. "I was like, 'Hey man, if this is how you feel, this is easily correctable.'"

With his unique combination of size, skills, and basketball IQ, Anthony also brought out the best in Boeheim as a basketball tactician. Boeheim utilized Anthony as the queen piece in Syracuse's offense, first establishing him about 12 feet away from the basket, and then pushing him behind the three-point line when the defense started collapsing. Inevitably the defense gave Anthony too much attention, at which point Boeheim turned him into a passer. Such was the case during the first half of the NCAA championship game against Kansas, when the Jayhawks were so intent on crowding Anthony's space that they repeatedly left McNamara wide open. McNamara hit six three-point baskets in the first half, three of which were on assists from Anthony.

Boeheim closed that game with some savvy maneuvers. With just under three minutes to play and Syracuse leading by eight points, Orange center Craig Forth picked up his fifth foul. Normally, Boeheim would have replaced Forth with the backup center, Jeremy McNeil, but he knew that Kansas would have to make some threes to get back into the game. So he replaced Forth with 6'4" freshman guard Billy Edelin in order to apply more pressure to Kansas's shooters. The problem was that meant moving 6'9" sophomore forward Hakim Warrick to the center spot, even though he had not played that position all season.

At first the strategy appeared to backfire. Syracuse's zone looked disjointed, and Kansas scored a couple of easy baskets to trim the lead to three with a minute to play. From there, Warrick made the two biggest plays of the game. The first came with 13.5 seconds left, when he snared a huge defensive rebound and was fouled. The next came after he missed the front end of a one-and-one, giving Kansas the ball and a chance to tie.

The Jayhawks worked the ball around the perimeter as the clock ticked toward zero. When KU guard Kirk Hinrich caught the ball behind the top of the key, Duany, who was at the forward spot, rushed out to contest him. Hinrich pump faked and swung the ball to sophomore guard Michael Lee, who was wide open in the corner. Warrick, who had been standing directly under the basket, sprinted in Lee's direction, jumped in the air, and, utilizing his long arms, blocked the shot out of bounds to seal the win. Had the stronger but slower McNeil been at center as he had all season, it is highly unlikely he would have been able to cover that ground so quickly.

The final score was Syracuse 81, Kansas 78. Jim Boeheim, mortician's son, was an underachiever no more. That the triumph came in New Orleans, the same city where Syracuse's championship dreams were buried by Keith Smart sixteen years before, made it all the more poetic. He had returned to the scene of his most painful temporary death and gotten to *Us* in emphatic fashion.

As soon as the game was over, Boeheim's wife and ex-wife shared an embrace. "This is as much yours as it is mine," Juli told Elaine. About twenty minutes after the final buzzer sounded, Juli stood on the platform with Jim and indulged in the celebration. The championship had been won. The confetti had fallen. The trophy had been presented. The wait was over. "What do we do now?" she said.

Boeheim gave her a weary smile and replied, "Let's go home."

When Jason Hart flew from Los Angeles to take his official recruiting visit to Syracuse during the 1995–96 season, one of the team's players, a 6′8″ forward from Rochester named John Wallace, warned that if he couldn't stand up to the head coach, he shouldn't bother going there. It didn't take long for Hart to figure out why. "Coach doesn't have time for bullshit," he says. "Look at the guys he's had there that have done well. They wasn't pussies. They were tough-asses. They stood up for themselves. That's how you have to be to have success there. Coach don't like no punks."

Hart grew up in the inner-city neighborhood of Inglewood, so he was not unfamiliar with confrontation. Still, he was put off by Boeheim's aloof manner. "I was like, *Damn, how do I penetrate this? This dude don't even know me,*" Hart says. He voiced his displeasure to Mike Hopkins, who suggested that he make a habit of stopping by Boeheim's office every day to check in. Hart took that advice, spending hours of one-on-one time with his coach, peppering Boeheim with questions about all those uniformed men whose framed pictures adorned his walls. He discovered that Boeheim was a lot more empathetic than he let on. "He's not a guy who's going to build a relationship with you," Hopkins says. "You have to build it with him."

Boeheim likes to keep things simple. His office is not a buzz of activity. He does not spend gobs of time pursuing ancillary projects. On most days, Boeheim can be found in there leisurely reading the newspaper and watching the Golf Channel, or chatting on the telephone. He loves watching basketball on television, but he is not one to stay up until three in the morning studying video of his next opponent. During practice, he delegates much of the early drill work to his assistants, wandering upstairs to his office sometimes until they are ready to start playing five-on-five. He's not a note taker, he doesn't hoard his practice plans, and he doesn't have drawers full of files bearing intricate plays. He scoffs at the whole analytics craze that has been embraced by so many of his younger colleagues. "I think a lot of that is nonsense," he says. "I don't need numbers to tell me which plays are working and which ones aren't."

Likewise, Boeheim prefers to give his players the bare minimum of information about their next opponent. He wants them playing with a free mind. "When we went into a game, we knew who the shooters were and who the offensive rebounders were. That's it," Hart says. While just about every coach puts their teams through game-day shootarounds several hours before tipoff, Boeheim has never done so. "We can show what we need to show them without leaving the hotel. I'd rather they get more rest," Boeheim says. When I ask whether that gives opponents an edge, he replies, "We had the only winning road record in the history of the Big East. We won 61 percent of our road games. Nobody knows that."

All of which is not to say that Boeheim doesn't prepare. He just does it differently from most coaches. "I'm always thinking about basketball," he says. "So even though I may not be having meetings, I'm thinking about things." By the time he is done with all this thinking, he usually finds the smartest solution. "He can take the most complicated situation and simplify it," McNamara says. "He has a unique ability to go over to someone whose head is spinning, calm him down, and say, 'All you need is to do *this*.'"

As Boeheim watches his team play, slowly pacing the sideline with arms folded and his tie askew, you can see the wheels turning in his mind. It's as if each game, each season, were one long hand of bridge. "He's always trying to figure out the next move," Hopkins says. For example, during a game at Providence in 2001, Boeheim's starters were playing poorly and the team fell behind, so he put in the subs. Syracuse came back and took the lead, but instead of riding the hot hands, Boeheim put his starters back in the game. Hopkins was incredulous, but the Orangemen won. When Hopkins asked his boss afterward why he made the substitutions, Boeheim reminded him that they only needed the reserves to win that particular game, but they'd need the starters the rest of the year. He was already several moves ahead.

As the years went on, Boeheim merged his knowledge with his authenticity and landed on a method of coaching that uniquely empowered his team. For much of his career, he utilized the 2-3 zone defense more than many of his peers. The zone works so well for Boeheim because it is malleable. Though it is nominally a 2-3 formation, with two guards on top and three forwards along the baseline, it is actually an ever-shape-shifting alignment that is uniquely crafted to castrate an opponent's strengths. When his team is on defense, Boeheim can study the intricate movements, discern the opposing coach's strategy, and try to devise the appropriate countermeasure. "I like to say, if you have the pencil last, you're gonna win," he says. "If I have the pencil last, I'm gonna win."

Boeheim's teams don't thrive because the zone is a better defense than man-to-man. They thrive because it's a better defense for *him*.

At the start of the 2009–10 season, Boeheim made a momentous decision to commit to the zone full-time. It came as the result of an exhibition game the Orange played against LeMoyne College, a Division II school located across town. Syracuse played man-to-man defense that night, and even though it wasn't going well, Boeheim stayed with it so he could see whether his guys could play it. Turns out they couldn't. The Orange lost in a shocker, 82–79. After the game, Boeheim told his assistants that they would play nothing but the 2-3 zone the rest of the season. No switching, no wavering, no man-to-man, no matter what.

It is not a stretch to say that Boeheim is the most knowledgeable zone coach in the history of the game. He has studied it so much, thought about it for so long, and made so many adjustments over so many games that he will usually come up with the proper tweak that leads to a win. His peers certainly respect his knowledge. Over the years, Boeheim has estimated he has conducted more than two hundred clinics about his zone defense. "It's the only thing I lecture on," he says. Friends from all over call to pick his brain, and he loves nothing more than to spend long periods of time discussing the various intricacies of his creation. Problem is, other coaches may be able to get some ideas, but they cannot replicate the brain that maneuvers the amoeba.

Miami head coach Jim Larrañaga is a close peer of Boeheim's, but even he didn't appreciate the depths of Boeheim's knowledge until he tried to adopt it for his program at Miami. Larrañaga and his assistants studied many hours of Boeheim's zone carefully. "I couldn't believe how many adjustments he makes," Larrañaga says. "At one point I turned to my wife and said, 'This guy's a genius.'" Larrañaga recalls an instance where his own team was victimized. He knew from studying video that when an offensive center drifted toward the top of Syracuse's zone, his defender usually followed. So heading into his game against Syracuse, Larrañaga directed his center to set some high ball screens in hopes of clearing out space. It worked, for a half. As the second half started, those passes were suddenly unavailable because Boeheim told his own center to stop taking the bait and remain under the basket. "I heard him telling his guys, 'Leave him alone. He won't make that shot,'" Larrañaga says. "And he was right. My big guys couldn't shoot from there." Syracuse won.

Mike Hopkins's favorite example comes from the 2013 East Regional final against Marquette. It was an ugly first half, with Syracuse holding a 24–18 lead at intermission. In the halftime locker room, Boeheim spoke of how Marquette was using its 6′11″ center, Chris Otule, as a decoy to contract the zone, which left a smaller forward, Davante Gardner, open for midrange jump shots. Gardner had nine of Marquette's 18 points in the first half. So Boeheim told his forwards that they should play in front of Otule instead of behind him, which would allow the Orange's guards to push out and crowd Marquette's space. The tweak sent Syracuse to the Final Four with a 55–39 win.

B oeheim may not be fond of long talks in private settings, but that doesn't mean he is not empathetic. There would not have been so many players over so many years who have played so hard and so well for him if they didn't believe he genuinely cared. Even Seikaly got over his hurt feelings, eventually. The two have been snippy with each other over the years—Seikaly once publicly questioned Boeheim's coaching, to which his former coach replied that Seikaly "has been an idiot all his life and continues to be one"—but Seikaly is also the first to admit that the knowledge he gained at Syracuse propelled him to a successful twelve-year NBA career. And when the Orange won the championship in 2003, Seikaly, who was playing for the Miami Heat, chartered a jet to New Orleans, cheered on his alma mater, boarded the bus after the game to congratulate the guys, and then flew home. You don't do that for a coach who lacks empathy.

Boeheim knows he is not good at dishing out compliments. This is part flaw, part design. "I'm not great at it," he says, "but when I do it, they know it. If you do it all the time, they'll expect it." On the other hand, heaven forbid if someone else says something negative about one of his players. Boeheim will sometimes criticize a player to Juli, but as soon as she starts to agree and chime in, he'll flip the script and say, "Well, he's not *that* bad." One of his more epic rants came in February 2007, when the Syracuse student newspaper published an article that included an anonymous quote from a Big East assistant saying that McNamara was "overrated." With McNamara sitting beside him on the dais, Boeheim addressed the matter during a postgame press conference at the conference tournament at Madison Square Garden in a most authentic manner. "Without

Gerry McNamara we wouldn't have won *ten fucking games* this year. Okay? Not *ten!*" he said. "That's the most bullshit thing I've seen in thirty years." McNamara's mother later told him that hearing Boeheim defend her son like that validated his decision to go to Syracuse.

Making himself literally and emotionally distant from his players might make for good basketball, but there have been times when Boeheim separated himself too much from the operations of his program, and it cost him. He can be quite lax, for example, when it comes to enforcing discipline off the court. He argues that it is not his job to be the program's policeman, but whether he likes it or not, his responsibilities to his players, his program, and his university do not end when practice does. This fault led to a second postseason ban in 2015, which the NCAA handed down at the end of an exhaustive ten-year investigation into Boeheim's program.

Those episodes, however, paled in comparison to the storm Boeheim endured in November 2011, when his longtime assistant Bernie Fine was accused of sexually molesting two former Syracuse ball boys more than a decade before. The allegations came at the worst possible time, just two weeks after a more wide-ranging pedophile scandal exploded at Penn State, where a football assistant coach, Jerry Sandusky, was revealed to be a serial child molester, eventually ending the tenure of legendary coach Joe Paterno. Boeheim reacted emotionally to the charges against Fine. He simply refused to believe that this person whom he had known so long and so well was capable of performing these heinous acts, and he said so publicly. He might have been on safe ground if he had stopped there, but he went on to tell numerous media outlets that he believed the accusers were "trying to get money" by capitalizing on what was happening at Penn State. He later tried to walk back his comments, acknowledging he should never have questioned the motives of the accusers, but he did not apologize for supporting his friend. "I'm proud I did. I've known him for forty-six years," he said a few days later. "We went to school together. I think I owed him a debt of allegiance."

In the end, Fine was never formally charged with a crime. One of the accusers, a third man who spoke up after the ball boys came forward, later recanted, admitting he was a "sociopath" who took "a lot of pride in lying" and had never even met Fine. Boeheim no longer has any contact with Fine, who lives in Florida. He is understandably cagey when I broach this subject, but it is clear he believes Fine was innocent. "Nobody ever proved anything, so we still don't know what happened," he says. "But if he didn't do anything, then he lost everything."

All these punches to the gut would have floored a less persistent man, but Boeheim never lost his balance. He grudgingly went along with Syracuse's wishes to announce that he would retire following the 2017–18 season and be succeeded by Hopkins. The plan got upended in March 2017, when Hopkins told Boeheim he was going to accept the head coaching job at the University of Washington. Boeheim was surprised but not exactly unhappy. "I feel good, better than ever, actually, and it's still fun coaching for me," he tells me. "I was fine with retirement, but I feel a little better about this moving forward than I did about being retired."

It turns out he isn't ready to be buried quite yet.

I'm a contradiction in some ways, probably," Boeheim says with a contented sigh. "I can be very sensitive with things. Very sensitive."

This is what passes as profound introspection for him. It is now past midnight in that hotel conference room in Colorado Springs, and Boeheim is exhausted, yawning often and reaching under his glasses to rub his eyes. But he doesn't seem to mind. He is, after all, a night owl. He's happy to talk about basketball, about politics, about life, even about himself a little. Anything to keep his mind occupied.

While most of Boeheim's colleagues are spending their summer recruiting or enjoying some downtime, Boeheim is leading a committee for USA Basketball that will choose a team of young basketball players to compete at the FIBA Americas Under-18 World Championships in Chile. This is how Boeheim relaxes—in a gym, evaluating players, lending his knowledge to build a team that another man will coach. "This is good therapy for me," he says. "August is for vacation, anyway, so it's not like I'm giving up time on my job."

"But you're giving up your vacation," I say.

"Oh, I don't mind that. Vacations are overrated. Anything more than a week is too much."

He still loves to win, but he realizes he has mellowed. "The hardest thing in coaching is to be flexible but not weak," he says. "Things are not always so black and white." Those who know him best have noticed this change. "I've seen him evolve so much," Coleman says. "His whole demeanor has changed, man. Even the way he dresses. And he's so different at practice. When I was there, I didn't even know my name at practice. I thought it was 'You Fucking Asshole.' He knows he can't be as aggressive as he used to be."

He still takes losses hard, of course. Juli tells the story of a particularly painful defeat that sent Boeheim skulking into the basement, where he spent a sleepless night reviewing the game in his head while playing mindlessly on his favorite pinball machine. He emerged the following morning, bleary-eyed and still wearing dress clothes, and joined the family for breakfast. When it comes to dealing with today's players, however, Boeheim is not quite as aloof as he used to be. "The newer kids need more neck rubs," Hopkins says. "He's been able to adapt to that."

Boeheim experienced a health scare in 2001, when he was

diagnosed with prostate cancer. His doctor told him they caught it early, but it was still a disquieting moment. Boeheim's mother had died of leukemia when she was just fifty-eight years old. His father, who was never one to maintain his health, also developed prostate cancer, but because it was so far along by the time it was discovered, he was unable to recover. Jim Sr. died in 1986 at the age of sixty-eight. He and Jim Jr. had learned to relate to each other well enough over the years, but only to a point. "He was a hard guy," Boeheim says. "We were okay by the end, but we were never close. He was just a very stubborn, competitive, opinionated guy."

It is a delicate balancing act, this constant teetering between his dad's hardness and his mom's softness, his understanding about life acquired while surrounded by death, the hard shell and the thin skin, the competitive edge and the empathetic intuition, the ability to suffer the losses but not the fools, all while enjoying a level of success and longevity rarely seen in the coaching profession. His persistence has proven out over time. "You don't want to go through life not feeling things," he tells me. "But coaches above all else have to be resilient. I mean, I've had bad things happen to me during the season. My divorce was right during the season. You've got to keep going. You have to be able to get through things. You're always trying to convince your players that they have to go forward, no matter what happens. It's like I tell them every year. When we're winning and things are going good, you don't find out anything about yourself. When you lose, that's when you find out."

There is no better example than Boeheim's 2015–16 team, which lost five of the nine games when he was serving his NCAA-mandated suspension, began the season 0–4 in the ACC, lost five of their last six games, squeaked into the NCAA Tournament as a No. 10 seed . . . and somehow managed to get back to the Final Four, Boeheim's fifth. It was a simple offensive tweak that sent them on their way. The Orange had ended the 2012–13 regular season with a horrific offensive performance, losing 61–39 at Georgetown. When they struggled again in their Big East tournament quarterfinal game against Pittsburgh, Boeheim called time out. He spun his wheels and arrived at a very simple notion: When your team is having a hard time making shots, run some plays for your best shooter.

Boeheim drew up some off-ball screening action to get 6′8″ junior forward James Southerland open. Southerland responded by hitting two quick three-pointers. That forced Pittsburgh to rotate more aggressively on him, which in turn spaced the floor and opened up driving lanes for the team's two big, sturdy guards, Michael Carter-Williams and Brandon Triche. "It changed everyone's mindset because they were in attack mode again," McNamara says. "The beauty was in the simplicity of it."

Syracuse won the game, reached the Big East final, where the Orange lost to Louisville, and ended the season, remarkably, at the Final Four in Atlanta, where they lost to Michigan in the semifinal.

Sitting in that conference room in Colorado a few months later, Boeheim delights in pointing out that his most recent team reached the Final Four with more losses than any other school in history. It's all about losing, right? Later in our conversation, he repeats that he "can be very sensitive with things." Now it is my turn to snicker condescendingly. No, really, he says, it's true. Why, just recently he got teary-eyed watching the coverage of Muhammad Ali's death. He also tells me that he often cries during movies. "Did you see *Love Story*?" he asks. I tell him I haven't. "Really? That was a tearjerker. You should see it."

This genuinely surprises me. "What's the thing that makes you cry the most at movies?" I ask. Boeheim pauses to spin his wheels. He yawns. He rubs his eyes. He smiles, maybe a little, I think.

"I cry when somebody dies," he says.

Geno Auriemma

H e couldn't understand a word she was saying, yet he understood her perfectly. The nun at St. Francis of Assisi School sat across from him, behind a desk. His aunt, who served as his interpreter, was by his side. Luigi Auriemma was seven years old and fresh off the boat from Italy. He didn't speak a word of English. Even worse, he was already two months late in joining the second grade.

The message from the nun was simple: If the boy performed well enough in the classroom, he would move to the third grade at the end of the school year. If he didn't, he would repeat. The aunt translated. Luigi nodded. *Yup, got it. Smart ones move up, dumb ones stay back.* "And there was no English-as-a-second-language lessons after school, or anything like that. No private tutors," Auriemma says. "No any of that stuff. You just had to figure it out."

The nun was neither mean nor nice about the situation faced by Luigi, whom everyone called by his nickname, Geno. She simply told him the truth. So he went back to his aunt's house, where he lived with her family as well as his parents and two siblings, and he started to figure it out. He studied the backs of cereal boxes. His older cousins, both girls, read him books. His aunt helped him with his lessons. Geno's mom, Marsiella, didn't speak English either, but she helped make that household run. His father was around too, but he worked long hours at the local steel mill and showed scant interest in his kids' Americanized lives, preferring to spend his idle time smoking cigarettes and sipping espresso at the Italian club in town.

Fortunately for Geno, he had a sharp mind. Somehow, some way, he made it through the second grade. Socially, however, things were not easy. The kids made fun of his clothes, his accent, even his lunch. They ate peanut butter and jelly, while his sandwiches teemed with sausages and peppers, the oil leaking embarrassingly through his brown paper bag. Fortunately for Geno, he did not have to get through it alone. Each time he stumbled, each time he struggled, there was a strong woman there to help him figure it out.

Like Sister Joseph Theresa, for example. He'll never forget the first day of class when she displayed a cardboard box that had been cut to look like a television. She warned the students that if they misbehaved, she would turn the box around and put on a special show: "You Asked For It." Geno did his best not to ask for it. "We were in a constant state of fear, like, 'Shit, this TV better not go on today,'" he recalls with a chuckle.

Later on, his favorite high school teacher was Sister Rose Patrice. If she hadn't helped him pass tenth-grade geometry, he wouldn't have stayed eligible to play basketball, just at the point when he was falling in love with the game. He felt her empathy before he truly understood what that was. "She just saw a weakness in me," Auriemma says. "You can tell when someone likes you."

The culture was a carryover from the country Auriemma left, where generations of strong women supported their families while the men were off fighting wars. From the very beginnings of his life,

Auriemma understood that women were to be feared and respected, and ultimately loved. "Since I can remember, I have never ever ever had any doubt that the role of women in the life of everybody that I knew was overpowering," he says. "You understood they were people that you listened to, that they would be stern, they would discipline you, but they would love you. They would tell you, 'This is what you need to do to be better.' They would criticize you when you were wrong. They would praise you when you were good. They would reward you, they would scold you, they made you work for everything. So this idea of women being the weaker sex, that's just so foreign to me. Whenever I hear that I'm like, 'What world did those people grow up in?'"

The seeds of Luigi Auriemma's PEAK profile were planted by strong feminine hands. It took persistence to return to that school day after day, despite the deep fear that he would be one of the dumb ones who got left back. He developed an innate insecurity that provided him with an empathetic core. He embraced his Italian heritage even when it put him at a disadvantage, because that's who he was. And he acquired knowledge that begat the overriding skill he would use to navigate in this strange new world: the ability to read people. Geno didn't always understand what people were saying, so he studied *how* they were saying it. He didn't read the native language, so he learned how to read body language. That skill now enables him to get to *Us* as a women's college basketball coach. He was never book smart, but he has great emotional intelligence. He sizes up rooms, analyzes situations, reads people, and reacts accordingly.

He learned this without any real male role model aside from his high school basketball coach. And yet Geno figured it out. His is a quintessentially American tale, centered around a young immigrant navigating the transition from one world to the next, achieving great success without ever quite fitting in. Every traveler needs a bridge, and for Geno, that bridge was built by women. They did more than help him learn. They showed him how to teach.

He laughed. Of course he laughed. All season long, Geno Auriemma had been waiting for his talented but young UConn Lady Huskies to cough up a game. Even as their epic winning streak climbed past 100 games, he believed it was inevitable. So when it happened in the most dramatic fashion possible—with a basket at the buzzer to deliver a 66–64 overtime win for Mississippi State at the 2017 Final Four—there was Auriemma on the UConn bench sideline, smiling like he had just been elected class president.

The loss was seismic, not just for Auriemma's program but for the sport of women's basketball. It broke UConn's 111-game win streak, the second time one of Auriemma's teams had eclipsed the 88-game men's record set by John Wooden's UCLA Bruins. When I bring up Auriemma's reaction to him a few months later, he concedes that in his younger days, the last thing he would have done after getting beat like that was laugh. He didn't react that way because he wants to win any less now than he did then. It was because he knows so much more.

"I've seen people get beat who are big-time winners over the years, and their reaction was totally disgusting. Like, 'How dare you beat us?'" he tells me. "I mean, c'mon. Maybe no one in the history of sports has won as much as we've won. What are you gonna do, be an asshole when you lose? You're gonna live up to everybody's expectation of you? It took five freaking months for what I thought was gonna happen to happen. The moment just got a little too big for us. That's all."

Even when you beat him, Auriemma gives you the feeling that he still knows just a little bit more than you do. The annoying part is he's probably right. My favorite all-time quote about him came from Rebecca Lobo, the cornerstone of his first NCAA championship team at the University of Connecticut. "Geno's natural walk," Lobo said, "is a strut."

Lobo first noticed it when she was a senior in high school and Auriemma was recruiting her. There was no logical reason for him to be so confident. He was a relatively inexperienced coach with a relatively unestablished program. But he strutted anyway, and she found it irresistible. "He just had that air about him. I guess today they would call it swag," Lobo says. "It can come across as arrogance, but I thought it was enticing more than off-putting. It made me want to play for him."

Phil Martelli noticed the same thing when he met Auriemma while the two of them were working a basketball camp in Philadelphia. Auriemma was a no-name part-time assistant coach at a local high school, yet to Martelli he appeared to have every belief he belonged. "He was magnetic even back then," Martelli says. "Like, he could *hang*. He had that Philadelphia edge. He was a ballbuster like all of us were. If you didn't think you were the best, then you weren't in second, you were not even in the running. So you had to think and carry yourself like you were the best."

Debbie Ryan noticed it too, right after she hired Auriemma to be her assistant women's coach at the University of Virginia in 1981. To that point, Auriemma's only coaching experience was a few years as a high school assistant plus one season as a men's assistant at Saint Joseph's University in Philadelphia. But from the time he arrived in Charlottesville, Auriemma had a swagger that belied his résumé. "For someone as young as he was, he had an amazing vision for what he wanted to do," Ryan says. "He never feared sticking his nose into anything. He could drop into any conversation and hold his own."

We see that strut today while Auriemma prowls the sidelines for UConn—hair finely combed, tie perfectly loosened, ass back, chest out, a perpetual look on his face as if he's thinking, *Can you believe how fucking dumb these people are?* Underneath, however, the story is much different. Auriemma may have strutted through life like he's the baddest dude in the gym, but his insecurities practically ooze from his pores, like olive oil soaking through a brown paper bag.

For example, when his UConn teams started winning and the crowds swelled, Auriemma learned to hate the long walk across the floor to his team's locker room in the opposite corner. He felt naked with all those eyes on him. He'd call over a couple of players so he would have someone to accompany him. When the school built a new arena, Auriemma told his wife, Kathy, that the best thing about the new place was that his team's locker room was next to the bench.

Ask Auriemma why he drives his players so hard, and he replies, "We have to win every game, because I have to prove that I can coach." This from a man who has won eleven NCAA championships and counting.

He doesn't strut so he can fool the rest of us. He's fooling himself as well. He's also carrying a lot of guilt—Catholic guilt, no less. He knows damn well his parents never had it this good. Geno may have been teased when he was a boy, but at least he was in a safe, promising environment. When Auriemma's mom was that age, her family sent her away to work on a farm because they couldn't afford to feed all five kids. She had no time for school, no time for learning. Geno's mom never learned to read or write.

Auriemma's father, Donato, didn't even want to come to America in the first place. He immigrated in 1960 because he felt he had to be with his brother, who had settled in Norristown, Pennsylvania, just outside Philadelphia. A year later, Donato sent for his wife and three children. Geno and his family left their tiny village of Montella, traveled on a boat for thirteen days, and eventually arrived in Norristown.

Between his illiterate mom and his indifferent dad, there was no one to push Geno in school. He did just enough to get by, and then he signed his own report cards. He loved playing baseball at first, but he soon fell into basketball, and when the coach at his high school took a liking to him, Geno was all in. Sports was the one area where he felt validated. He certainly had no "game" with the ladies. "I didn't have a car," he says, laughing. "So where was I going?"

Needless to say, he wasn't making grand plans back then. He wasn't making *any* plans. He was too busy helping his mom buy groceries, cash checks, pay bills. They took taxicabs to the store. He rode the city bus to school. He made a few friends, especially his teammates, but there was a part of him that felt as if he would always be an outsider. "When you're an immigrant, you're caught between two worlds," he says. "You've got to fake it a little bit. So you develop an attitude of embracing the difference, but still trying to prove you belong."

By the time high school ended, Auriemma hadn't given much thought to his future. His coach tried to persuade him to go to a four-year college and keep playing basketball. He wasn't good enough to earn a scholarship, but maybe he could walk on at Saint Joseph's or LaSalle, and in four years he would have a degree. Auriemma pretended to consider it, but deep down he sensed he wasn't good enough. So he decided to go with the flow and join some buddies who were headed for a local community college. Some strutter, this guy.

She first spotted him shooting hoops in an empty gym, wearing sweatpants and no shirt. He was easy on the eyes, that's for sure. Kathy Ostler, a cheerleader at Montgomery County Community College in Pottstown, Pennsylvania, mentioned to her girlfriend that she thought the guy was cute, so her friend conspired to arrange for Geno to give her a ride home after a game. Along the way, Kathy asked what he planned to do with his life. Geno said he wanted to be a lawyer. "I thought, *Oh really? We're in community college*," Kathy says. "The quality that I first recognized in him was that he seemed a little older than other guys, a little more serious. I felt like there was texture to him, this depth that I just found really cool."

She directed him through her hometown of Cheltenham, a well-to-do suburb of Philly located on the Main Line. He liked what he saw. This girl was cute, she seemed cool, and she came from money. That is, until they reached her home, a tiny apartment above a drugstore next to a railroad track.

At least they could empathize with each other. Like Geno, Kathy knew about assuming responsibilities at a young age. She also understood what it was like to have an absent father—in her case literally so, since her dad died of illness when she was a young girl. "I grew up fast," she says. "I had a single mother, so I was really responsible in my household. I had to pay bills and start dinner. I knew how to go to the grocery store."

He liked her looks, her spunk, her wit, and that she wasn't a "girly girl," as he puts it. Even though she was raised without a father, Kathy was a big sports fan. They dated for the remainder of their time at Montgomery County and became engaged after graduation. She found a job as a teacher but was laid off before they got married. It was not an extravagant wedding, to say the least.

Geno may have dreamed of having a law degree, but he didn't pursue it. He didn't pursue anything, really. Knowledge was not his thing, at least not the classroom kind. After finishing up his two years at Montgomery College, he enrolled at West Chester (Pennsylvania) University, but he dropped out a few credits shy of graduation because he had a chance to take a job as a teacher and athletic director at a local high school, and he needed the dough. (He went back and finished up his degree several years later.) Then one day a friend from college, Jim Foster, asked him to be his assistant coach for the girls' basketball team at Bishop McDevitt High School in Harrisburg. The pay for the entire season was around $600. Auriemma thought it was a silly idea—coaching girls' basketball?—but Foster talked him into it.

Auriemma coached for two seasons, and he liked it more than he anticipated. Basketball was the one thing he knew something about. He had a knack for motivating those girls. He liked that they respected him. "I knew a little more than they did, and they seemed to be responding," he says. "Whenever I showed 'em something, they thought it was pretty cool."

Auriemma had to leave his athletic director job to coach, so he needed another way to make ends meet. Fortunately, Kathy had a friend whose father owned a grocery store. She got Geno a job stocking shelves from 11 p.m. to 7 a.m. Having found something he enjoyed doing, Auriemma rediscovered his childhood persistence. It was an odd way to begin marital life—no plans, no prospects, no real logic in place. Had he been any different, and had he married someone who didn't think like he did, then he probably would have chucked the whole thing long beforehand. To outsiders it may have seemed foolish, but to Geno it felt authentic.

"The breadwinner in our house was a guy stocking shelves in the supermarket so he could coach basketball in the afternoon. That's pretty scary," he says. "If either of us had traditional parents, they would have looked at us and said, 'What the hell are you doing?' I mean, basketball coach? Where the hell are we going with that? The whole time I'm chasing basketball, and for no reason whatsoever. It made zero sense because it didn't have any future to it. I'm taking all these part-time jobs so I can coach and make six hundred dollars? Like, what the hell is wrong with you? I wouldn't recommend that as a life journey to anybody."

To Auriemma's surprise, Foster got hired in 1978 to coach the women's team at Saint Joseph's. When he asked Auriemma to come with him, it was an easy call, even though it still wasn't a full-time job and didn't pay all that much more than the one he had at Bishop McDevitt.

Working at Saint Joseph's was a great experience, but the real benefit was the invitation that came with it to Cathy Rush's basketball camp. Rush had won three national championships as the women's coach at Immaculata University, a small private girls' school outside of Philadelphia. Her camp presented Auriemma with a golden opportunity to learn about the game and network with local coaches. Philly was an incredible hotbed back then. Two future NBA coaches, Jack McKinney and Jim Lynam, worked at Saint Joseph's. Paul Westhead, the future Lakers and Loyola Marymount coach, was at La Salle. The head coach at Penn was a guy named Chuck Daly. Auriemma worked alongside those guys during the day and joined them for beers at night. They dropped some serious knowledge on him.

One of the men whom Auriemma bonded with at the camp was Phil Martelli. He had just gotten hired as the head boys' coach at Auriemma's old high school, Bishop Kenrick. When Martelli invited Auriemma to be his assistant in 1978, Auriemma thought he had it made. The job still didn't pay much, but it had some cachet. He was back coaching boys, and in the hypercompetitive Philadelphia Catholic League. "I'm thinking, *Okay, this is it*," Auriemma says. "I'm gonna get a teaching job in high school and coach boys' basketball. This is gonna be my life."

He spent two happy years working by Martelli's side. They were a couple of Italian Americans from Philly, busting balls, coaching hoops, having a blast. It could have gone on forever, except in the spring of 1981, Martelli got a call from Debbie Ryan, who was the head women's coach at the University of Virginia. Ryan knew Martelli from the Cathy Rush camp, so she reached out and asked if he would be interested in coming on board as her assistant. Martelli had no desire to leave Philadelphia, but he suggested she consider Auriemma, given his experience in coaching high school girls. Once again, the notion made little sense to Geno, but Ryan persuaded him to come to Charlottesville for a visit.

He was blown away. The rolling, leafy campus, the classic red-brick buildings, the aura of Thomas Jefferson, the passion and spirit of ACC basketball—it was as if a brand-new world had opened up for him. Geno returned home from the trip sky high. Kathy didn't need much convincing that they should make the move.

From day one, Ryan gave Auriemma responsibilities that touched every aspect of the program. He was an eager learner and a relentless assistant. "Geno was the type who was always challenging you," Ryan says. "If you wanted to do something, he'd say, 'Why?' He really made you think about what you were doing."

Though he was living in the South, Auriemma stayed in touch with his old Philly crew, traipsing up to the Poconos to work camps each summer. He'll never forget the day Jim Lynam came up to him while he was working a defensive drill station and said, "I really like what you're teaching over there." For the first time, he was starting to believe he could really hang.

As it happened, Auriemma's career arc was dovetailing with the ascent of women's college basketball. Nine years before he got hired at Virginia, the U.S. government passed Title IX as part of a package of amendments to the 1964 Civil Rights Act. That law effectively forced universities to offer equal opportunities in athletics for men and women. It took ten years, but in 1982, the year after Auriemma got hired as an assistant at Virginia, the NCAA finally decided to begin holding its own national championship in women's basketball. (The men's version had been around since 1939.) Virginia qualified for the tournament in Auriemma's third and fourth seasons there. As the team kept winning, and as Ryan leaned on him more heavily, Auriemma became increasingly confident that he was ready for his own gig. Following his third season, he was interviewed for the women's head coaching position at DePaul. He didn't get it, but the experience emboldened him. At the start of the 1984–85 season, he predicted to Kathy that in one year's time he would have his own team.

Sure enough, at the end of that season, Auriemma got a call from the University of Connecticut. The school's search committee was hoping to hire a woman, but it was having a hard time finding any takers—and for good reason. The university was located in the small town of Storrs, thirty miles east of Hartford, seemingly in the middle of nowhere. The program had only been around for eleven years and had yet to produce a winning season. The outgoing coach had won just nine games in each of her previous four years. The team played in the Hugh S. Greer Field House, a shabby facility that could not even hold 5,000 fans, though size wasn't much of an issue since the games were so sparsely attended.

Where others saw squalor, Auriemma saw potential. He saw a chance to return to his northern roots and run his own program. He strutted into that interview, sized up the room, and blew away the committee. The school's athletic director, John Toner, took him to a local Dunkin' Donuts and offered him the job at a salary of $29,000. Auriemma accepted. Then he told Kathy the news and flew home to pack up and start a new life. He raved to his wife about the people he met at UConn but added, "The gym must be a piece of shit, because they never showed it to me."

How in the world was he going to win at a place with no facilities and no tradition, with no head coaching experience to draw from? Hell if he knew. He would just get there and strut around like he knew what he was doing. One way or another, he would have to figure it out.

. . .

One of the ways Auriemma convinced UConn's search committee that he should get the job was by promising he would bring in a prominent young assistant named Chris Dailey. She was working at Rutgers, where she had won an NCAA championship as a player in 1982.

There was only one problem. Auriemma never told Dailey his plan.

They weren't even all that close. Sure, they had hung out on the recruiting trail and served on a coaches' committee, but they had never talked about working together. Auriemma called Dailey shortly after he got hired and offered her the job. "What are you going to accomplish at Rutgers that hasn't already been done?" he said. "Come work for me and we'll build this thing together." Dailey was intrigued, but she made him wait until later that summer for her boss, Theresa Grentz, to return to the country from her stint coaching for USA Basketball. Eventually, she succumbed to his persistence. "He challenged me, which is one of his great assets," Dailey says.

Auriemma was right. The gym was a piece of shit. His players had to share locker room space with the men's soccer team. Auriemma and Dailey were crammed into a tiny office, where they used a rotary phone and shared a line with the track coach. If he was on a call, the basketball coaches would have to wait until he was done before dialing.

On more than one occasion that first season, Dailey wondered what she had done—and who she had done it for. In the very first game of the very first season, Auriemma bitched at the refs so much that he was whistled for two technical fouls. That did not warrant an automatic ejection in those days, but it did not bode well. Dailey's dad was one of the few spectators in the gym that day. He reminded her, and not for the last time, that she was welcome to come home anytime.

Sure, Auriemma could be hotheaded (not to mention hard-headed), but Dailey noticed something else. "The closer the game, the calmer he was," she says. "You could see he had a great feel. He has a vision of how it's supposed to look in his head, and he is unwilling to stop until it looks like that."

Auriemma let Dailey handle all the aspects of the program he either didn't enjoy or wasn't good at—tickets, recruiting, practice schedules, academics, marketing, community outreach. Meanwhile, it took everyone a while to get accustomed to Auriemma's temperamental ways. During his second season, he walked into the locker room during halftime and blew his stack. As he chastised his "guys"—that's how he refers to his players—he slapped his top freshman, guard Kris Lamb, on the elbow. Auriemma didn't think anything of it until three months later when he learned that the older players, the ones who had been recruited by his predecessor, complained to the athletic director that he had been abusive. If that had happened much later in his career, Auriemma might have been in trouble. In this case, Lamb stuck up for him and the AD backed him. It was a harrowing episode, but it also gave Auriemma an important piece of knowledge. From then on, he recruited players who could deal with his style of coaching. If he failed at that part of the job, then he wasn't going to last very long.

It was not in him to sweet talk recruits anyway. That would be inauthentic. When a highly regarded 6′1″ forward from New Hampshire named Kerry Bascom asked him during a phone call what she would get out of playing for him, Auriemma replied, "Whatever you put into it." Bascom later said that of all the coaches who recruited her, Auriemma was the only one who didn't promise her anything. He had, instead, a different message: Don't come here unless you can hang. She ended up becoming his first breakthrough recruit and left UConn in 1991 as the school's all-time leading scorer.

It made no difference to Auriemma that his players were women.

He would coach them just as hard as he would coach men. Lots of women's coaches said that, but in 1985, very few believed it as deeply as Auriemma did. He had learned firsthand that women could be as persistent as men, in many cases more so. He could be as tough and mean as he wanted and still trust they understood he empathized with what they were thinking and feeling. He could also have fun with them, like he did with his boys back in Philly. Just because they were ladies didn't mean he couldn't bust their balls.

For example, early in Auriemma's career, he was cautioned against criticizing his players if they gained too much weight. He thought this was ludicrous. To be a great player, you need to be in proper shape. He's not supposed to say that just because they might get their feelings hurt, or perhaps develop an eating disorder? That's bullshit, man. "What's hard about playing here is that there's no looking the other way and saying, 'That's all right, sweetheart, we'll get 'em next time,'" Auriemma says. "That pisses me off when I hear that, because they never do that with guys. When a boy screws up in sports and he's fifteen, there's no 'It's all right, sweetheart, we'll get 'em next time.' But for a girl the same age, that's what they hear."

After the Lady Huskies went 12–15 his first season, the wins started coming: 14 in year two, 17 in year three. In year four, UConn went 24–6 and won the Big East championship. Two years later, they broke through and reached the game's biggest stage, the Final Four in New Orleans, where they lost to Virginia, coached by his old boss Debbie Ryan.

Reaching the Final Four was a remarkable achievement for Auriemma's program. The question was whether he could sustain that success. The answer came in the form of a 6'4" center from Massachusetts named Rebecca Lobo. She was a consensus All-American, by far the best player Auriemma had tried to recruit. Lobo's parents were teachers, and they were enamored with the idea of their daughter going to Stanford or Notre Dame. Yet Lobo was convinced from the start that Auriemma was the man she wanted to play for. During their conversations, Auriemma stressed that she would only play as many minutes as she earned. "I really liked that honesty," she says. "With some coaches, when you talked to them on the phone, you were kind of waiting to get off. But with him, it wasn't that way. I actually looked forward to the chance to talk with him. He had something in his personality that made me want to play for him."

Once again, Auriemma benefited from some propitious timing. Just as he was starting to recruit Lobo, UConn was putting the finishing touches on Gampel Pavilion, a sleek 10,000-seat arena that began hosting games in 1990. The men's basketball program was also enjoying a rise to national prominence under Jim Calhoun, who was hired away from Northeastern the year after Auriemma came on board. Aside from the NHL's Hartford Whalers, the state of Connecticut had no professional teams, so the citizenry was passionate about UConn basketball. It was difficult for fans to get tickets to the men's game, but tickets to the women's game were plentiful—and free. And the team was fun to watch.

With facilities and players finally in place, Auriemma went about fulfilling his vision. When CBS offered him the chance to play Tennessee on national television during Lobo's senior season, he jumped at it. Tennessee was the premium brand in women's basketball, led by the brilliant, stern southerner Pat Summitt. When the teams tipped off on January 16, 1995, Tennessee was ranked No. 1 in the country, UConn was No. 2, and both were undefeated. Auriemma's Huskies won, 77–66. By Monday morning, they were, amazingly, the No. 1 team in America.

From there, the Lady Huskies completed their historic romp, finishing with a perfect 35–0 record and a six-point win over Tennessee in the NCAA championship game. A few hours after capturing the title, the players, coaches, families, and friends were gathered in their hotel watching a replay of the game. Everybody was hooting and hollering, until at one point Auriemma barked something from the back of the room. He had spied a defensive breakdown and asked the person playing the video to run back the play. He stood up and pointed out the miscue to his players. At first, they looked at each other, unsure whether he was serious. Finally, a reserve guard named Missy Rose spoke up and said, "Hey, Coach, relax for once. We won."

The room burst out in hysterics. Auriemma laughed, too. He had to admit she had done a good job of busting his balls.

It wasn't quite a nervous breakdown, but it was pretty damn close. Having run out of words—which is remarkable in its own right—Auriemma stalked off the practice floor in a fit of rage and frustration. He figured he would just keep going and exit the building, but he decided instead to crawl under the bleachers, sit up against a wall, and close his eyes. Dailey continued to run the practice, but the players were confused, and not a little bit worried.

After about twenty minutes, Nykesha Sales, a former player who had been visiting that day, poked her head under the bleachers and asked if he was all right.

"Leave me alone," Auriemma said.

"Uh, Coach, everyone is getting concerned. Maybe you should come out now."

This was Auriemma at his most authentic—driven, exacting, deeply insecure. But he still had much to learn. It was early in the 1998–99 season, four years after that first championship. In the wake of that triumph, Auriemma had strutted too close to the sun. He had convinced himself that the championship resulted from the sheer force of his will, intellect, and creativity. Yet even though the top recruits were now annually lining up to play for him, he could not recapture that magic. Every time it looked like his team was going back over the top, it got hit with a bad injury, and the season would end with a loss.

Now Auriemma had just brought in what was being called the greatest recruiting class in the history of women's collegiate basketball. He was grossly unrealistic about how quickly his newbies would make the transition from high school. It was only a few weeks into the preseason, but he was at his wit's end. His meltdown was not rooted in anger. It was rooted in self-doubt. "I really questioned whether I was good enough to do this," he says.

It was a total reversal. When Auriemma first got to UConn, he was convinced that whatever challenge his upstarts faced, they would figure it out and beat more talented teams. Once his teams became heavy favorites, however, he found himself consumed by worry, certain that whatever could go wrong, would.

This was the price he paid for chasing perfection. It wasn't enough to win. They had to win by playing the *right* way. Auriemma wasn't just facing opponents, he was chasing an ideal—and an unreachable one at that. No practice plan could compete with that vision. Auriemma might schedule a two-line layup drill for ten minutes, but it would go on for well over an hour if his guys didn't do it exactly how he wanted. His goal was to make those workouts so taxing that the games seemed easy by comparison. "The players know he's always watching," Dailey says. "Even when you think he's not watching, he's watching."

To be fair, Auriemma held himself to the same high standards. He was an eager student of the game, always learning and tinkering in an effort to maintain his edge. He possessed a wonderfully creative basketball mind, especially on the offensive end. He wants his teams to play artistically and selflessly. That's why they don't have names on the back of their jerseys, and it's also why he has resisted the trend toward isolation pick-and-roll offenses that have overtaken the NBA and men's college basketball in recent years. Auriemma would rather stick with a pass-happy offense that involves all five players.

Auriemma fancies himself a seat-of-the-pants coach. He doesn't like plans. He may drive Dailey mad with his penchant for tardiness, but even she has to admit that he has a knack for figuring things out. When I suggest to Dailey that Auriemma must understand women at a level that most men don't, she brushes me off. "I don't know that I would say that," she replies. "Here's what I would say: Geno gets people. He knows how to read people, he knows how to relate to people, he knows what buttons to push. And it annoys me to no end, because he usually knows when something is amiss with one of our players. He has a sixth sense. He'll say, 'Something's not right,' and I hate to admit it, but he has never been wrong when he says that."

That empathetic instinct, that keen emotional intelligence, provides Auriemma with the blueprint he needs. Sure, he can get under a player's skin, but he also knows the way into her heart. "He inspires those kids every single day," Ryan says. "That's what he does better than anybody else. From the very first day of practice, he inspires them to be better than they think they can be. He would have been great as a Navy SEAL because he can pivot on a dime and go in another direction just like that, and he's not afraid to give that to his kids."

It is not easy playing for this man, but that is what his guys sign up for. During recruiting, he asks them what their goals are. Once they tell him they want to be NCAA champions, All-Americans, professional players . . . well, then he's got 'em by the balls. If they complain, he reminds them that he is only helping them get to where they said they wanted to go. That's why his players are so loyal to him long after they're through at UConn. Kara Wolters, who played at UConn from 1993 to 1997, has said that Auriemma is the best coach she ever played for, despite the time her freshman season when he kicked her out of practice by throwing a basketball at her head.

"He's like the puppetmaster. If he wasn't coaching basketball, he would be great at psychology," says Swin Cash, a 6′1″ forward from the Pittsburgh area and a member of that vaunted freshman class. "I had this habit that whenever he would start yelling at me, I would always look up at the sky. Nothing's up there but our banners. So one day I was doing that and he goes, 'Okay, I guess Swin is pissed off. She's looking up at the banners.' I just busted out laughing."

Lobo got the full Geno treatment early in her junior year. She had been complaining so much to her mother about Auriemma's badgering that her mom persuaded her to go into his office and discuss it. When she did, Auriemma pulled out the team's media guide and read the part where Lobo said she wanted to be an Olympian. Auriemma explained that if he let her standards fall to the point where she didn't reach her goal, it would be his fault. At the end of what Lobo thought was a private and intimate conversation, she felt much better.

That is, until two days later, when in the midst of a lousy practice Auriemma exploded and shouted toward Dailey, "She comes into my office complaining I'm too tough on her, and now she plays like *this*?" Lobo was mortified. But she got the message. "He wasn't just saying he was going to hold me accountable. He wanted my teammates to hold me accountable, too," she says. "If you're playing for him, he makes sure you're as mentally strong as you can be."

Surprisingly, Auriemma's demands for excellence extend to the classroom, even though by his own admission he was a lazy student. "That's what teachers do," he says. "We always expect more out of our students than we ever did from ourselves."

There is, alas, a fine line between being demanding and being unreasonable, between possessing drive and suffering from impatience. Between a confident stride and an insecure strut. That was the tension that broke Auriemma down that day in practice, leaving him distraught, dysfunctional, and hiding under the bleachers. He had finally lost his swag. His drive had driven him crazy.

The breakdown also added to his knowledge. "It was a real lesson for me. Like, *What are you doing?*" he says. "All this internal pressure, all this angst and beating yourself up. What's that getting you? I don't know if I'm so much better now, but I think I understand it more because I know there are a lot of things out of your control. I used to think I can control the outcome, but I learned that I can't. I can only control how we prepare."

Auriemma eventually crawled out from under those bleachers, returned to practice, took a deep breath, tapped into his well of persistence, and resumed teaching. The episode didn't cause him to lose his strut. It just taught him to step a little more carefully.

I f Auriemma was being authentic that day under the bleachers, he was also being empathetic. By letting his players see just how badly he could lose his confidence, he was showing he understood what they were feeling when it happened to them. He doesn't get to *Us* by teaching his players not to feel scared. Rather, he strives to convince them that the only way to persist through the fear is by relying on each other.

"I live with self-doubt every day, so I can empathize with the players I'm coaching," Auriemma says. "I *know* these guys are filled with self-doubt. How can they not be? You're putting yourself out there in front of thousands of people. You're being judged and you're eighteen, nineteen years old. So you're thinking, *Am I good enough to do this? What happens if I play shitty?* So this is a part of daily life. I try to tell them, 'It's good for you to have self-doubt, because it forces you to look at yourself objectively.'"

Auriemma's players don't typically arrive with a lot of insecurities.

They were all among the best high school players in the country. They are used to being feted and featured. The way he sees it, his job is to put them in situations where they have to deal with failure. Oftentimes this will happen organically as they move up to face tougher competition. Other times, Auriemma will look to manufacture the stress himself. "Kind of like tossing a rattlesnake onto the middle of the court," he says. "I want to see how they react."

For example, when Diana Taurasi, a 6'0″ All-American guard from California, was having a particularly good practice her freshman year, Auriemma ordered her into a drill that required her to defend two players at opposite ends of the lane. Taurasi shuttled back and forth as each offensive player caught a pass and tried to score. The only way to get out of the drill is to get two stops in a row. It is a diabolical exercise, because the longer it takes, the more tired the defender gets, and thus the more unlikely she is to get a stop. As Taurasi failed again and again, she started fouling more blatantly. Finally, Auriemma told her to step out of the drill, making sure to let her know she had failed. Taurasi was angry, but she fought her way through the rest of practice.

Auriemma didn't have to throw a rattlesnake at Breanna Stewart. The Baylor Lady Bears did it for him. It happened during a game in Waco early in her career. Stewart, who would go on to become arguably the best player Auriemma ever had, played just seven minutes off the bench that night. During that time, the woman she was guarding scored twelve points. UConn lost by six. Auriemma prodded her as they talked about it afterward. "Stewie, you're scared. I know you are. Just come out and say it," he said. It took a while, but she finally admitted it. She realized Auriemma knew what she was feeling better than she did.

The blunt talk starts at the very beginning of the relationship. When Auriemma first called Shea Ralph, a highly coveted guard from Raleigh, North Carolina, she asked him how much playing time she would get. "I don't know," Auriemma replied. "If you come here and you suck, you're not gonna play." Ralph hung up the phone and told her mother she wanted to go to UConn. "To that point in the recruiting process, I couldn't remember coaches and their names because they all sounded the same to me," Ralph says. "They all said how great I was and what I could do for them, but I knew in the back of my mind that it wasn't that easy. I knew that I wanted to be challenged."

Ralph got a little more challenge than she bargained for. Like many players, she did not enjoy practice. This created considerable tension with Auriemma, but Ralph thought she was doing okay. During a game her freshman year at Rhode Island, however, she sat for the entire first half, even though UConn was winning by more than 40 points. Auriemma even put in a walk-on while leaving Ralph to stew on the bench. By the time she got into the locker room for halftime, she was fighting back tears. Auriemma walked in and immediately called her out in front of everyone. "Shea, how many points did you have in that half?"

Ralph shook her head, indicating she had none.

"How many rebounds?" he asked.

She shook her head again.

Auriemma continued to go down the list. How many assists? How many steals? Then he made his point. "The answer is zero, because that's exactly how you've been practicing the last two weeks. And if you don't learn to practice better, you're not gonna play in games."

The words were harsh, but Ralph knew he was right. More important, she knew he was saying them because he cared about her. "How many people do you have in your life that will tell you the truth no matter what? Not many," she says. "It's not easy to hear all the time, but it's exactly what you need."

Auriemma was equally direct when it came to the delicate topic of Ralph's issues with food. But he was also discreet. Ralph had battled anorexia when she was in high school, which everyone knew because she had discussed it publicly with reporters. Auriemma made it clear to her that there was no way she could be a successful player at UConn if she was severely underweight. "You will eat, or you won't play," he told her. When Ralph fell back on bad habits like eating a bagel and a couple of diet sodas to get her through the day, Auriemma would walk by her during practice and say quietly, "Yeah, I guess those diet sodas didn't work so well for you today." On the few occasions when he was more concerned, he called her into his office and let her know what he was seeing. He never once said anything in front of her teammates. "I don't know that I would have heard it the right way, had he not done it like that," Ralph says.

It is remarkable enough that Auriemma is this intuitive with players of a different gender. He also pulls it off without delving into their personal lives. "You hear some players talk about their coach like, 'He's like a dad to me.' I've never heard anyone say that about Coach Auriemma," Cash says. As a rule, Auriemma is willing to discuss personal matters with his players, but only if they ask him to. Otherwise, he respects those barriers. But whenever one of his players finally does buckle under all the stress, Auriemma unleashes all the dimensions of his PEAK profile. "That's when I do what I think I'm really good at, which is blow so much smoke up their butt that they feel like they're the king of the world," he says. "So by the time we get into the NCAA Tournament, it's a done deal."

Like all highly successful coaches, Auriemma is a skilled tactician, thanks to the expansive basketball knowledge he has accumulated over the years. He is compulsively fearful of stagnation. Ralph, now an assistant coach at UConn, will sometimes get text messages from her boss early on a Sunday morning in June with ideas about something they can add to the offense. Even when he is coming off an undefeated championship season, Auriemma fights the urge to "stick with what's working." He is always on the lookout for new things to try.

Auriemma knows that there is no single system that gets a team to *Us*. What matters is whether a coach can tailor his tactics to his personnel, and then get his players to follow his instructions with total belief. He won his first NCAA championship in 1995 using the triangle offense made popular by Michael Jordan's Chicago Bulls teams. Five years later, he claimed his second behind a perimeter-oriented offense that emphasized three-point shooting, which he had installed because his tallest player was only 6′5″. After the Lady Huskies made the 2007 Final Four, Auriemma scrapped his offense and implemented a "drag screen" series, which begins with a big man setting a ball screen for a guard early in the shot clock. Auriemma got a thick playbook from then–New York Knicks coach Mike D'Antoni and worked on it throughout the preseason. The players were awful the first time they tried it in a game, but Auriemma stuck with it, and the Lady Huskies went undefeated and won the 2009 NCAA title. "We've had years we won a national championship, and we're on the bus afterwards and he's asking me, 'Okay, how are we going to be better next year?'" Dailey says. "It's not about, 'How can we win more games?' It's about, 'How can we get better?'"

Of course, an offensive system is only as good as the players who run it, and Auriemma is the first to acknowledge that he has great players. Then again, he also points out that he is not the only coach who can say that. After all, there are twenty high school players good enough to be named McDonald's All-Americans each year, and he routinely signs about three of them. "So what happened to the other seventeen?" he asks.

That remark represents his PEAK profile in full bloom. Auriemma struts persistently despite being racked with self-doubt. He empathizes with his players even as he is crushing their spirits.

He is unapologetic about who he is and where he came from, but he is always on the lookout for ways to bust up what's working and try something new. He was an unmotivated student who barely found time to graduate college, yet he insists his players go to class and get good grades. His thirst for knowledge is never quenched. He loves to win, yet when a shot goes in to beat his team in the most dramatic way possible, he is able to laugh at the absurdity of it all. That's because he knows something the rest of us don't: Getting to *Us* and winning aren't the same thing.

Not everyone cottons to Auriemma's bluntness, of course. Over the years, he has provoked many feuds with the media as well as the sport's most prominent names, from Boston College coach Cathy Inglese to Notre Dame coach Muffet McGraw to the iconic, late Tennessee coach Pat Summitt. As a man coaching (and dominating) the women's game, Auriemma is subject to a lot of petty grievances. He doesn't suffer them gladly. "I did a lot for these people that resent me. I'm one of the reasons why they make so much money," he says. "I don't say that in an arrogant way, but the bottom line is that we've done more than anybody ever, ever has [for the sport]."

Indeed, during his three-plus decades at UConn, Auriemma has never hired a male full-time assistant coach. Instead, he has given jobs mostly to his former players, affording them opportunities that many women did not have when he first got into the business in 1985. "I wish other men would do what Geno has done in developing women for jobs," Stanford coach Tara VanDerveer says. "He mentors a lot of women and helps them stay in the game."

Dailey, for one, has turned down several offers over the years to run her own program. She and Auriemma are arguably the most successful head coach–assistant coach combination in the history of college sports. Cash says they're like a "functioning married couple," but it's not always clear who wears the pants. More than anyone, Dailey knows how to cut through Auriemma's skin-deep arrogance by questioning the tie he is wearing. When I tease Auriemma that working as his assistant for more than thirty years should earn Dailey an automatic pass into heaven, he replies, "And when she gets there, she's gonna tell Saint Peter everything he's been doing wrong for the last two thousand years. It's a running gag up here in Connecticut. Everybody knows Chris Dailey is the brains behind this outfit. Women take all the credit, trust me."

As Auriemma's career blossomed, he also engendered the enmity of UConn's men's basketball coach Jim Calhoun. It wasn't long before their sniping spilled out into the public. Their clashes were great fodder for Connecticut's newspaper writers. Calhoun's disdain gnawed at Auriemma because it was of a piece with the most constant dig he has heard over his career. "It's this whole bullshit about, well, I'm a guy coaching women's basketball. 'If you were any good you'd be coaching men,'" he says. "You know how many times I've heard that?" He raises his voice and repeats, "*You know how many times I've heard that?*"

It was only natural that Auriemma would fall prey to that line of thinking. Maybe people who asked that question had a point. He found himself at a crossroads in 2006, when he all but said yes to an offer from a university—he won't say which one—to coach its men's team. He eventually passed, however, because his daughter Jenna, who had just taken a teaching job near UConn, was heartbroken at the prospect. "Kathy has always been a big believer that you don't move away from your kids. Your kids are supposed to move away from you," Auriemma says.

Rather than being haunted by regret over turning down that men's job, Kathy believes the decision settled her husband in a way he wasn't before. "He knew that he could have had a men's job if he wanted one, but he didn't," Kathy says. "Not that it legitimized him, but in a way it took the edge off what he was doing." In many ways, the decision to stay at UConn, to stay in the women's game, marked the completion of Auriemma's immigration, the realization that he was living out the American dream. It forced him to acknowledge that he had taken two worlds, braided them into one, and made it authentically his own.

I magine the look on that nun's face back at St. Francis of Assisi if someone had told her that the immigrant boy sitting across from her would someday be able to compare and contrast his experiences hanging out with three different U.S. presidents.

It is an annual tradition for the NCAA men's and women's basketball champions to be honored with a ceremony at the White House. Auriemma, a student of history, has paid particular attention to the habits of the various presidents. Bill Clinton came late and stayed late. George W. Bush arrived exactly on time and left exactly on time. Barack Obama was somewhere in between.

The ultimate highlight came when Auriemma brought his mother on one of the visits. He took her picture under the official portrait of John F. Kennedy, the ultimate honor for a Catholic mother. "Growing up, there were only two pictures in my house— John Kennedy and Pope John XXIII," he says. When Obama came into the room, Auriemma introduced his mom, and the president of the United States leaned over and gave her a big hug. "Here she was, couldn't read or write. Came from Italy, lived through the war. The Americans liberated her town. Seeing the look on her face when he gave her that hug, it was a truly great moment in my life."

Does it surprise you that he is not a man of vanity? When Auriemma is out and about in his neighborhood or on vacation at his beach house, you will never catch him wearing a UConn shirt. Nor does he have a single picture or piece of memorabilia on display in his home that would indicate what he does for a living. He published a memoir in 2009 recounting his upbringing and his championship seasons, but he vows never to write one of those motivational tomes imparting his secrets of success. "That's such bullshit, man. I don't get it. That's not who I am."

Geno never got much closure with his dad. In 1996, when his parents came to visit him for Thanksgiving, he and Donato went for a walk outside. Donato had been fighting lung cancer, so he could no longer smoke his beloved cigarettes. Geno puffed on a cigar and blew the smoke his way so his dad could taste it. They talked as they strolled. It was one of the few times when Geno felt he and his father had genuinely connected, and he wondered if it might signal a new beginning. Alas, Donato passed away a year later, his son and his son's country forever a mystery to him.

If Auriemma puts a lot of pressure on himself to win championships for UConn, imagine how he feels when he is representing the entire United States. In 2010, he was named the head coach of the U.S. national program. His teams won two FIBA World Championships and two Olympic gold medals—including at the 2016 Rio Games, where his squad, which included three of his former UConn players, trounced the competition by an average of nearly 30 points.

One of the games was a 105–62 victory over China. Even though it was a laugher, Auriemma still insisted that his players chase perfection. They ended up with 40 assists on 46 made field goals. Watching from his office back at Saint Joseph's, where he has been the head men's coach since 1995, Phil Martelli marveled at how much had changed—and yet how little. "My brain was racing because I'm thinking he's the same guy who was standing on the sideline as the jayvee coach at Bishop Kenrick High School," he says. "Think about that number—forty assists in a game of basketball. I don't care if it was Connecticut playing a Division III school. Forty assists! So it's not about women's basketball with him, it's about basketball. He wants his teams to play the absolute perfect game. That's the separation between him and his competition."

One of the players on that gold medal team was Diana Taurasi. Auriemma first coached her when she was in high school playing for Team USA at the Under-18 championships. They went on to win three NCAA championships together along with two World Championships and two Olympic gold medals. Like Auriemma, Taurasi is the child of immigrants. Her father was born in Italy, her mother in Argentina. After they won the gold in Rio, they shared a quiet embrace. "If it weren't for you, I wouldn't have accomplished nearly as much as I have," he told her. She told him she felt the same way about him. There they were, two first-generation Americans, speaking the same language, the language of basketball. It was not a moment for strutting, but rather for disbelief and gratitude at the path Auriemma has traveled since he stepped off that boat. It's remarkable where that bouncing ball has taken him. He certainly never planned it this way.

Doc Rivers

"YOU CAN GET A GREAT SPEECH FROM A THERAPIST."

He didn't want a hug. His house had just collapsed in a heap. Everything he had was gone. The pets had been trapped inside and were presumed dead. The police told him it was arson. Racially motivated, maybe. He was shocked and angry, but he was already in game mode. He needed to find a new place to live, get his kids enrolled in school, start dealing with the insurance companies. What did his father always tell him? *There will be no victims in this house.* His house may have been gone and there was no doubt he had been victimized, but there was nothing he could do to change that now. The only thing he could do was keep moving.

On that morning after the worst night of his life, Glenn "Doc" Rivers stood on the street outside what used to be his house. The fire had shocked his peaceful, well-appointed neighborhood in San Antonio, Texas. As he stood there with the wheels turning in his mind, an older woman from the neighborhood walked up to him with tears in her eyes. "I'm so sorry," she said. Without asking, she hugged him. He appreciated the gesture, but it was an unwelcome interruption. "I was too shocked to be hugging anybody," Rivers told me. "I was just thinking about all the shit I had to do."

He didn't want to be rude, so he hugged the lady back, sort of. Then he sat down on the curb and began filling out insurance forms, the ruins of what used to be his house still smoldering behind him.

This was in June 1997. Rivers had been playing in a charity golf tournament in Seattle that morning when he got the news that his house was on fire. He flew home just in time to see it collapse. Fortunately, his wife and four kids were vacationing with his in-laws in Milwaukee, so they never saw a thing. He was determined to get the mess cleared before they returned. He didn't want his children to see their home reduced to charred ruins. By the time they got there the next day, a stone slab was all that remained.

Looking back at that awful day, Rivers is not so sure he was in the healthiest frame of mind. His ability to keep moving when bad things happen has long been one of his greatest strengths. But as is so often the case when it comes to the human character, his greatest strength can also be his biggest flaw. "There are times when I'm ruthlessly cold," he says. "That was one of those times when I wish I could have a do-over. My wife needed to see me more emotional about the fire, but I was more emotional about getting our life back."

Still, Rivers knows full well that life, and basketball, can come at you fast. His ability to recover from adversity, coupled with the empathy and knowledge he accrued during a thirteen-year NBA playing career, have enabled him to become one of the most venerated head coaches in the NBA. There is a great deal of friction generated inside an NBA locker room, and if those sparks are not properly managed, they can set even the most talented teams ablaze. During his stints with the Orlando Magic, Boston Celtics (where he won the 2008 NBA title), and Los Angeles Clippers, Rivers has proven to be uniquely deft at managing egos, routinely calling upon his PEAK profile to build winning cultures and foment a common agenda. By minimizing his emotions, even to the point of being ruthlessly cold, he teaches his players how to be persistent. By calling upon his experiences as a player, he empathizes with their frustrations and fears, feels their aches, their pains, their tired legs. By showing them how comfortable he is in his own skin, he convinces them to sacrifice their individual glory for the greater good. By proving that he has expert knowledge, he gets them to trust his instructions and his vision, which he tends to impart with a theatrical flourish.

It is through this balance between coldness and empathy that Doc Rivers gets his teams to *Us*. When critical moments arise, he doesn't play the victim and doesn't want a hug. He'd rather pivot and get moving, trusting that his players will follow.

He couldn't go left. Thirteen years as an NBA point guard—the one position on the floor where ball handling is paramount—and his left hand was basically useless. The players knew it, the fans knew it, the media knew it, the coaches knew it. And still he persisted.

One night, right before tipoff of a game in Milwaukee, one of the opposing players shouted at him, "You're not going right tonight!" Rivers smiled, shrugged, and replied, "Well, I'm not going left."

He was not necessarily the most talented guy on the court. Just the most determined. That had been true ever since he started playing as a grade schooler on the courts at Tenth Avenue and Washington Boulevard in Maywood, Illinois, a downtrodden suburb twelve miles west of downtown Chicago. During the summertime, Glenn and his older brother would play until the lights went out at 10 p.m. He never thought of it as "working on his game." He just thought he was playing.

The rules on a basketball court were clear enough, but life could be confusing outside the lines. Glenn was in the second grade when his neighborhood was overrun by race riots in the late 1960s. The violence got so bad that the police had to patrol the streets so the black students could walk on one side to school while the white kids walked on the other. Glenn remembers bottles flying back and forth. It was an unsettling time.

But then something amazing happened. In 1969, when Rivers was eight years old, the Proviso East High School basketball team, which included his uncle, Jim Brewer, reached the Illinois semifinals. The whole community went "downstate" to Champaign to watch them play. The following year, Proviso won the title. One white kid was in the starting lineup; his sister dated a black player. For all the tumult on the streets, Glenn noticed that once the folks were inside the gym, everyone cheered for the Pirates. That left a profound impression. "It was like the team unified the town and the school again," he says. "That showed me the power of sports."

He was lucky to have both parents at home, which was not the case with many of his friends. His dad, Grady, was a beat cop. Sometimes he would take Glenn and his brother, Grady Jr., with him on the night shift. That's when the bad guys came out. When their dad took his boys with him to the station, Grady Sr. would point to the holding pen and warn them, "If you ever get thrown in there, don't think I'm gonna get you out." Talk about ruthlessly cold.

In those days, Glenn had a bad habit of getting in fights in school and mouthing off to his teachers. He'll never forget the day his dad came down to school, walked into Glenn's classroom, took off his belt, and whupped Glenn right in front of his friends. Then there was the night when Grady heard that the little record shop he owned in town had been robbed. He took his wife and two boys to the store to see what was going on. When Glenn's mom found the burglar hiding in a closet, Grady dragged the offender out and proceeded to beat the living shit out of him. He threw the guy out of the store and told the cops not to arrest him. He wanted the poor fellow to spread the word that the owner of the Night Time Record Shop was not to be fucked with.

But Grady was tender too, in his own way. He didn't give out hugs and compliments, but when he was down at the barbershop, Glenn could hear him bragging about his boys. Grady was the loudest guy at family get-togethers, cracking jokes and keeping everyone laughing. He was also highly educated. He was an avid reader who did the crossword puzzles every morning. That was his way of teaching his sons that knowledge was important.

Grady gave great advice—"Trust everyone, but cut the cards"— and coached Glenn's baseball teams when he was young. He would leave his police car near the field so if he got called on the scanner, he could hop in, flip on his police lights, and take off. Grady made sure every kid played, but he still managed the team to four consecutive Little League championships. "He was disciplined, but he was also a lot of fun," Rivers recalls. "And you believed that he believed in you. To me, that was his gift."

Glenn's mother, Bettye, was an optimistic, devout Baptist who had a Bible verse for every occasion, but she could be tough, too. If one of her boys said he was too injured to play ball, she sent him right back out there. She had the early shift at a local assembly line, so she would get up at 4:30 a.m. and make the boys breakfast. After Glenn and Grady Jr. ate, they would go back to bed until their father came home from the night beat.

For all the discipline being enforced, the Rivers house was an empathetic one as well. The door was always open to the neighborhood kids. Glenn and Grady Jr. never quite knew who was coming to dinner, but when they came, they were welcome to sit and eat, to pray and play ball. It was not uncommon for Grady and Bettye to take in a boy or two for weeks at a time. One of them, a boy named

Casso, lived with the Riverses for several years. "My brother saw at an early age that it's okay to help people," Grady Jr. says.

It was evident from the start that Glenn was a basketball prodigy, but he still needed an occasional lesson in persistence. When he was in sixth grade, he attended a high school basketball camp where every other kid was white. When one of the other campers called him a nigger, Glenn got into a nasty fight and was sent home. The camp directors were fine with him coming back the next day, but Glenn didn't want to go. His pops was having none of it. "I paid. You're going," Grady said. "There will be no victims in this house." Glenn returned to the camp, and at the end of the week he was named Most Valuable Player.

He grew into an elite player at Proviso East, where as a senior he was named a McDonald's All-American. He had his pick of colleges and eventually chose Marquette, partly because he had become familiar with the coaching staff while attending a couple of summer basketball camps there. On the first day of the first camp he attended, Rivers showed up wearing a Dr. J T-shirt. Rick Majerus, a portly, Falstaffian assistant, started calling him "Doc." The nickname stuck. When he began his freshman season at Marquette, he was listed on the roster as Glenn "Doc" Rivers. As the years went on, the nickname would come to supersede his given name, but his close friends and family back in Maywood would always call him Glenn.

They met during a study hall his freshman year at Marquette. She was working two jobs so she could pay for her education, so she wasn't exactly dolled up that day. "You'd look good if you washed your hair," he said by way of introduction. Only later did Kris Campion discover that the boy who had insulted her was a much-ballyhooed basketball player. They soon became good friends. She dated one of his teammates for a while, but he traveled abroad during the summer before Glenn's junior season. While the boy-friend was away, Glenn and Kris fell in love. That made for some bad blood in the locker room that year, but Glenn couldn't resist. She was cool, she was smart, she was cute, she was fun, she was un-derstanding, she was supportive, she was his best friend.

She was also white.

Her parents were immediately accepting of the situation. They were ultra-progressive, having participated in peace marches in Milwaukee during the 1960s. Rivers's family, however, was wary. "It was difficult for our family, to be honest with you. We never had anybody in our family go out with a white girl," Grady Jr. says. "Once we met Kris and her family, though, we let it all go. They were such great people, it really changed the way I viewed things. It helped me see that you can't coat everybody with one brush."

Outsiders were far less tolerant. Glenn and Kris faced all kinds of harassment. One day, they arrived at her apartment and found the words "Nigger Lover" spray-painted on the sidewalk. On another occasion, they returned to her car and discovered her tires had been slashed. Her parents' house in Milwaukee was spray-painted with epithets as well, and a few hate letters arrived in their mailbox. "I come from a family of blond-haired, blue-eyed people. I had never experienced anything like that," Kris says. "One of Glenn's strengths, and I think this carries over into coaching, is he doesn't overreact. He's pretty calm in uncomfortable situations. He just kept saying, 'We have our family and friends. Who cares what strangers think?'"

Rivers was angry, but he wouldn't let the hate dissuade him. "That's just how it is with him. Once he made up his mind he was gonna do something, nobody could stop him," Grady Jr. says. It also helped that Marquette coach Hank Raymonds was in his corner. He called Rivers into his office one day and asked, "Do you love her?" When Rivers said yes, Raymonds told him, "Then to hell with everybody."

Rivers grew in many important ways during his time at Marquette. During his freshman year, one of his history professors returned a paper marked up with red ink. The information was correct, but Rivers's grammar and spelling were awful. He resented this at first, believing he was being singled out because he was an athlete, but he persisted anyway, even agreeing to extra help at the professor's home. He eventually got the paper right. "That changed me in a lot of ways," he says. "It taught me that you can be very smart and not well educated."

Still, Rivers's junior season was not a happy time. Though he had played well his first two seasons, his production fell off, which made the harassment he endured because of his white girlfriend even worse. The strife between him and Kris's ex-boyfriend was also an ongoing issue. For the first time in his life, basketball was not fun. That led him to the foolish decision to enter the NBA draft before he was ready. He was shocked when he didn't get selected in the first round, instead being plucked by the Atlanta Hawks with the seventh pick in round two. He cried that night and vowed to exact revenge on every point guard who was selected ahead of him.

He arrived at the Hawks' training camp seething with anger. At one point, he got into a fight with another guard, Wes Matthews, who had elbowed him in the mouth. He came to camp without a guaranteed roster spot, but he earned one through sheer determination. The Hawks had a bevy of talented scorers, including Dominique Wilkins, Dan Roundfield, and Eddie Johnson. Problem was, there was only one ball, and Rivers spent much of the games handling it. "I didn't look to be a leader, but I became one," he says. "I learned as a player that if you're going to lead, you're not going to make everybody happy. *No* can be a very positive word."

That was just one of many bits of knowledge that Rivers collected that he would later call upon as a coach. He learned a great deal about defense from Atlanta coach Mike Fratello. Rivers had always been taught that when going up against a superior athlete, the best tactic was to give him space so it would be harder for him to blow by. Fratello, on the other hand, wanted Rivers to crowd his man. It made it harder for his opponent to move anywhere.

Doc and Kris were married on May 31, 1986, following his third season with the Hawks. He wore pink canvas basketball shoes to the wedding. He was at the peak of his abilities, having just played in the one and only All-Star Game of his career. While Doc settled into a steady career, their family tree grew. They had a son, Jeremiah, in 1987 and a daughter, Callie, in 1989. Glenn also spent some time doing work for Turner Broadcasting, which was based in Atlanta. He was a natural at calling games. Those repetitions enhanced his communication skills and gave him peace of mind knowing that he would have good options once his playing days were done.

In 1991, Rivers was traded to the Los Angeles Clippers, where he played one season for Larry Brown. Rivers had never seen a coach who was so passionate and meticulous about practice. A year later, he was traded to the New York Knicks, which put him under the sway of the Knicks' intense, exacting head coach, Pat Riley. Rivers was spellbound by Riley's aura. When Riley preached the importance of conditioning, Rivers tried everything he could, including running with a parachute, to get his body into tip-top shape. Mostly, he remembers the way Riley was able to come up with so many stirring motivational speeches. "He was eighty-two for eighty-two," Rivers says. Very few coaches in the history of sports have been better than Riley when it came to getting his team to *Us*. Rivers soaked it all in. "I learned from Riley that the key to coaching is to get a group of players to believe there's one agenda, and that you have the same agenda as them," he says. "If you can do that, your players are going to do whatever they can for you."

Eventually, Rivers could feel his usefulness in New York wearing out, and he started asking Riley to waive him. It took a few shouting matches, but eventually the coach acquiesced. Rivers was thirty-four years old when the Knicks released him a month into the 1994–95 season. When they shared an emotional goodbye, Riley said to his now-former player, "You're gonna coach someday."

"No way," Doc replied.

"We'll see," Riley mumbled, and with that Rivers's time as a Knick was done.

After playing his last two years with the San Antonio Spurs, Rivers retired in 1996 at the age of thirty-five and took a job as a color analyst on the Spurs' TV games. He liked the gig, enjoyed spending time with his kids, and fell in love with golf, but it was clear to Kris that he was not long for that profession. "He was bored out of his mind," she says. "I knew he would end up coaching. He needed more grit in his life."

For the most part, Rivers enjoyed his time in San Antonio. That is, until the morning of June 29, 1997, when his house burned down. As the story goes, a couple of local kids had broken in to have a party. They started a bonfire, intentionally or not, but it had gone awry. It has never been firmly established that the boys acted out of hostility toward the mixed-race couple, but Doc and Kris believe they did. The Riverses were even more disheartened to learn that even though police believed they knew who the perpetrators were, they were not able to collect enough forensic evidence to bring charges against the juveniles.

"It shook me to my core," Kris says. "My first reaction was to flee. I wanted to leave San Antonio in the worst way. Glenn was an announcer, so he could fly where he needed to get to. But he was adamant. 'We're not doing that, we did nothing wrong, we're gonna teach our kids that when something bad happens, you look it in the eye and move forward.' Looking back, I'm very grateful that we did that. We ended up with another three great years in San Antonio."

As the Spurs struggled to win, speculation swirled that the team would fire its coach, Gregg Popovich, and replace him with Rivers. That caused some tension between the two men, though it would not last. By that time, Rivers knew he wanted to coach. At the end of his third year calling games for the Spurs, an opportunity arose to coach the Orlando Magic. So he picked up his family and moved them yet again.

The Magic were in dire straits. They had just traded away their best player, Anfernee "Penny" Hardaway, leaving a depleted roster that included just two players who had been drafted. The first thing Rivers did was to make sure his players understood there would be no victims in that locker room. He spent the summer meeting with them individually and sending them one-page sheets by express mail that included a single quote or statement designed to inspire. Darrell Armstrong, a six-year veteran guard who had been undrafted coming out of Fayetteville State University, got one such overnight letter just a few weeks after Rivers took the job, even though Rivers only lived a fifteen-minute drive from Armstrong's house.

One of the smartest things Rivers did was heed the advice of the previous coach, Chuck Daly, that he should retain Daly's personal assistant, Annemarie Loflin. To this day, Loflin works for Rivers with the Clippers under the title of chief of staff, basketball operations. She is his window into what is going on within the organization, providing him with information that is critical to a coach's ability to empathize with his players.

Three players who were on that first Magic team—Tariq Abdul-Wahad, Armen Gilliam, and Chris Gatling—came in with reputations as being problem children. Rivers learned right away how unfair that was. "Coaches need to learn that just because you don't get along with someone, it does not make him a bad guy," he says. He noticed that when he gathered his players for the Lord's Prayer before taking the court, Abdul-Wahad stood to the side with an unhappy look on his face. When Rivers later asked him privately what was wrong, Abdul-Wahad said that he had felt ostracized because he was Muslim. So before the following game, Rivers invited his players to stand in a circle, hold hands, and quietly pray to the God of their choice. It is a ritual he continues to this day.

Rivers was a force of nature during that first season in Orlando. His players bought into his vision and played their asses off for him. The team earned the label "Heart and Hustle" and somehow clawed its way to a .500 record, barely missing the playoffs. No team Rivers ever coached got to *Us* better than his first one. As a result, he was named the NBA's Coach of the Year.

Alas, the Magic were never able to build on that early momentum. The team had developed an undrafted power forward named Ben Wallace into a ferocious rebounder, but then it inexplicably traded him to the Detroit Pistons, where he blossomed into a four-time All-Star and won an NBA title. The Magic appeared to land a huge free agent coup when it signed forward Grant Hill to a seven-year, $93 million contract in the summer of 2000. But Hill's career quickly went awry due to a serious ankle injury that never quite healed. Despite such setbacks, Rivers managed to squeak the Magic into the playoffs for the next two years. Each time, they were eliminated in the first round, which is what typically happens to the No. 8 seed when matched against the best team in the conference.

Rivers's methods of communication, taught to him by his beat-cop dad, did not always go over well. He knows he can be blunt to a fault, as well as impatient when it comes to idle chatter. Sometimes, when Kris is telling him a lengthy story, he will draw a circle in the air with his index finger, as if to say, "Get to the point." While riding the team plane, he almost came to blows with Horace Grant, a 6´10˝, 245-pound power forward. He was particularly harsh on the Magic's young superstar, Tracy McGrady, who had been drafted straight out of high school. "I pushed the shit out of Tracy," Doc says. "Tracy was good at basketball. My job was to make him great at it. In the end, it probably cost me my job because he didn't like being corrected."

The losing took a toll. Rivers lost sleep and developed ulcers. His tenure collapsed in a hurry when the Magic began the 2003–04 season by dropping 10 of their first 11 games. Rivers was fired on November 18, 2003. He was relatively sanguine when he broke the news to Kris. Of course he was disappointed, but he knew it was coming, understood why it happened, recognized it was part of the profession, and believed that he would coach again. He also heard from his dad, who always called when something bad happened. It was not a long conversation. "Getting fired doesn't mean you're a bad coach," he told his son. "Getting fired just means you got fired. If you want to believe you're a bad coach, that's on you."

Three days later, Rivers signed a contract with ABC Sports to serve as a color analyst on NBA games alongside Al Michaels. He got to work the NBA Finals and could have been an elite broadcaster for the rest of his life. But there was never a doubt he wanted to coach again, and though he thought he might bide his time behind the mic for a couple of years, he changed his mind when the general manager of the Boston Celtics, Danny Ainge, asked Rivers if he would like to interview for their vacancy. Rivers left such a good impression on the team's owners that they canceled their other interviews and instructed Ainge to make the hire.

Basketball-wise, the decision to go to Boston was easy. On the home front, however, things were more complicated. Kris and Doc now had four children—their youngest, Austin, was born in 1992, and Spencer was born three years later—and the oldest two were in high school. Kris and Doc did not want to uproot them again, so they made the difficult decision that when Doc went to Boston, the family would stay behind in Orlando. It wasn't going to be easy, but in the end, he didn't have much choice. A job awaited. He had to keep moving.

L ike many coaches, Rivers has often sought the company of coaches in other sports to enhance his knowledge. When he was in Orlando, he spent time with Jon Gruden, who at the time was the coach of the NFL's Tampa Bay Buccaneers. Rivers was fascinated by how a pro football team is organized, with the head coach delegating huge responsibilities to his offensive and defensive coordinators. He recalls walking with Gruden into a defensive meeting, only to hear the players razzing the head coach, who specialized in offense, that he was only there to impress his guest. "My belief is we coach wrong in basketball," Rivers says. "In football, the head coach doesn't have to be the voice on everything."

Rivers assembled his staff in Boston accordingly. Getting through to the players, however, would be a tougher challenge. That started with the franchise's cornerstone, small forward Paul Pierce, who was entering his seventh season in the NBA with little to show for it. Soon after he took over, Rivers met with Pierce and addressed the situation with his usual bluntness. "Do you think you're a great shooter?" he asked.

"Yes," Pierce replied with confidence.

"Then why are your percentages so awful?"

It was a fair question given that Pierce was coming off a season in which he had made a career-low 40.2 percent from the field. The year before, he had made a career-low 41.6 percent. As Rivers saw it, the answer was simple: Either Pierce wasn't a great shooter or he was taking bad shots. So he encouraged Pierce to move better without the ball, and to learn how to pass up good shots so he could get better ones. Pierce, however, insisted on holding on to the ball and jacking it up like he always did. Rivers started to pull him late in games, which led to some unpleasant exchanges on the court. Finally, it boiled over in the locker room. "Let's get one thing straight," Rivers told Pierce in front of the entire team after a loss. "I am not fucking changing."

Pierce laughed when I recounted this story. If he didn't recall this specific confrontation, it's because there were so many of them. "I probably said to him, 'I'm not changing, either.' We're both pretty hardheaded." He added, "Doc has a unique ability to get guys to buy into what he's teaching every day. He played in the NBA, so he understands players better than a lot of other coaches who didn't have the chance to do that. He understands how to come at you tough, how to back off a little bit. He understands when you're tired, when you're emotionally there and when you're not."

The Celtics won 45 games his first season and lost in the first round of the playoffs. They failed to make the postseason the next two years, and once again there were rumblings that maybe Rivers wouldn't make it. At one point during his third season, the Celtics lost 18 consecutive games. Meanwhile, he was dedicating every free hour to flying back and forth to Orlando to see his kids. He paid for the private air travel out of his own pocket.

There were no ulcers this time, just a resolute persistence to keep moving forward. "Every day during that losing streak, he came in and he would never say anything negative to the players," says Armond Hill, Rivers's longtime assistant coach. "Even when the coaches were alone, he wouldn't rip the players. He might get frustrated about what was happening, but he would always say, 'We gotta make them better.'"

The Celtics' fortunes changed dramatically during the summer of 2007, when the team acquired two future Hall of Famers, Ray Allen and Kevin Garnett. Immediately, a franchise that had missed the playoffs two years in a row was being pegged for an NBA title—but only if Rivers could get them to *Us*.

Having played alongside so many talented and ego-driven players—during those early years in Atlanta, for example—Rivers understood the pitfalls ahead. So he dipped back into his Pat Riley playbook and invited his three best players to meet him one morning by the Charles River. There was a crisp chill in the air, and Garnett, for one, was none too pleased. Pierce, however, had lived in Boston for a while, so he understood what was happening.

As the four of them stood on the dock, a duck boat pulled up, and Rivers led them on board. The boat was similar to the one the Boston Red Sox rode for the championship parade celebrating their 2004 World Series triumph. Rivers played tour guide that morning, showing Garnett, Allen, and Pierce all the spots along the route they would pass after they won the title. But he cautioned that it would not be easy getting there. "Everybody is going to have to sacrifice," he said. "It may be notoriety, it may be shots, it may be pats on the back. The media's not going to be at your locker all the time. But you've got to trust me, and you've gotta let me coach you. Because if I can coach you three, I've got everybody else."

Two days after the regular season began, Rivers's father died in Chicago. A lifelong smoker, Grady had been suffering from lung cancer for several years, yet he told no one, not even his wife, until he was near the end. Doc missed just one game to go to the funeral.

Besides being eager to resume the work of getting to *Us* with his Big Three, he also faced the challenge of blending them with the team's talented yet enigmatic second-year point guard, Rajon Rondo. Rondo was a gifted distributor, which was necessary because he couldn't shoot a lick. He also had a tendency to pout when things didn't go his way, and that especially created problems with Ray

Allen. "Ray wanted to handle the ball more, and I didn't think at that point in his career he should. I never gave in on that," Rivers says.

Rivers called out Rondo several times in front of the whole team, but he also thought Rondo was a borderline genius when it came to making instantaneous decisions. So he gave him a lot of decision-making responsibilities, especially when he drew up plays out of time outs, a Rivers specialty. Technical skills aside, Rivers's greatest gift is as a visionary. "I'm a good speaker when I'm talking about the vision of the season, not necessarily an individual game," he says. "I try to come up with things that connect our team to our journey and our goals."

That was never more evident than the night the Celtics lost a tough road game to the Los Angeles Lakers. Upon seeing how disconsolate the players were, Rivers asked each man to give him $100. Then he hid the wad of cash in the ceiling of the visitors' locker room at Staples Center. "We're coming back for this," he said, which could only happen if the Celtics and the Lakers reached the NBA Finals.

And that is exactly what happened. The Celtics steamrolled through the Eastern Conference playoffs, met the Lakers in the Finals (Rivers made good on his promise to grab that cash out of the ceiling), and clinched the title in the series's sixth game at TD Garden in Boston. When the buzzer sounded, Rivers exulted on the court as his players doused him in Gatorade. He participated in the trophy ceremony and took a bunch of photos. Then he retreated into his office and sat for a while—exhausted, emotionally empty, perhaps a little bit shocked. His wife sat with him, as did his mother and brother. He left to do his postgame press conference and then came back and sat for another long while. When he was finally ready, he told Kris he wanted to go home.

It wasn't until later that Rivers realized he had never gone into the locker room. He didn't get one drop of champagne on him. All that work, all that stress, all those hours spent figuring out a way to get to *Us* . . . the least he could have done was celebrate with his players and staff. Even his kids went in there and whooped it up.

To this day, he is not sure why he didn't go in there. But he regrets it deeply. "I should've enjoyed it more. I mean, every celebration you see, the coach is in the goddamn locker room," he says. "It didn't even cross my mind to go in there. I had a huge pride, it was awesome, but I also had the idea that, 'Okay, we've done that now. It's time to get the next one.'"

He continues, "What makes winning special is that it's hard. That's what I realized in that moment. All those years I chased it and couldn't get it. It *should* be hard. So many things have to go right for you to win a title. I had the ultimate high inside, but at the same time I'm thinking, *Okay, we gotta win this motherfucker again. This is the best feeling in the world.* So that was my version of elation."

The more he thinks about it, the more he guesses it might have something to do with his pops. He had never allowed himself to properly grieve when Grady died, because he dove so quickly and coldly back into the season. Doc shed a few tears that night, however, knowing how happy his dad would have been. Kris had mentioned that she wanted to make a big breakfast for everyone the following morning, so on the way home, Rivers stopped at the local grocery store. The cashier was shocked to see him there, just a couple hours after winning the NBA title, his collar still stained with red Gatorade.

In the weeks that followed, Rivers realized how foolish he had been not to go into the locker room. In his mind, he started planning how he would celebrate the next time his team won an NBA title. He pictured renting out a big hotel ballroom, inviting everyone he knew, and throwing a party that nobody would forget. There would be lots of hugging, too. It was a lovely thought, but the party never happened.

· · ·

There was nothing in the coaches' manual that told him what to
do, but in many ways, Rivers had spent a lifetime preparing for
the surreal moment.

It happened during the playoffs, naturally. He had been sitting
in a hotel room in San Francisco, going over video with his staff in
preparation for the Los Angeles Clippers' game against the Golden
State Warriors. He had taken the Clippers job in 2013 after it became evident the Celtics were headed for a rebuild. Rivers had no
interest in doing that, so he convinced Ainge to let him out of his
contract and sign with the Clippers in exchange for a first-round
draft pick. Now in his second season, he had a veteran team headed
by point guard Chris Paul and power forward Blake Griffin. He
believed his team could do some damage, maybe even contend for a
title.

The coaches' meeting was interrupted by one of the Clippers'
media relations executives. He said something about a controversial
videotape concerning the team's longtime owner, Donald Sterling.
Rivers brushed him off. A half hour later, the guy returned and said
he was hearing bad things about the tape and maybe Rivers should
come and hear it. Again, Rivers told him to handle it. Then, after
the media exec heard what was actually on the tape that was about
to be posted by TMZ, he barged back in and insisted that Rivers
end the meeting immediately and listen.

Rivers was disheartened to hear his team's owner make dispar-
aging, racist remarks that had been secretly recorded by his much
younger girlfriend, but he was hardly shocked. He had never personally heard Sterling say something bigoted, but he knew the man's
reputation. Besides, given the way Rivers grew up, the specter of an
old white guy secretly harboring racist stereotypes was hardly earth-
shattering. Perhaps that's why he so badly underestimated what was

happening. "I totally miscalculated the scope of the story—like, I mean, completely," he says.

That changed when he saw the collection of satellite trucks parked outside their practice gym. When he walked inside, he was stunned at the size of the horde. It really hit him when he spotted Bob Schieffer, the venerated CBS News anchor. Rivers had to find a place to sit quietly by himself for about twenty minutes so he could gather his thoughts before addressing the media.

The more critical test had occurred a few hours before, when he addressed his players as a group for the first time since the tape was released. His main concern was that they not pop off and say something that would make the situation worse. He wanted the team to speak with one voice—and that voice should be his. As he began to talk to them, he could sense that his players were distant. Their arms were crossed, their heads were down. They didn't like that he was asking them essentially to stay quiet. For a moment, he saw himself through their eyes, as if he were a member of the establishment trying to keep them down. And it pissed him off.

This was one of those moments when a coach must rely upon his PEAK profile. Rivers's players needed to trust that he would persist in doing what was right no matter what pressure, internal or external, came his way. They needed to believe he could empathize with how they were feeling. They needed to know that he wouldn't say one thing to their faces and another to the public or to team executives. And they needed to accept that his lifetime of experience—as a player, a coach, and a broadcaster—instilled in him the knowledge to make the best decisions, not just for himself but for the group.

So he seized the moment like he always did—with ruthlessly cold bluntness. "All right, you motherfuckers," he said. "My name is Glenn Rivers. I'm from Maywood, Illinois, and I'm black. Okay? So any of you motherfuckers here think you're more offended than me, you can kiss my fucking ass." Then he pointed to J. J. Redick, a white shooting guard. "And if you guys think J.J. is not as offended as you, then you're fucking wrong, too. So I don't know what we're gonna do, but I do know one thing—it has to be one voice. I'm asking you to let me be your voice. Tell me what you want me to say, and I'll say it. But the target has to be on Donald Sterling. We cannot say something that makes the story about us."

The next few days were a blur. Shortly before tipoff of their next game, the Clippers' players took off their warm-ups and left them in a pile at midcourt. NBA commissioner Adam Silver banned Sterling for life. The Clippers lost the series in seven games, but they played hard and for each other. They carried themselves like professionals and stuck to the script. They didn't win the series against Golden State, but they had pivoted and moved forward under the most difficult of circumstances. Much of that could be traced to their leader. Even in the worst of turmoil, Rivers had kept them at *Us*.

The ensuing years in L.A. have not been easy. Even with a new owner, the former Microsoft CEO Steve Ballmer, the Clippers remain one of the most star-crossed franchises in sports. During his first two years, the team had reached the Western Conference semifinals, but in 2016 they lost both Paul and Griffin to injury in game four of their first-round series against Portland and were eliminated. They lost in the first round again in 2017 to Utah, thanks partly to a toe injury that Blake Griffin sustained in the third game, which sidelined him for the remainder of the series. Of course, the worst misfortune of all was playing in the same conference as the Golden State Warriors, who have become a juggernaut of historic proportions, first winning an NBA-record 73 regular season games in 2015–16, and then claiming their second NBA championship in three years after signing former Oklahoma City Thunder superstar Kevin Durant.

Rivers, meanwhile, made a special kind of history on January 16, 2015, when he became the first NBA head coach to coach his son in a game. All of Doc and Kris's kids were college athletes, but Austin was the most successful—largely because he was the most driven. He was also entirely self-motivated. Doc lived in Boston for most of Austin's upbringing, and even when he made it to Austin's high school or AAU games, he didn't say much. He wanted Austin to love the game authentically, not because he was trying to please an overbearing father.

Likewise, Austin rarely went with his mom and siblings to visit his father in Boston. He preferred to stay back in Orlando and practice. "I didn't really grow up with my pops. I grew up with my mom," Austin says. "He was there when I needed him, but he didn't show his emotions too much. No matter what happened, his answer was, 'We gotta move on.' If I broke up with a girlfriend or I had a bad game, it was, 'We gotta move on.'"

By the time Austin reached his senior season at Winter Park High School, he was one of the top prospects in his class. He committed to Duke, where he was so good as a freshman that he was able to enter the NBA draft. The New Orleans Hornets selected him with the 10th pick, but it was not a happy situation for Austin. As a rookie, he was hobbled by hand and foot injuries, and the Hornets' coach, Monty Williams, was quick to pull him from games if he took a few bad shots. After his second season ended, the Hornets signed two talented combo guards. His father did not mince words. "They're writing you off," Doc said.

Midway through his third season in New Orleans, Austin thought the Hornets were getting close to trading him to the Celtics, of all places. Then he got word that the Clippers were a possibility. At first, he hated the idea. He had spent his life trying to escape his father's shadow. His mind changed after his dad told him the Clippers needed to replace their backup point guard, Jordan Farmar, who had just been waived. Doc's assistant, Sam Cassell, who had played fourteen years in the league as a point guard, was a fan of Austin's and wanted him to come. The only promise Doc made to Austin was that he would have a chance to prove what he could do. "That's all I needed to hear," Austin said.

The move drew plenty of backlash, not least because Austin was so unproven at that point. Even so, Kris was in favor of the idea. "My first thought was that no one is going to want Austin to be the best player he can be more than his dad," she says. When Austin started playing, he heard lots of teasing from opposing players. Those barbs subsided as he started to improve, thanks largely to the belief that was instilled in him by his new head coach. "The biggest thing with him is that he'll give a player an opportunity to show what he can do," Austin says. "A lot of coaches will say you have to earn freedom. He gives you freedom from the start, and if you play well with it, then you keep it."

Toward the end of his second season in Los Angeles, Austin was asked for the umpteenth time what it was like to play for his father. His answer caught many by surprise. "He doesn't really share his life outside of basketball with me," Austin said. "He and I don't know each other like that. We know each other as strictly basketball. A lot of people on the outside don't understand that because people think we have a relationship like every other father and son. We just don't. That's because he's been gone my whole life, and that's fine."

Doc says he believes Austin doesn't really feel that way, that he was just trying to defuse the awkwardness to reporters. Kris thinks otherwise. "Austin is not that manipulative. He says things off the cuff," she says. When I ask Kris what her reaction was to that quote, she replies, "To be really frank, sadness. If Austin had said that about me, that would break my heart."

Austin earned the respect of his teammates during the final game of that 2016 playoff series against Portland, when he took a nasty elbow to the face, left the court to get eleven stitches, and then returned to finish with 21 points, eight assists, and six rebounds in the season-ending loss. In game three of the 2015 Western Conference semifinals against Houston, when Austin went on a scoring tear, Chris Paul went up to Doc, slapped him on the chest, and said, "This is one time when you can be a dad and not just a coach." Doc was wearing a microphone and the exchange was aired on ESPN.

It was the kind of feel-good moment that led millions to share it on the Internet. But it didn't make Austin feel good. "Personally, I did not like that. I'm not into that lovey-dovey stuff, man," he tells me. "Maybe twenty or thirty years from now, I will look back and feel like that was pretty special to play for my pops, but right now I don't like that. I know Chris didn't mean any harm by it, but it took away from what I was doing. Made me look like a little kid out there. This is the playoffs, man. I don't want that shit. I'm hooping out here just like you."

It's a fair point. Austin put in a lot of hard, lonely hours to get himself to that point. He wanted the guys to respect him. He didn't want a hug.

It was a little too dark and overcast to see the Pacific Ocean on that cool spring evening, but I knew it was there. Doc Rivers led me to the backyard of his expansive house in the hills of West Hollywood. The dense, well-lit urban flatland blinked below. I joked that he was a long way from Maywood, Illinois. "Ain't it the truth," he said. Rivers loves that house, and yet he had spent much of his day off checking out properties in Malibu. Real estate had become a passion of his, and he figured three years living in the same place was long enough. He was ready for his next move.

Rivers might refer to himself as ruthlessly cold, but there are very few people around the NBA who would describe him that way.

He has long been a media favorite because he is so approachable, congenial, and fair. In many ways, he is still his father's son, the guy who cracks on everyone at the family gathering, keeping everything light and infusing the room with joy. I will never forget the time I took my oldest son to meet Rivers the night the Celtics eliminated Cleveland in game six of the 2010 Eastern Conference semifinals, in what turned out to be LeBron James's last game during his first stint in Cleveland. After it was over, Rivers's assistant, Armond Hill, brought us back to the coaches' locker room to say hello. It was a big night for the Celtics and he had a lot going on, but when Rivers saw us enter, he jumped up from his chair, walked over to where we were standing, shook our hands, and chatted us up like we were the most important people in the world. We hung out for about fifteen minutes, then he knelt down to take a picture with my son. He couldn't have been nicer.

After we left, my son remarked how impressed he was that I was such good friends with the Celtics' coach. I didn't have the heart to tell him it was the first time we had ever met.

On the night that I visited Rivers at his house, there was only a week remaining in the 2016–17 regular season, and he was understandably weary. It had been a rough few months, with a variety of injuries and other bad luck threatening the fortunes of this hapless, snakebitten franchise. There was also the reality that even at their absolute healthiest and most efficient, the Clippers were still bound to end up with everyone else in the Western Conference—which is to say, miles behind the Golden State Warriors.

"I'm only fifty-five. I'm not ready to retire or anything, but sometimes I wish I had a year off," Rivers said as he relaxed on his living room couch. "I've started eighteen straight training camps. [Spurs coach Gregg] Popovich is the only other one that's had that. But I still love it. I even love the hard years. I can tell you this has been a hard year. We've had so many injuries, so much bad stuff that happened. Sometimes I feel like the players just expect it now. You know what I mean? So my job is to try to get them out of that. I don't know if I will or not, but that's my job."

Bad luck aside, Rivers is doing his job as well as ever. With each passing year, he possesses greater knowledge and evinces deeper empathy. Unlike a lot of coaches, he does not do any conditioning work in practice. He figures if these guys are in the NBA, they're supposed to show up in shape. Nor does he tell them how much extra shooting work they need to put in. Rivers was self-aware in bailing on the Celtics when they were going into rebuilding mode. He does not have the patience for that anymore. But give him a locker room filled with veteran players who deeply, truly want to win, and he will coach his ass off.

"He's a player's coach in the best way," Austin says. "He has a good balance where he gives players a lot of freedom, he gives them responsibility, he's a good guy, but at the same time you better not get it twisted. People know not to fuck with him. They may be stars, but he is running the team."

Rivers is always on the lookout for opportunities to impose his won't-go-left persistence. He told me the story of a recent practice when he was practicing late-shot-clock plays with his starters, and he sensed they were being too timid. "I said to Chris [Paul], 'I know what shot you're going to take. You're gonna try to get to the elbow and fade away. So go get your fucking shot.'" To drive home the point, he informed the second unit what play the starters were running beforehand, and then he instructed the starters not to change a thing. "That's what happens in the playoffs," he said. "The other team knows what you're running. You still gotta run it."

He remains confident in the knowledge he brings to each practice and game. "I mean, I played for thirteen years and I've coached for eighteen. I gotta know *something.*"

Getting older means experiencing more moments of joy as well as sadness. His mother died on June 19, 2015, after a long battle with dementia. Her funeral took place six days later, which happened to be the same day as the NBA draft. Rivers buried his mom with his family and then flew to L.A. to be in the Clippers' war room. The move to Los Angeles has also had a predictable effect. A few years ago, Rivers took a course on Transcendental Meditation, and now he tries to give himself twenty-minute sessions once or twice a day to refresh his mind and even his keel. "I don't really go to church anymore—I think I've had enough church in my lifetime—but I'm definitely a spiritual person," he said. "I'm not into the Zen thing, but I do believe there's a spirit you have to have. I'm a seeker of knowledge. I believe in the basketball gods."

Most of all, Rivers is finally learning that for all his strong-willed stoicism, there is only so much a coach can control. After getting ejected three times in the season's first thirty-five games for yelling at referees, he scaled it back. "I thought, *Man, what am I doing?* That's not me," he said. "A lot of my guys are on the refs on every play, but I'm coaching better because I'm not worrying about that. At times I have to tell them, 'All right, guys, it was a bad call. What do you want me to do? The call was made already. We gotta move on.'" *There will be no victims in this house.*

When he feels the need to decompress, Rivers will drive to San Diego alone at night so he can wake up early and play golf at Torrey Pines. Or he will spend a day by himself at a spa in Newport Beach. He has even indulged in some occasional therapy, an idea he would never have entertained while he was playing. Sometimes during those sessions, his therapist will pass along a quote or a tidbit that Rivers will immediately type into his iPad so he can share it later with his team. "You can get a great speech from a therapist," he said.

"He spends so much of his life in the middle of this three-ring circus, he definitely has come to enjoy his quiet time," Kris said. "That side of him evolved when he was in Boston. He had to be alone a lot."

Once in a while, Kris will tell her husband a piece of news she has heard about the boys who allegedly burned down their house in San Antonio. Doc doesn't want to hear it. He has fantasized about accidentally running into them so he can give them a piece of his mind, but he has no desire to seek them out. He doesn't see this attitude as an act of amazing grace. He just doesn't want to pivot in that direction. As he put it, "Why would I waste one ounce of energy on bad people?"

Energy is one thing that is not a problem for him. It was now past midnight, and though we had already talked for nearly three hours, Doc looked like he could have kept going for a while. He has always been a night owl. He likes to sit by himself on the couch and watch game video. Or maybe he will read a little and flip through the channels mindlessly until around two in the morning before turning in. He sets his alarm, but he almost always wakes up before it goes off. "I tell people I'm a sun god. The light gives me energy," he said.

As he walked me to the front door, he showed me a few things around the house, including a large limited-edition book about his hero, Muhammad Ali, on a coffee table. Finally, he slapped my back and sent me on my way. As I heard the door close behind me, I pictured him going back to the couch, back to the solitude, back to the grind, and eventually back to bed. In a few hours, the sun would come up, and it would be time to get moving again.

Brad Stevens

"ALL THE GOOD ONES WANT TO BE COACHED."

Most every day that the Boston Celtics are scheduled to play a home game, their head coach, Brad Stevens, will take about fifteen minutes out of his game preparation to go into his basement and play a few games of Ms. Pac-Man. I say "most" because while Stevens is very much a child of routine, he is not anal about it. Nor is he superstitious. He just knows what works for him and what doesn't, and on most days, what works is some time at that console. He likes to call it his "moment of mindfulness," but there is a side benefit: It helps him get better at a game at which, in a rare moment of self-aggrandizement, he boasts, "I'm pretty good."

Stevens has always been old for his age and older than he looks. But don't let the smooth taste fool you. He is intensely competitive, which is why by the time he turned forty, he had already spent six years as the head coach at Butler University, taking his little-engine-that-could to consecutive NCAA championship games, and was in his fourth season as the head coach of the Boston Celtics. Mention these achievements to him, and Stevens is quick to deflect, evincing the classic self-effacement of the midwestern Methodist. No one who knows him, however, would be surprised that he's happy to point out his proficiency at a video game. That includes his eleven-year-old son, Brady, who once took a lead on his dad during a game of Ms. Pac-Man and started to let him know about it. After Brad dug in and vanquished his own progeny, his former player at Butler and current Celtics assistant Alex Barlow chided Brady for his premature celebration. "You should never have said anything to him," Barlow said. "You knew he was going to come back at some point."

It is not so much the joy of winning as a disdain for losing that drives Stevens. He is often called a genius, but that is not true. Rather, he is diligent and persistent and a synthesizer of information. His thorough, meticulous, disciplined preparation, and the knowledge he accumulates during that process, is what empowers him to get his team to *Us*. It's hard work but a labor of love.

Stevens dives into his game-day routine like he does all his endeavors, with quiet, burning, even-keeled intensity. He wakes up early, sees his kids off to school, grabs a cup of coffee, and secludes himself in his home office. He spends a lot of time during the season speaking one-on-one with his players, but he is not a big "meeting guy" when it comes to his staff. He will organize a conference call to start the season and assign everyone their responsibilities, but aside from a few confabs along the way, his assistants work in their own silos just like he does. For each opponent, one assistant scouts the offense and, one the defense, and a third evaluates personnel. The coaches email their written reports to Stevens and send him their video edits via Dropbox. These are due to him by noon the day before. He likes to stay a game ahead, if possible. That's why he almost never sleeps on airplanes. If he can get some work done late at night, he won't have to cram the next day.

Sitting at his desk and sipping his coffee, Stevens will pore over the information his assistants have compiled. Then he will watch that opponent's three previous games, start to finish. This takes about six hours. Next he will take all those videos, select a smaller handful of clips, and edit them on his laptop. That's the reel he will show his team later in the day. Stevens wants the video to be precise, with the plays in the exact right order. The last thing he ever wants to do is waste anyone's time, most of all his own. Unlike many NBA teams, the Celtics do not hold morning shootarounds. Stevens prefers that his players get their sleep. They will meet at the arena a few hours before tipoff, go over the game plan, get up some shots, and then get to work.

While he edits videos and analyzes the math, Stevens takes notes on a pad full of templates that he has developed over the years. Once all his watching and note taking is done, he will use his laptop to retype his notes onto another template, which has just enough room for the information that really matters—offensive and defensive sets, individual tendencies, plays to be executed in certain situations. He will also compile a list of plays that he can draw up according to the situation. The names are derived from the person or team he stole them from—"Minnesota" or "Chicago," for example. Another play might be called "Tibs" because he saw Timberwolves coach Tom Thibodeau run it, or "Spo" for something Miami coach Erik Spoelstra did, or "Mack" for a play run by the Israeli professional team Maccabi Tel Aviv. If one of Stevens's assistants saw that list of names, it would mean nothing to him. Each reference conjures for Stevens a corresponding action that he can draw up on a clipboard for his players.

When he is through typing his notes, Stevens will print out the sheet and stuff it into his back pocket. Most games, he won't even bother pulling it out. This is not because he has a photographic memory. It's because he has spent so much time poring over the information that it has entered his brain and stayed there.

He is able to maintain his routine without being enslaved by it. "I know what I need to accomplish," he says, "but it doesn't have to all go perfectly to plan." He doesn't work off a daily checklist, but about a dozen times a year he will sit down and fine-tune his methods to ensure the machine is humming properly. His wife, Tracy, is in awe of his persistence. "It is amazing to watch him do the same thing every day," she says. "The routine has evolved a little bit over the years, but the importance of having a routine that prepares him has stayed the same."

In the midst of all this work, Stevens will send several text messages to his players, both individually and as a group. Some of these he sends the night before, so as soon as they wake up they will have something from him. His teams tend to play the way he works—efficiently, intelligently, consistently, intensely, all the while maintaining their collective even keel.

An NBA season is a marathon, with 82 regular season games, a couple dozen more in the preseason and postseason, plus all the training and travel in between. Stevens knows that he needs to take a break and have a little fun once in a while. He allows himself intermittent breaks. He goes for a run. He eats lunch, usually an egg panini. (But not the same meal every time.)

And he plays fifteen minutes of Ms. Pac-Man. Tracy got him the tabletop console as a gift several years ago. Stevens could play different games on it (such as Galaga, Frogger, and Donkey Kong), but Ms. Pac-Man is the first in the sequence. He started there and stayed there. He doesn't study books or YouTube videos to get good at the game. That would be excessive. Rather, he learns by doing. He's a math guy at heart, and the way he figures it, fifteen minutes times 41 home games adds up to a lot of eaten power pellets and blinking ghosts, not to mention all those points-yielding fruits. His strategy, not surprisingly, is well thought out. "I play for score, not boards," he says.

The game is a perfect diversion for many reasons, but most of all this one: It always ends with a loss. Ms. Pac-Man always gets killed by a ghost. Stevens hates to lose, but that's okay because he owns the game and can simply hit the start button and try again. The pleasure's in the process. Each new game is a chance to get better.

His childhood was quite comfortable. He is almost apologetic about this. Even the name of the neighborhood where he grew up, Colony Woods, hints at an idyllic, Eden-like existence. Brad Stevens had two doting parents and no siblings, but he never thought of himself as an only child, because he had so many buddies living nearby. "Our house was always crawling with kids," his father, Mark, says.

Brad's parents were both professionals. Mark was an orthopedic surgeon; his mother, Jan, was an educator. They gave him their full attention and took him everywhere, so he was around adults a lot. Tracy says he was "the center of their universe," but Brad's parents also took measures to make sure he wasn't entitled. They were regular attendees at the Zionsville United Methodist Church in Indiana, and they sent Brad on mission trips to Louisiana and Texas, where he helped feed needy people in downtrodden neighborhoods. Brad also got a painful lesson on the fragility of life when the fifteen-year-old boy who lived next door was killed in an auto accident. Humility, gratitude, and faith were the core values in the Stevens household. He started there and stayed there.

Brad's first encounter with struggle came when he was a senior at DePauw University, a Division III school located in Greencastle, Indiana. He had been a very good basketball player at Zionsville Community High School, setting school career records in points, assists, steals, and three-pointers. He had hoped to play for Indiana, or any other Division I school for that matter, but he wasn't good enough. So he ended up at DePauw. He was a frequent starter during his first two years there, but midway through his junior season, with the team mired in a losing skid, he saw his playing time dwindle. He barely got off the bench as a senior. Tracy, then his college girlfriend, could see how hard it was for him. "We would talk about it a lot because he was really struggling," she says. "Basketball had been such a strong part of his identity. To have that change was really tough on him."

As he stewed over this turn of events, Stevens and a fellow senior turned their ire on the freshmen who were taking their minutes. After one particularly harsh practice, the coach, Bill Fenlon, called the two of them into his office and dressed them down. When Stevens objected—"What are we supposed to do, just lay down for these guys?"—Fenlon gave him his first lesson on leadership. "No, you should play hard," he said. "But do it in a way that brings them along. Don't create a divide."

Stevens felt ashamed. He also realized he had a choice. He could either quit the team or make the most of the situation. He chose to persist. "Nothing could have been better for my coaching career than that experience," he says. "I rode the roller coaster of emotions until my senior year, and then I became content when I came to the conclusion of, 'Hey, moron, it's not about you. It's about being as good of a teammate as you can be and putting your best foot forward every day.'"

Looking back, there really was no other option. Stevens loved basketball way too much to quit. Growing up in Indiana, he was naturally inculcated into the state religion. His parents used to record Indiana games on television, and they can remember him being transfixed by the action on the screen since before he was in kindergarten. Brad grew up reading the sports pages, digesting the box scores daily. He had a hoop in the driveway, of course, but much of his time was spent at the fully paved court located in the backyard of his friend's house. The neighborhood kids would play all day and then ride their bikes to the local Dairy Queen. Losers bought ice cream. "Those were fun days," Stevens says.

His life was a buzz of activity. Even as a young boy, Stevens always had to be playing games, running around the neighborhood, doing something. Like many of the coaches in this book, he suspects that had he been tested, he would have been diagnosed with attention deficit disorder. "I clearly have ADD—clearly," he tells me. "I've been told by specialists in that field that I would probably have been on some sort of medication." He is an avid reader, but he confesses that he usually puts the book away when he is about halfway through. If he gets a long email, he clicks out by the second paragraph. His wife calls him the "cruise director" because whenever he goes on vacation, he plans a full slate for the family. Jan recognized these patterns when Brad was young, but she was never concerned. "I loved the energy he had towards life," she says.

Tracy Wilhelmy met Brad through mutual friends when they got to DePauw, but it wasn't until they started dating as sophomores that she understood where his heart was. On their third date, he took her to a high school basketball game. The game was an hour's drive away, and Brad talked about Indiana high school basketball the whole way there and back. "A basketball nerd through and through," she says. "He was an encyclopedia. We had been friends for a year, but I didn't know he had this love. I didn't think it was weird. I actually thought it was really cool because he was so passionate about it."

Tracy also got an early lesson in her new boyfriend's hypercompetitiveness. A few months into their relationship, he invited her to Florida to take a vacation with his parents. She envisioned a few days of relaxing under the sun, but instead he engaged her in a series of competitions—at tennis, board games, shuffleboard, even running on the beach. He won everything. At one point during a tennis match, she finally got exasperated and said, "What is *wrong* with you?" She estimates that their lifelong series record in Scrabble is 500 to 2 in his favor. "I don't know why I keep playing," she says. "I guess I'm a tortured soul."

Temperamentally, Brad took after his mom more than his dad, but the family member he most favored was Jan's father, Jack Lothamer, a high school teacher, coach, and principal in Ohio. "He was a very commonsense guy, very practical. He was patient and calm and thought things through," Jan says. For a guy with no economics or business background, Jack also turned out to be a pretty savvy investor. He didn't have a lot of money, so he had to make his choices wisely. Jack gave Brad one heck of a tennis—and life—lesson when Brad was a kid. "You can win a lot of matches," Grandpa Jack said, "by staying patient and waiting for your opponent to make a mistake."

So when his college coach phased him out just as his playing career was winding down, Stevens's PEAK profile started to be forged. It taught him the value of persistence when things didn't go his way. It taught him to consider the thoughts and emotions of others. It forced him to decide who he was and what was important to him. And it imparted a very important piece of knowledge: No matter how much you plan, no matter how much you prepare, sometimes life is not fair. As much as he loved basketball, for the first time he understood there was a much larger game to be played. *Hey, moron, it's not about you.*

When they weren't playing their respective sports or hanging with friends at DePauw, Tracy and Brad spent a lot of time together in the library. He liked to work in a cubicle on the third floor; she was one floor below. Even though it seemed they spent about the same amount of time studying, Tracy noticed that by the time final exams came around, she would be up all night cramming, while Brad was always in bed at a decent hour. "He was never stressed out before a test," she says. "He was much more efficient than me."

Brad was an economics major in the Management Fellows Program, which was designed to combine an academic curriculum with real-world business experience. He does not remember much from the material he studied, but he did figure out his own best way to acquire knowledge. He wrote notes while he read his textbooks. When he was through, he rewrote those notes in cleaner, more organized form. He noticed that as he went through this process, the information magically entered his mind. This resulted from discipline, not genius. Once the test was over, he pretty much forgot the stuff.

His most salient moment of clarity came during an elective leadership seminar his senior year. The class exposed him to the teachings of Robert K. Greenleaf, an Indiana native who founded the notion of servant leadership. Stevens had done some volunteer basketball coaching in the past, but he had never seriously thought about entering the profession. The two coaching icons in his home state, Indiana's Bob Knight and Purdue's Gene Keady, were hot-tempered, old-school disciplinarians whose primary mode of communication was beratement. It never occurred to Stevens there was another way to go about leading. Learning about servant leadership was a life-changing lesson in the art of authenticity.

"I remember thinking, *This makes sense*," he tells me. "Do you want to be around somebody who lifts you up, or somebody that breaks you down? That's why whenever people ask me what's your leadership style, my answer is, 'It should be you.' There's an authenticity that is needed for leadership. If it's not real, then it's not going to work."

When Stevens was a junior at DePauw, he earned an internship at Eli Lilly and Company, the pharmaceutical conglomerate whose headquarters are located in Indianapolis. He was so impressive that he scored a full-time position upon graduation. The job suited his skill set, and it paid quite well, to the tune of about $44,000 per year. One of his primary responsibilities was to help set up a new incentive structure for the company's sales force, which he presented to a roomful of executives during a company retreat in Arizona. He was also in charge of planning that weekend. Figuring that all those people wouldn't want to come to Arizona and spend their time attending stuffy meetings, he budgeted periods for recreational activities like golf, horseback riding, and swimming. He also set up a group dinner off-site. It was a dream job for a natural-born cruise director.

Eli Lilly's most prominent drug at the time was Prozac, which treats depression. To that point, Stevens had not given much thought to mental wellness, but working on that account opened his eyes to just how many people were dealing with depression without their friends and family knowing it. He credits that experience for making him a better coach. "I think a lot of people in sports have missed the boat on mental health," he says. "You have to be empathetic in knowing that everybody has their own lives, and everybody has something tough going on. You need to make sure you understand that before you coach them."

It was a good gig with a bright future. Yet there was something missing: a scoreboard. To feed that jones, Stevens continued to do some coaching at local AAU teams and camps. He also made a few bucks working the basketball camp at Butler University, a private school in Indianapolis with a storied basketball tradition. It was an exciting, challenging environment. Stevens clung to a Butler assistant coach named Thad Matta and soaked up all the information he could. "He was always right by my side, asking questions, asking if I needed help," Matta tells me. "He was young, but you could see the wheels were turning."

It didn't take long for Stevens to come to an obvious, albeit unconventional career choice. He decided to leave his cushy office job with the stable future to take his shot at coaching. Neither his girlfriend nor his parents were surprised. One of the people whom Stevens called looking for advice was Matta, who had just been promoted to head coach at Butler. Matta suggested that Stevens come to work for him as a volunteer assistant. The job came with no salary, but it offered a foot in the door. Stevens had a couple of possibilities at Division II and Division III schools, but he had always dreamed of being in the NCAA Tournament. He felt like he underachieved as a player, so his only chance was to get there as a coach.

Stevens moved into a friend's basement and found a part-time job at Applebee's. Before he started at the restaurant, a position opened up on Matta's staff. Stevens moved into the full-time but low-paying role of director of basketball operations. Tracy was thrilled for him—that is, until Matta asked him to accompany the team on a trip to Finland that forced Brad to miss Tracy's brother's wedding. She was furious. "We broke up for about two hours," Tracy says. "It turned out to be a good thing, though, because at least I knew what I was getting into."

The idea to change careers might have seemed risky, but Stevens never felt that way. He felt authentic. Each day, he walked into work and passed a statue honoring Tony Hinkle, the legendary coach at Butler whose career spanned five decades. Beside the statue was a stone plaque listing the five principles that constitute the "Butler Way." Among those tenets was the word *Servanthood*. Whenever Stevens saw that word etched in stone, he knew he was in the right place.

The first thing he learned at his new job was how little he knew. "I remember sitting in that first meeting with Thad and his guys and thinking, *I have no idea what I'm doing*," Stevens says. "I played this game my whole life, but everything was foreign. I could see I had a lot to learn."

In many ways, Matta was the perfect boss for Stevens. Whereas Brad was by nature reserved, Matta was a ball of fire. At thirty-two, he was pretty young himself, and the two of them spent a lot of time together on and off the court. If Matta gave Stevens a small assignment like reorganizing the personnel book, Stevens would attack it like it was the most important thing he had ever done. With Tracy relocating to Ohio for law school, Brad was free to devote as many hours as he wanted to watching video, studying numbers, and learning the craft of coaching. It was basketball nerd heaven.

The best thing Matta did for Stevens was assign him to work with Matta's top assistant, Todd Lickliter. Lickliter had spent twelve years as a high school coach in Indiana before coming to Butler two years before. Stevens considered himself to be thorough and meticulous, but Lickliter took those habits to the extreme. He asked Stevens to go over box scores and statistics in search of any bit of information that might give Butler an edge. He instructed Stevens to type up his scouting reports and edit video packages. If the video wasn't in the proper sequence, he would tell Stevens to cut it again. Back in the days when coaches performed this task using three videotape machines, it might take Stevens two hours to reorder a ten-minute clip. Looking back, Lickliter says if he realized how much time was involved, he might not have asked Stevens to make those minor changes. "But that's the beauty about Brad. He's not going to say anything," Lickliter says. "You knew you could trust him. He wasn't going to try to cut a corner."

There was an important principle at work. Lickliter liked to cite an age-old line from the man who apologizes for writing a long letter because he didn't have time to write a shorter one. He understood that a coach's time with his players is finite, so it's important to make every moment count. Stevens noticed that the players tended to gravitate toward Lickliter during practice. Such was the power of knowledge.

In 2001, his first year at Butler, Stevens reached his dream of being part of the NCAA Tournament when the Bulldogs made the field and advanced to the second round. As a result, Matta was hired away by Xavier, and Lickliter was promoted to head coach. Lickliter worked efficiently and wanted his teams to play that way. If he had ninety minutes to practice but got his work done in fifty, then practice would end early. He wanted his players to be prepared, but he also wanted their minds clear and their legs fresh. In 2003, when the Bulldogs were in Birmingham preparing for an NCAA Tournament first-round game against Mississippi State, Lickliter spent an hour teaching the guys how to play zone defense, which they had not done all season. Then he took everyone to the zoo. The next day, Butler squeaked by Mississippi State, 47–46, and two days after that they beat Louisville to reach the Sweet Sixteen.

By that time, Tracy had returned to Indianapolis to finish up her law degree. She and Brad were married in the summer of 2003. In 2007, Lickliter again led Butler to the Sweet Sixteen. As a result, he was hired to be the head coach at Iowa. Lickliter had a young coaching staff, and most schools in that situation would look elsewhere to hire a successor. Butler, however, is not most schools. It has a culture of excellence that dates back to the early twentieth century. The athletic director, Barry Collier, is a Butler graduate who was the head basketball coach there for eleven years. He appreciated the value of hiring from within.

The only question was whether any of Lickliter's young assistants were ready. For his part, Stevens didn't think he would be seriously considered. He had already packed his suitcases into the trunk of his car and was prepared to follow Lickliter to Iowa. When Collier called to say he wanted to interview him for the head job, Stevens pulled over, fished a suit out of his trunk, and got dressed

standing by the side of the road. ("I probably could have gotten arrested for public indecency," he says.) During two long interviews,
Collier was taken by how thoroughly Stevens had thought things
through. "He had some coaching materials that he had organized
and drawn up and shared with me that were indicative of his orga-
nizational skills," Collier recalls. "All the assistants were impressive,
but Brad stuck out. He seemed to be the most ready, and the way he
expressed himself gave me confidence he could do the job."

On April 4, 2007, Stevens was introduced to the public as the
new head coach at Butler University. He would be the second-
youngest basketball coach in all of Division I, and by far the
youngest-looking. His wife believed he could handle the coaching
part, but she was less sure about how he would conduct himself with
the media. That changed as soon as Brad stepped to the microphone. As he spoke, Tracy stood a few feet away and marveled at her
husband's poise, eloquence, and confidence. It was as if he had been
doing it his whole life.

Like most coaches, Stevens remembers his losses more vividly than
his wins, so it's no surprise that he credits his very first loss for
delivering another important piece of knowledge.

It happened in the Bulldogs' eighth game. The Bulldogs were
undefeated heading into their first Horizon League matchup at
Wright State. As his players struggled to put the Raiders away in the
second half, Stevens let his temper get away from him. They lost,
43–42. "That one was on me," he says. "I was on edge, and our players were playing tight because of that. I told myself afterwards, *You
can't be like that.* So that was a good learning experience."

One of the best pieces of advice Stevens got that first season
came from Sean Miller, who had the unenviable job of following
Matta at Xavier after he was hired away by Ohio State. "You've got

to be yourself," Miller said. That was good advice, but it wasn't easy to follow. Butler had been to two Sweet Sixteens in the previous five years, which was astounding for a school from a "midmajor" conference with a sparse recruiting budget and limited television exposure. Though the team's arena, Hinkle Fieldhouse, is a shrine that is listed as a national historic landmark, it was a far cry from the gleaming modern arenas that the big-time schools were building. In many respects, however, Stevens saw this as a benefit. If a recruit could walk through Hinkle Fieldhouse and still want to play for Butler, Stevens knew he was coming for the proper reasons.

Stevens and his staff were forced to use their shoestring budget to scavenge for just the right players. "We tried to identify kids with intrinsic motivation," he says. In his never-ending quest for knowledge, he read Malcolm Gladwell's book *Outliers,* which includes a chapter explaining that the best hockey players in Canada tend to be born in the first three months of the year. That meant they were the oldest among their peers, which gave them early access to quality competition and coaching. Stevens piggybacked on that notion and looked for recruits who were born between March and June, making them the youngest of their grades. He figured that meant they had more potential to grow into their bodies. While emphasizing that he does not have enough data to fully validate his theory, he does point to two success stories: Kam Woods, who was born on April 22 and went on to become the school's second all-time leading rebounder; and Gordon Hayward, who was born on March 23 and was the ninth player selected in the 2010 NBA draft.

Stevens had come a long way from being the wide-eyed greenhorn at that first meeting with Matta. Stevens's father remembers watching a practice that first season in which Brad was preparing his Bulldogs for a game at Wisconsin–Milwaukee. Mark did not understand most of what Stevens was saying, except for a sequence in which he instructed his guys to leave one of the Wisconsin–Milwaukee shooters alone because "he is only shooting 18 percent from the corner." Sure enough, the next day, the players did as their coach instructed and won the game.

Stevens's first team won 30 games and lost in overtime to Tennessee in the second round of the NCAA Tournament, but that was with an older roster full of players whom Lickliter had recruited. The real challenge came when Stevens had to replenish the program himself. His first recruiting class as a head coach featured Hayward, a skinny but skilled 6´8˝ forward from Brownsburg, Indiana; Shelvin Mack, a tough-minded point guard from Lexington, Kentucky; and Ronald Nored, a 6´0˝ guard from Homewood, Alabama. Nored was a preacher's son who was drawn to Stevens after he drove 480 miles from Indianapolis to give his pitch and drove back to Indy later that same day.

Nored had told Stevens he wanted to be a basketball coach someday, and he sensed from the start that Stevens would help him achieve that goal. Nored will never forget the time he walked by Stevens's office during his senior year and the coach invited him to sit with him and study how to manage two-for-one situations, when a team takes a quick shot in the final minute to ensure that it will get a second possession before time runs out. "The best thing about him is that he's so real. It's not like he's trying to fake his way through just to get you to like him," Nored says. "And he's such a great communicator that he doesn't have to scream and yell. He's not going to hide the truth, but he's going to do it in a way that builds you up and makes you want to get better."

On the other hand, Nored can offer testimony on Stevens's competitive intensity. Nored was a limited offensive player, so Stevens needed him to be his toughest, most resilient defender. During a first-round game against Murray State in the 2010 NCAA Tournament, Stevens called time out because Nored was getting lit up by the Racers' outstanding shooting guard, Isaiah Canaan. Holding a clipboard that listed Murray State's players, Stevens turned to his assistants in the huddle and shouted, "Is there *anybody* on this board who Ron Nored can guard?"

Butler is a rigorous academic school, but unlike many college coaches, Stevens did not steer his players into easy majors. Their schedules were so loaded with physics labs and engineering exams that the only time he could get them together for practice was at six o'clock in the morning. Hinkle being Hinkle, the place was freezing in the winter at that time of day. The players could often see their breath. When they complained, Stevens would remind them that being tired was no excuse for not performing. "Someday you're all going to be fathers," he said. "Your baby is going to be crying at three in the morning, and your wife is going to want you to feed him. You may be tired, but you still have to be a good dad."

Another player who enjoyed significant growth under Stevens's tutelage was Matt Howard, a 6′8″ power forward from Connersville, Indiana. Howard was good enough to earn a scholarship offer from Purdue, a Big Ten power, but not good enough for the Purdue staff to prioritize him. Stevens was all in from the start, and his persistence eventually won Howard over. Stevens was used to having to utilize undersized big men, so he tapped into Howard's agility and toughness. He also loved Howard's intrinsic motivation. Howard was the kind of player who would dive into the stands to try to save a ball from going out of bounds even if his team was winning by 24 points in the second half, which he did.

Stevens encouraged his players to grow by straying out of their comfort zones, so much so that he often ended individual workouts with ten minutes where they could try funky things they'd never think of doing in games. The coaches referred to those periods as "dream time," and in Howard's case, that meant hoisting three-pointers. He went from not taking a single attempt as a freshman to shooting nearly 40 percent on 133 attempts as a senior. Show up, work hard, get better, persist. That was the Butler Way.

An opposing coach inside the Horizon League once described Stevens's teams to me as having "Ivy League smarts combined with military academy toughness." Stevens likes to refer to Lickliter's quote that "toughness is doing the next right thing," but his players wouldn't have had that quality if he didn't emphasize it each day. He even had the letters TGHT stitched onto their game shorts. They stood for "The Game Honors Toughness." During his first season as head coach, he named all five seniors as co-captains. It was the right thing to do for that team, but as the years progressed Stevens believed that naming a few players as captains disempowered the rest of the team. He rarely assigned captains again.

Butler steamrolled through the 2009–10 Horizon League with an 18–0 record, but though they entered the NCAA Tournament as a No. 5 seed, few so-called experts (including yours truly) pegged them as a serious Final Four threat. That started to change as they defeated UTEP, Murray State, and No. 1–seeded Syracuse to reach the Elite Eight. The Bulldogs' collective authenticity was a major advantage in those games. They knew they weren't going to "out-athlete" their opponents, so they would have to outsmart them and out-tough them. They managed tempo and guarded with intelligent ferocity. In the Elite Eight, they faced a Kansas State team that had averaged 79.7 points on 45 percent shooting during the season. Butler held the Wildcats to 56 points on 39 percent and won by seven points. That made the thirty-three-year-old Stevens the youngest coach to take his team to the Final Four since Bob Knight took Indiana there in 1973 at the age of thirty-two.

It was remarkable enough that this humble little midmajor program with the baby-faced coach could make it to the game's biggest stage. Adding to the Hollywood storyline was that the Final Four was being held that year in Indianapolis. After the team got home, Stevens had the team bus cruise by Lucas Oil Stadium so his players could savor the moment. From there, he fell back into his routine, running early-morning practices and bivouacking himself in his office so he could study the video and stats. Even after his team edged Michigan State in a dramatic win in Saturday's semifinal, Stevens stuck to the script. On the morning of the title-game matchup against Duke, his players attended classes, just like always.

The final game was a classic. Butler appeared poised to prevail right up until Hayward's halfcourt attempt clanked off the rim at the buzzer, enabling Duke to escape with a 61–59 win.

Much of Butler's team's core returned for the 2010–11 season, which was a blessing and a curse. The team may still have been technically a midmajor one in the Horizon League, but the Bulldogs were faced with big-time expectations. That took a toll. The season appeared to be headed off the rails after they lost three out of four games to fall to 14–9. After the team arrived at their hotel in Cleveland for a road game, Mack asked the coaches to leave so he could address his teammates. "Okay," Stevens said, "but make sure whatever you say, you better start with yourself." Mack challenged everyone to rediscover their underdog, aggressive mentality. Stevens, meanwhile, looked for ways to alleviate the pressure. In early February, he called Howard into his office to remind him that whatever happened the rest of the season, his legacy as the best four-year player in school history was secured. He invoked the metaphor of the trampoline, where the lowest point catapults the jumper to his highest level. "Let's just enjoy this last month," Stevens told him. From there, the team went on a 14-game win streak that didn't end until the NCAA championship game, where Butler lost to UConn.

Despite that ending, the consecutive championship game appearances constituted one of the most unlikely achievements in the history of the sport. Lots of people figured their coach was some kind of genius, but it takes much more than that to get a team to *Us*. Stevens made it happen because he worked hard, demonstrated character, empathized with his players, acquired the requisite knowledge, and applied an authentic servant's leadership. He may have been young, but he was very good at what he did. And he really, really hated to lose.

Stevens could have had just about any college job he wanted. Collier gave him several new contracts with pay raises—Stevens had no agent besides Tracy, a contract lawyer—but Brad never really felt the pull of the big time. When he turned down UCLA in 2013, Tracy started to believe he really was never going to leave.

It is quite possible that if Stevens had stayed at Butler, he would have taken the Indiana job after the school fired its head coach, Tom Crean, in the spring of 2017. That aside, the only times he let his mind wander to other destinations were when he thought about the NBA. He had been intrigued by the pro game ever since he attended a coaching clinic conducted by then Florida coach Billy Donovan shortly after Stevens was named head coach at Butler. The clinic featured several NBA assistants. As they started to explain how they scouted opponents and developed players, Stevens was amazed by their advanced methods. The pros were way ahead of anything he had seen at the college level. For a basketball nerd like him, coaching in the NBA seemed like the ultimate learning experience.

After Hayward and Mack entered the league, Stevens bought the NBA's television package so he could keep track of his guys. He grew ever more fascinated by the pro game and looked for ways to bring an NBA methodology to his own program. In 2012, he became the first college coach to hire a full-time staffer devoted to analytics, Drew Cannon. He had discovered Cannon's work while

Cannon was living in his parents' basement in Raleigh, North Carolina, and working for a national recruiting service. Stevens made Cannon his graduate manager. Though Stevens bristles when people call him an "analytics guy"—"99.9 percent of the time, the numbers don't drive decisions, they validate them"—he also concedes that most of the time he trusts the data. Alex Barlow recalls a game at Saint Joseph's during the 2012–13 season when Hawks guard Chris Wilson made four three-pointers in the first five minutes. Stevens had told his guys to leave Wilson unguarded because he came into the game shooting 28 percent from behind the arc. Rather than making an adjustment, Stevens opted to stick to the game plan and wait for Wilson to revert to the mean. Sure enough, Wilson only made one three-pointer the rest of the game, and Butler went on to win by six.

This pro-style approach caught the eye of several NBA executives, but each time one of them reached out to gauge his interest, Stevens shooed them away. He had a different reply when Boston Celtics general manager Danny Ainge called in the spring of 2013. Ainge had become impressed with Stevens while scouting Hayward. When Doc Rivers decided to leave the Celtics, Ainge asked whether Stevens was interested in taking his place. He was. The NBA can be a much colder business than college, but if there was one franchise that had echoes of the Butler Way, it was the Celtics. Plus, the timing couldn't have been better. Brad and Tracy had decided to move to a different community now that their children, Brady and Kinsley, were eight and five years old, respectively. They had sold their house and were staying with Brad's mother while looking for a new place to live. Had they settled on a house and a new neighborhood, Brad might have been reluctant.

Brad sat at Jan's kitchen table, which was covered in plastic to protect it from the kids' arts-and-crafts projects, and listened as Ainge, two of the Celtics' co-owners, and the team's assistant general manager, Mike Zarren, made their pitch. The money was nice, of course, but Stevens was more swayed by Ainge's offer to give him a six-year contract. In the face of such a drastic rebuild, that long-term commitment spoke volumes. Brad thought it through as he always does. Then he walked into his office at Butler where Tracy was signing payroll checks for the basketball camp and told her, "I'm going to do it."

There was much to learn. NBA basketball is much different from the college version, with a 24-second clock and an additional eight minutes of playing time. That equates to a lot more possessions and substitutions for the head coach to manage. Plus, for the first time Stevens was coaching players of comparable size and speed. That forced him to challenge some long-held assumptions.

For example, he had always instructed his big men to aggressively trap opposing guards while defending a ball screen. When he got to the Celtics, he hired assistants with extensive NBA experience. They argued that now that he had big men who were actually big, he should have them "drop" to the baseline instead of "blitzing" the dribbler. It took some convincing, but Stevens eventually went along. "That was really hard for me," he said. "I've never dropped in my life. Thirteen straight years of hard showing and blitzing."

In an effort to accrue all the information he could, Stevens brought Cannon to Boston to work as his basketball operations analyst. He uprooted the team's video and analytics systems to put in place an infrastructure that best suited his ways of learning. At the same time, Stevens has figured out how to study the numbers without being consumed by them. When he gets bogged down, Austin Ainge, the Celtics' director of player personnel, will tell him, "Just use your eyes. You're good."

The egalitarian ethos at Butler was a relic of the past. Pro players work under contracts of varying length and compensation. A team's roster turns over every season, oftentimes within the same season. And yet the fundamentals of the job—the give-and-take, the relationships, the personal development, the empathy—remain very much the same. Stevens realized early on that if he demonstrated to his players that he possessed knowledge that could make them better, he could get them to play the way he wanted, just like they did at Butler. "All the good ones want to be coached," he says.

At no time is this more true than when Stevens is drawing up a play during a time out. His players have the utmost confidence in his decision making. "I just think I enjoy that. It's a puzzle, right?" he says. "It's figuring out how you can score in a given moment. I watch a lot to prepare for those moments, but it's not like I'm a savant. All I do is steal from everybody else based on how I watched other teams guard things. I mean, how many tricks can there be at the end of the day?"

Temperamentally, Stevens was well suited to the task of rebuilding a proud franchise. The Celtics had lost the Hall of Fame trio of Ray Allen, Kevin Garnett, and Paul Pierce that had won the NBA title five years before. It was left to Stevens to sweep up the morning after the party. The Celtics went 25–57 his first season, but they steadily improved thereafter, winning 40 and 48 games respectively the next two years.

Stevens truly distinguished himself during the 2016–17 season. Though the Eastern Conference was supposed to be dominated by the LeBron James–led Cleveland Cavaliers, Stevens's slow-and-steady-wins-the-race approach enabled the Celtics to win 53 games, sneak up on the Cavs from behind, and snare the No. 1 seed in the playoffs. It was fitting that the team's success was fueled by a pint-sized point guard named Isaiah Thomas, who was selected with the final pick in the 2011 NBA draft. Thomas was undersized and overlooked, so he played with a healthy chip on his shoulder. He would have been a great fit at Butler.

The Celtics' season was tragically upended when Thomas's sister was killed in an auto accident the day before their first-round playoff series with the Chicago Bulls was to begin. Stevens was all too prepared to play the role of empathetic grief counselor. He had dealt with family deaths several times during his tenure at Butler. Over the previous fifteen months, two of his former players had passed away, one after a lengthy battle with cancer, the other from sudden heart failure. After Thomas learned the news about his sister at the end of the team's afternoon practice, Stevens went to his house to console him. He encouraged Thomas to spend as much time away from the team as he needed.

Thomas went home for his sister's funeral but did not miss any games. When the Celtics lost the first two at home, the Boston media was aflame, but the team's locker room maintained a detached serenity. "Our perspective was not on basketball at that moment," Stevens says. "People start throwing around the term *adversity*, but nobody got caught up in that. I'm telling you, that kind of noise could never have been more unimportant to us."

Many teams in that circumstance would have wilted, but those Celtics had gotten to *Us* long before the playoffs began. They stuck together and rebounded to win four straight and eliminate the Bulls. Then they got by the Washington Wizards in the conference semifinals in seven games before coming face-to-face with the reigning NBA champion Cavaliers in the final. After Cleveland walloped the Celtics by 44 points in game two, Stevens asked Barlow to research the records of how teams performed in the game following a 40-point-plus loss in the playoffs. Barlow found they were 4–3. Stevens relayed the information to his players in hopes of boosting their confidence. Sure enough, in game three the Celtics managed to come back from a 21-point deficit and scrape out a three-point win despite playing without Thomas, who had sustained a hip injury. The team fought gamely but eventually succumbed to the Cavaliers in five.

As his circumstances, fame, and net worth have changed dramatically over the past decade, there is one thing about Stevens that has remained consistent: his demeanor. Sure, he tends to be a little more animated on the NBA sideline than he was at Butler, and now that he is coaching grown men he is more inclined to drop an F-bomb when he wants to make his point. For the most part, however, he strikes a serene pose on the bench that is distinctly at odds with that of most of his peers. Many people, including Stevens, have suggested that his cool exterior masks a painful churning within, but I'm not buying it. That would be inauthentic, not to mention inhuman. A person cannot fake who he is for this long. If Stevens appears cool on the outside, I believe it's because he really is that cool on the inside. He does not discipline himself this way because he is trying to be a good guy. He does it because he wants to win so badly. As he puts it, "I can't be wild and crazy and think."

Besides, it's not just the difficult moments when Stevens maintains his equipoise. He seems constitutionally incapable of experiencing elation as well. He constantly amazes his Celtics players and assistants when he bypasses any semblance of celebration following dramatic wins. He's immediately on to the next thing.

My particular favorite Brad Stevens moment occurred on January 20, 2013. Butler was hosting Gonzaga on a Saturday night in a much-hyped game between powerhouse midmajors. ESPN had manufactured the matchup and sent its *GameDay* studio crew to lend it a big-time environment. The game more than lived up to the hype as Butler sophomore guard Roosevelt Jones lofted up a runner at the buzzer to give the Bulldogs a dramatic win. The shot unleashed a wild scene with fans rushing the court, but Stevens betrayed no emotion at all. Not only did he decline to celebrate, he didn't even bother to unfold his arms. Rather, he simply lowered his head and walked toward the opposing bench, where he shook hands with Gonzaga coach Mark Few as if they had casually met on the street.

When I bring this up to Stevens, he tells me he was just doing what came natural. "I think the bigger the moment, the more I get focused on what's next," he says. "If you can keep perspective in a moment like that, you can really get to your team. Because something big just happened and everybody's locked in."

"But didn't you miss out on the jubilation?" I ask.

"Oh, I don't care about that," he replies. "The satisfaction I get is more internal. For me, jumping up and down is not the same as just going in your office, leaning back in your chair, and being like, *That was special. That was a pretty cool moment.*"

When Alex Barlow was a high school senior in Cincinnati, he wasn't good enough to earn a Division I scholarship. But he had ambitions to be a head coach, so he tried to find a place where he could walk on and maybe get a chance to play. Barlow visited a few different schools, but only one head coach took the time to meet him when he arrived, show him around campus for a couple of hours, and then sit with him to discuss his potential within the program. That coach was Brad Stevens. "And this was just two weeks after they had lost to UConn [in the championship game]," Barlow told me. "I had visited some Division II schools. All of them sent out a director of basketball operations or an assistant coach to greet me. And here's this dude who just coached in two straight national championship games, and he's greeting me at the door. That made me think that he was about what he said he was about."

Stevens had a record of playing his walk-ons, and he told Barlow that he would have every chance to compete for minutes. Stevens was true to his word. Barlow moved into the starting lineup early in his sophomore season. He made a game-winning shot over No. 1–ranked Indiana that forever earned him a part of Butler lore. A few weeks later, Stevens put him on scholarship.

After Barlow graduated in 2015, Stevens hired him to be the Celtics' assistant video coordinator. Late one night, Barlow was riding the team plane. It was about three in the morning, and everyone on board was asleep—or so he thought. Barlow woke up momentarily and looked over to see the team's head coach watching game video on his laptop. He was still very much the same guy who first greeted him at the door of Hinkle Fieldhouse. "Sometimes people think it comes easy to him," Barlow says. "That's because they underestimate how much time and preparation he puts into everything. He's obviously very smart, but he prepares better than anybody I've ever been around."

And yet unlike many coaches who fall victim to the grind, Stevens has a deft instinct for when he needs to pull back and recenter himself. That instinct came in handy after the Celtics lost back-to-back games late in the 2016–17 season. When they landed in San Francisco for a date with the Golden State Warriors—not exactly the opponent an NBA coach wants to see when his team is on a losing skid—Stevens took a couple of his assistants on an impromptu bike ride across the Golden Gate Bridge. "When I was twenty-eight, I probably would have poured over more film that was meaningless and confused myself," he says. Maybe it's coincidental that the Celtics won that night, but I doubt it.

His humility remains his most enduring and endearing trait. When referring to a difficult loss, he tries never to say it was a game his team "should have" won. He says it "could have" won, because "it's not fair to the other team. I believe that wholeheartedly." On a recent visit to Ohio State, where Matta served as head basketball coach for thirteen years, Matta invited Stevens to a football prac-tice so he could watch Urban Meyer in action. When they got to the practice field, Stevens asked Matta where he could stand so he wouldn't be in the way. "I'm like, 'Dude, you're the head coach of the Boston Celtics. You'll be fine,'" Matta says. Stevens stood off to the side anyway and quietly took notes.

Stevens loves spending time with his family, but he loathes being idle. The idea of sitting through a movie in a theater is anathema to him. "I don't ever relax in that setting," he says. When the kids have games of their own, he will often jog one or both ways. It helps him to expend energy and make good use of his time. On the morning after the Celtics were eliminated from the 2017 NBA playoffs, he sat next to his wife at their kitchen table and started to go over the summer calendar. For Tracy, this was a little too much persistence. "Can I at least finish my coffee?" she asked.

Their home is in Boston, but in many ways their hearts are still in Indiana. They have a summer lake house in the northern part of the state. In 2014, Tracy was appointed to the board of trustees at Butler. They go back there frequently to attend functions, and they meet with high school students in Massachusetts who are consider-ing Butler. The school's basketball program has come a long way, largely because of the success Stevens had there. Before the start of his final season, Butler was invited to join the Atlantic 10 Confer-ence. The following year, it became part of the newfangled Big East. Hinkle Fieldhouse has undergone a $36 million renovation, which added a video board plus a refurbished locker room and offices. The Stevenses' ties will remain strong in the wake of Butler's decision in June 2017 to hire LaVall Jordan, a former Butler player who worked as an assistant with Stevens for Lickliter. Ironically, the job had become vacant because the previous coach, Chris Holtmann, was hired by Ohio State to replace Matta, who had just been fired.

His old and new worlds merged in an uncanny way during the

summer of 2017, when Gordon Hayward, who had grown to become a stellar player with the Utah Jazz, signed a four-year, $128 million contract with the Celtics. Stevens told me it was "surreal" to be wooing Hayward all over again. "We recruited him when he was seventeen, and then we recruited him again when he was twenty-seven," he said. Later that summer, the Celtics pulled off another blockbuster when they traded Thomas for Cleveland Cavaliers point guard Kyrie Irving. The 2017–18 campaign started in horrific fashion when Hayward sustained a gruesome ankle injury in the very first game and was lost for the season. That will make it even more difficult for the Celtics to get past LeBron and his Cavaliers, not to mention those Golden State Warriors. Stevens understands the challenge he has taken on, knows all the pitfalls, realizes the season could still very well end again with a loss, but that's okay, because the next morning he can wake up, grab some coffee, pull up a chair, lay out his calendar, and start preparing for what's next. The pleasure's in the process. Each new season is a chance to get better.

Dabo Swinney

"GOD NEVER SAYS, 'OOPS.'"

Nobody ever said Dabo Swinney was a man of few words. His speeches become stem-winders. His tangents have tangents. Ask him a simple question, and he will embark upon a lengthy, meandering, disjointed, flighty disquisition that touches on a variety of topics, most of which you never asked him about, yet somehow ends up driving home his original point with remarkable eloquence. As the football coach at Clemson University, Swinney is constantly buttonholing people, holding forth at meetings, chatting up employees, addressing his players on in team meetings. His gift of gab keeps on giving. "He can just talk and talk and talk forever," says Hunter Renfrow, a wide receiver who came to Clemson in 2014 as an invited walk-on and later became a starter. "Every single day, we're getting hammered with messages about how we can become better people, how we can become better football players. He can go on for hours sometimes, just because it means so much to him."

And yet Swinney is also highly organized, focused, and disciplined. He has an impressive ability to harvest a high volume of information and funnel it into a single cogent message. To reinforce this skill, he conducts an exercise each summer in which he chooses a single word that will serve as his theme for the coming season. It is an idea he got from Jon Gordon, whom Swinney befriended after reading his bestselling motivational book *One Word That Will Change Your Life*. Swinney asks his players to do this same exercise. His hope is that they too will find the one word that inspires them to do the small things that make the biggest difference.

When Swinney sat down to choose his word for the 2016 season, he was doing so at a weighty moment. His Clemson Tigers were coming off a 45–40 loss to Alabama in the College Football Playoff National Championship. Most of his starters, including star quarterback Deshaun Watson, were returning. A coach can spend an entire lifetime without having that kind of a chance to make history, so Swinney felt a greater urgency to find the exact right word. After ruminating on the possibilities for a while, he made his choice. The word was *love*.

When I asked Swinney a year later why he made that choice, he was uncharacteristically at a loss for words. "I can't answer that," he said. "That's just something that's put on my spirit. I write down a bunch of words, and one of 'em always jumps out. I just kept coming back to that word. Like, 'Guys, we gotta love what we do, love the grind, love each other, love your school, be passionate.' When you love something, you want to give that little extra."

Swinney is not one to choose a message and let it drop. He must hammer it over and over again, putting it on signs, inserting it into playbooks, dropping it into presentations and conversations. So when a really big moment comes, like when his team faced a seven-point deficit to Alabama during halftime of the 2017 BCS National Championship Game, he knows just where to turn.

"Jay, you love Deshaun, right?" he asked Jay Guillermo, the team's starting center.

"Yessir," Guillermo replied.

"Deshaun," he said, "you love when [senior running back] Wayne Gallman lines up behind you, right?"

"Yessir."

Swinney called out a few more of his players, and then he drove the point home. "Guys, we know we're good enough to win this game," he said. "We got this far because we love each other. Let's just go out there and finish it."

That is not a message we are accustomed to hearing from the macho men who coach Vince Lombardi's game, but in this case it was fitting. Clemson came back to beat the Crimson Tide with a dramatic final drive to win, 35–31. Though I would like to say the victory happened because of Swinney's stirring words, that is not really true. Locker room speeches are way overrated. Whatever emotions are generated when a coach says "win one for the Gipper" usually wear off after a couple of plays. A coach's words only work when they are of a piece with the thousands he has spoken during the course of the season. There is a reason why Swinney hammers his guys with such numbing repetition. Each time he invokes a life lesson or turns a clever phrase, he is lighting one tiny pixel that, when placed alongside the thousands of others, projects a clear and colorful message onto a big screen. In other words, Clemson doesn't win games because of Swinney's eloquence so much as because of his persistence. He uses words to get to *Us*.

Swinney is a man of faith, and he brings to his program the spirit of the tent revival, under which he preaches the gospel of football. His clarity, alas, has been hard-won. When he was in high school, his life was ripped apart, throwing his family into emotional disarray and financial hardship. The adversity gave him the foundation for his PEAK profile, and while it made his journey to *Us* winding and painful, it also provided him with important tools he would need to become a championship football coach. Many people who have endured such private pain feel ashamed and try to keep it private, but that is not Swinney's way. He processes the difficult events of his family's past the same way he deals with everything else.

He talks about it.

The persistence, he gets from his mama.

Carol McGraw was born the youngest of four children in 1944, in Clanton, Alabama. She was a robust, plump, healthy ten-pound baby, but she contracted polio shortly before her second birthday. Saddled by paralysis and high fevers, Carol was admitted to a university hospital in Birmingham and placed into isolation. She survived the fevers, but for several months she needed an iron lung to help her breathe. She was later moved to the Crippled Children's Clinic and Hospital, where she went about the long, arduous process of rehabilitating her withered muscles and damaged nerves.

When Carol was six years old, her doctors noticed that her spine was starting to curve. It was a bad case of scoliosis, no doubt caused by the polio. She spent an entire year in a head-to-toe body cast, followed by another year in a shorter one. She also had two spinal fusion surgeries during that span. Once she graduated from the casts, the doctors gave her a big, clunky metal brace, which she was not allowed to remove, not even to bathe. The brace came off a year later, after which she was pushed around the hospital in a wheelchair.

Teachers gave Carol school lessons by her bedside. When she grew strong enough, they wheeled her down to the hall to a make-shift classroom. Her right arm was so weak that she had to use her left hand to hold it up so she could write on the chalkboard.

The only thing that rivaled her physical pain was the psychological trauma of her isolation. Aside from occasional visits to her home in Alabaster, Carol spent virtually her entire childhood cut off from family and friends. "Basically, I didn't know my own siblings," she says. "It was a very rough ordeal."

Carol was finally well enough to leave the hospital just before her thirteenth birthday. After a year of homeschooling, she entered her local public high school as a ninth grader. The doctors told her mother that Carol needed to stay as active as possible, so she signed her up for dance classes. One day, Carol saw another girl twirling her baton and decided she wanted to learn how. It took her a while, but eventually, using the same arm she used to lift with assistance from her other hand because it was so weak, she became a lead majorette in the school's marching band. The *Birmingham News*'s Sunday magazine put her photograph on its cover and published an article about the lovely majorette who survived polio and grew up to twirl a mean baton.

Looking at her today, you'd never know that Carol's spine remains severely curved, bending grotesquely toward her right shoulder as it travels upward from her lower back. "If you could see the X-ray of my spine now, it would take your breath away. It's absolutely terrifying," she says. As rough as her ordeal was, it also formed her character—stiffened her spine, so to speak. "It made me a survivor," she says. "No matter what happens to me, I always think I can adapt."

She would need every bit of that persistence in order to survive the rough ordeals to come. When she wavered, she relied on her youngest son, the future football coach, to pull her through. Says Carol, "It frightens me sometimes to see how he's so much like me."

O n the night Clemson lost the 2016 championship game to Alabama, Swinney returned to his hotel room around 2 a.m. He had a few hours before his early flight, but he was too wired to sleep. So he hopped into bed and flipped on the TV . . . just in time to see a replay of the game getting ready to kick off.

Many coaches who suffer such a painful loss would never want to watch the game again, much less a few hours after its conclusion.

Swinney sat there and watched it all the way through. He second-guessed himself a few times, winced at a few mistakes that could have altered the outcome. Mostly, though, he was in awe of his players' effort and competitiveness, and he felt gratitude for the opportunity to coach a game of that magnitude. Even though his Tigers lost, he believed they had gotten to *Us*. When the replay ended, he packed his bag and left the room. No regrets.

"It definitely hurts to lose, don't get me wrong, but I try to teach our team not to let one moment make us lose sight of all the good," Swinney told me. "I live by the belief that God never says, 'Oops.' My life has given me a clear perspective on what real problems are."

He has certainly had his fair share of those, but fortunately he was well equipped to handle them. From the very beginning, Swinney excelled at everything he tried. As a grade schooler growing up in Pelham, Alabama, he was one of those gifted students who could memorize and process information with ease. He loved to acquire knowledge. Not only was he smart, but he was conscientious. Carol remembers him doing his first-grade homework over again because he didn't get it quite right the first time.

Socially, things flowed just as smoothly. Dabo was funny and outgoing and always had lots of friends. His teachers adored him. "He won everything in school. He was Mr. This, Mr. That," Carol says. "He was exactly the same way he is now—very outgoing, very organized, very driven. Everyone loved Dabo."

And he was great at sports, "always just a little bit better than everyone else," as his older brother, Tracy, puts it. He played basketball, football, and baseball. Dabo loved the camaraderie that came with being on a team. He was always tagging along to Tracy's Little League practices. When Tracy went off to play football and baseball for Marion Military Institute, Dabo would visit him before games and slap high fives with the players as they took the field. The locker room felt like home.

Tracy and Dabo have a younger brother, Tripp. When he was sixteen years old, he was in a horrific car accident in which he was thrown from the passenger seat through the windshield. Tripp spent two weeks in a coma. When he awoke, he had near-total memory loss. He eventually recovered his memory, but he was never quite right after that.

Dabo had tons of friends, but one was special. Her name was Kathleen Bassett, and she was a year younger. They first clicked when they were barely out of kindergarten, and later became boyfriend and girlfriend in junior high. Dabo and Kathleen were the sweethearts of Pelham High School—he the star athlete, she the adorable cheerleader. Aside from a brief "break" in college, they have always been together. When they tied the knot in 1994, Dabo said he felt like he was marrying his sister.

To outsiders, the Swinneys looked like the perfect family. Beneath the surface, however, the picture was very different. If the Swinneys' neighbors and friends could have seen an X-ray of what was really happening inside that house, it would have taken their breath away.

Ervil Swinney was a good man. Doted on his wife. Coached his boys in Little League. Owned a pair of appliance businesses in town. And like just about every red-blooded male in that state who didn't root for Auburn, he worshipped the Crimson Tide. His three sons loved nothing more than to watch Bear Bryant's TV show with him on Sunday mornings during the fall. For Tracy, Dabo, and Tripp, football was their religion, and their dad was their preacher.

Things started to change in the mid-1980s, when Ervil's businesses faltered. He grew fearful that he could not provide the type of lifestyle he thought his family needed, and his debts were only getting larger. Rather than being frank with his family, making hard choices, and figuring a way out of the mess, Ervil withdrew and succumbed to his personal weakness—beer. He drank it like it was water, and it made him mean. He started hanging out with other men in town who loved to drink as much as he did. Then he'd stumble home in the middle of the night and pitch a fit. When he was really worked up, he would throw things around the house. Sometimes, when Carol would confront him, the boys would have to hold Ervil back so he couldn't hurt her.

By the time Ervil's drinking got really bad, Tracy was almost through with college. Tripp had also left for the University of Montevallo, where he himself struggled with alcohol. So Dabo was the only boy at home as his father lost his businesses and plunged deeper into his addiction. At his worst, Ervil would go on benders that kept him away from home for days at a time. "It was scary every time the phone would ring," Carol says. "We wouldn't know where he was. I would just wait and hope that he would come back." Problem was, when he did come back, he'd sometimes toss lamps, punch walls, and break windows. One time he threw a Christmas tree clear across the living room. Carol would have no choice but to grab Dabo and drive away. Sometimes they spent the night in a motel. Sometimes they slept in the car.

It was an awful and humiliating way for a boy to spend his adolescence. "I saw things that kids shouldn't see," Dabo says. "Police showing up at your house, running out of the house at night, knocking on neighbors' doors, jumping in a car with your mom. It was bad. My dad would give you the shirt off his back, but when he drank it just took over and cost him everything."

Dabo leaned hard on Kathleen in those days. She came from a "normal" family, and she offered some stability. That helped him stay focused on school and sports. "He was so busy. He went from football to basketball to baseball year round," Kathleen says. "He was an honor student, he had tons of friends, he was close to his coaches. So he didn't have time to dwell on anything. If he had been a loner, it would have been a lot harder."

Finally, Carol had enough. She decided to leave Ervil. When she broke the news to Dabo, he cried in the high school gymnasium. Carol had always been a stay-at-home mom while Ervil ran his businesses, but she managed to find work behind the counter at a Birmingham department store for $8 an hour. At first, they rented an apartment in town, but after about six months they fell behind on payments and were evicted. Carol stayed at her mother's house in Birmingham for a while, and Dabo crashed at his friends' houses a few weeks at a time, but for the duration of his senior year, they were essentially homeless.

Through it all, Dabo found the strength to persist, soldiering off to school, pulling down excellent grades, and trying to build a life for himself. He was embarrassed, hurt, angry, confused—all those things. But he was never defeated. "So many times he'd say, 'Mama, don't worry. We'll be okay. It's gonna work out,'" Carol says. "I always knew he was different. He always had that little personality and that little attitude. From the time he was born, he was a fighter."

His dream was to be a pediatrician. He was interested in science, he knew he was smart enough, and he liked the idea of helping kids feel better. So he enrolled at the University of Alabama as a pre-med biology major. As a freshman, Swinney was happy in school and did well in his classes, but for the first time in his life, he was not on a team. And it was killing him.

In the fall of 1988, Swinney was sitting in Bryant–Denny Stadium and watching an Alabama football game with Kathleen, who was in the midst of her senior year at Pelham High. She noticed that something was bugging him. Finally, he turned to Kathleen and told her he wanted to try out for the team. It was too late to join for that season, but the walk-on coordinator told Swinney that he could come on board in the spring.

First, however, Swinney had to complete a rigorous two-month conditioning program. Some forty Crimson Tide wannabes were put through their paces under the eye of Alabama's merciless strength coach, Rich Wingo. One of Wingo's favorite "drills" entailed bringing the players into a practice gym on the lower level of the basketball arena, cranking up the heat, and forcing everyone to run sprints around garbage cans until they puked. One of Swinney's best friends from high school, Norm Saia, also tried out, and he remembers Wingo getting so ticked off at Swinney one day that he spent the entire afternoon personally running him through torturous exercises. "Dabo had to be carried off the field," Saia says, "but he didn't quit."

Only about a half dozen players survived, and Swinney and Saia were among them. "I wasn't a walk-on, I was a *crawl*-on," Swinney says. He was thrilled when he got in for a few plays during the spring game the following April. He practiced with the varsity over the summer and was excited to begin his second year at Alabama, especially since Kathleen would be enrolling as a freshman.

When he went to Coleman Coliseum to sign up for fall classes, however, he got some awful news. His paperwork had not been properly processed for him to receive the Pell Grant money he needed to reenroll as a sophomore. He tried to explain that his finances were disorganized because of his father's problems, but that did not change his situation. If he didn't come up with half of his $1,100 tuition for the semester, his class schedule would be canceled. Meanwhile, he also owed his landlord $400 in back rent.

Swinney had made a little money over the summer cleaning gutters with his buddies back in Pelham, but he didn't have anywhere near that kind of dough. He was devastated. He went back to his apartment, called his mom, and told her what was happening. The two of them cried on the phone together. Swinney sank to the floor and prayed. Resigning himself to the situation, he figured he would go back to Pelham, take some classes at a local college, try to make some money, and hopefully get back to Tuscaloosa in the spring. But there would be no football for him that fall, despite all the hard work he had put in.

He went to get the mail, like he always did. He was shuffling through the envelopes when he came across one with the Discover Card logo on it. Curious, he opened the envelope to find two blank checks and a letter addressed to him. The letter congratulated him on being a Discover Card member, and it informed him that he could start drawing money right away. He read the letter a few times and figured it was a hoax, but he dialed the phone number anyway.

The woman who answered told him that yes, this was a privilege Discover was extending to its new cardholders. Swinney told her he didn't have a card. She asked him to hold, and a few minutes later came back to say that he had in fact been sent a card a few months before but it was returned. "If you give me your address, we'll send you another one," she said. "In the meantime, you can use those checks to draw on your account."

"You're telling me I can take these right now and use them like it's a checking account?" he asked.

"Yes," she replied. "Up until your credit limit."

"What's my credit limit?"

"A thousand dollars."

Swinney let out a holler. It was a bona fide miracle. He broke out in tears all over again. The woman on the line thought he was certifiable. Swinney called his mother back, not twenty minutes after they had just hung up in such despair, to share the glorious news. He went back to Coleman Coliseum, wrote the check to the school registrar, and then went to his landlord's office and handed him the other one. "I was a thousand bucks in debt," he says, "but I was *good*."

. . .

Swinney was still a young man, but he had lived long enough to see the benefits of having a sound PEAK profile in place. Sure, he had had some lousy things happen to him, but as long as he persisted, things had a way of getting just a little bit better. Watching his family unravel gave him a deep sense of empathy for people who struggle with addiction or other problems. He may have been the poor son of an alcoholic father, but his mom taught him to be proud of who he was, which fortified his authenticity. And he was learning some hard truths that very few people his age have to face. That knowledge about what people were like and how to handle setbacks was far more important than anything he would ever learn about the technical aspects of football.

As Swinney was getting set to begin his redshirt freshman season at Alabama, Carol was still having a tough time making ends meet. Dabo suggested that she should just move into his apartment in Tuscaloosa. Space was tight, so they shared not just a bedroom—they shared a queen-sized bed. They stuck a broomstick in the closet so they would have some place to hang their clothes.

It may seem like those were tough times, but Carol looks back and calls them some of the best days of her life. "We didn't have anything, but we were making it," she says. "We could go to sleep at night and we didn't have to worry." Swinney's roommates called her Mama Swinney, and from time to time the other players would come by to ask her to sew a button or wash some clothes or serve up her homemade brownies. Every Sunday, she'd cook a huge chicken-and-dumplings dinner. The leftovers lasted for days.

With his girlfriend enrolled in school and his mother living as his roommate, Swinney dove into his life as a college student and walk-on wide receiver. He did not appear in any games during his redshirt freshman season, but he endeared himself to the coaching staff, particularly Tommy Bowden, the wide receivers coach. However, he was blindsided at the end of the season when Alabama's head coach, Bill Curry, was dismissed along with his entire staff. With the new coach, Gene Stallings, at the helm, Swinney did not set foot on the field during the 1990 spring game. He was profoundly discouraged.

Still, Dabo being Dabo, he persisted, working hard throughout the summer and fall in hopes someone would notice. He felt invisible until one day in October, when the new receivers coach, Woody Mc-Corvey, called him over during practice. To that point, Swinney had barely heard McCorvey say his name, but the coach was watching more closely than he realized. "I was impressed with the way he went about his business. He was always trying to do things correctly," Mc-Corvey says. "You couldn't help but notice him." On this day, Mc-Corvey was fed up with his varsity receivers. He told Swinney that if he had a good practice, he would suit up that Saturday at Ole Miss.

Swinney sprinted back to the locker room and put on a white jersey. He paused for a few moments of prayer. Then he charged onto the field and practiced his tail off. He was rewarded with a coveted spot on the travel roster. After the roster was posted, Swinney took down the sheet of paper and kept it as a souvenir. Today it hangs in a frame in the basement of his house in Clemson.

Once he got that chance to compete, Swinney never let up. Eventually, Stallings rewarded him with a scholarship. Swinney wasn't all that big or quick, but Stallings's teams hardly ever threw the ball anyway. His primary responsibility was to serve as a blocker. That was something he knew he could do.

After playing in four games and catching one pass as a redshirt sophomore, Swinney played in nine games and caught two balls as a junior. As a senior, he caught a total of four passes for 48 yards. When Alabama took the field on January 1, 1993, to play for the national championship in the Sugar Bowl against Miami, Swinney was a starting wide receiver. The Tide's quarterback, Jay Barker,

threw just 13 passes in the game (Swinney had no catches), and the
Tide won in a rout, 34–13. From crawl-on to walk-on to national
champ—that's what Dabo Swinney did.

He was named to the SEC's all-academic team, but he gained
his most important knowledge on the field. "I tell people I have a
ton of education, but the education I got between those lines, I can't
put a price on that," he says. "The things I learned about myself, the
challenges, the sacrifices, the team aspect, the work ethic I had to
bring every day was just powerful in shaping me into who I am today, not just to coach my players but be a dad to my three boys. It
was an amazing experience."

By that time, Swinney had given up on the idea of becoming a
doctor, mostly because he did not want to endure a long residency.
So he switched his major to commerce and business administration
and aspired to run a hospital someday. After graduation, he started
working as an intern for a health care company in Birmingham and
had accepted a full-time position for the fall. Later that summer,
however, he got a call from Stallings, who said he wanted to hire
Dabo as a graduate assistant coach. To that point, Swinney had
never considered a career in coaching, but he liked the idea of having his education paid for while he pursued an MBA. Besides, when
Gene Stallings tells an Alabama boy to do something, it's hard to
say no. So Swinney accepted the offer, moved back to Tuscaloosa,
and showed up for practice.

Immediately, it felt like home.

Unfortunately, things were not going nearly as well for his father.
Ervil had remarried and found a business partner to open a
hardware store with him in Alabaster. He and his new wife lived in
a trailer behind the store. He scaled back his drinking to a few days
a week, but when he drank, he still got drunk. Chain-smoked, too.

Ervil was estranged from Carol, Tripp was nowhere to be found, and while Tracy had moved back to Pelham to join the police force, he had basically washed his hands of his dad. Dabo was the only one who stayed in touch, encouraging Ervil to make different choices. It was to little avail.

Carol also remarried shortly after Dabo's graduation from Alabama. Her new husband, Larry McIntosh, worked for State Farm insurance in Birmingham. Meanwhile, Dabo poured himself into coaching. He was a natural. All those years of squeezing out every drop of his own potential translated beautifully into working with young men who were far more gifted than he ever was. He was inexhaustible when it came to accumulating information, filling up countless notebooks with ideas, diagrams, and ruminations on all the things the Alabama coaches were doing, good and bad. He never threw a single notebook away.

When his two years in graduate school were up, Swinney was given a full-time job on the staff, first as tight ends coach and later as wide receivers coach. And then, just like that, he was out of work. In 2000, head coach Mike DuBose, who had succeeded Stallings three years before, was fired. His whole staff was swept out the door with him. Swinney hardly had time to contemplate his next move before he got an offer from a most surprising source—Rich Wingo, the former strength coach at Alabama who had tortured him so badly during walk-on tryouts. Swinney hadn't heard from Wingo in more than ten years. Turns out Wingo was now president of a large company based in Birmingham called AIG Baker Real Estate, and he wanted to offer Swinney a job. Swinney was skeptical, but he was unemployed and the job came with an $80,000 salary. He accepted the offer. A few days later, he was flying to Las Vegas to help negotiate leases on a local shopping center.

Swinney loved that job. He enjoyed reading through demographic reports and sales figures, absorbing and processing the information in order to discern opportunities. He was savvy when it came to cutting deals. He was also making good money and living a normal life, the kind where a man leaves the house at a decent hour and comes back in time for dinner. Still, it wasn't football, so when his old receivers coach, Tommy Bowden, who had taken the head coaching job at Clemson four years before, called in 2003 and asked if he wanted to be his wide receivers coach, Swinney jumped at the chance—even though Kathleen was pregnant with their third child, they were two weeks away from moving into a new house, and everyone knew Bowden was on very thin ice.

Swinney's brief tenure in the business world is barely a footnote on his curriculum vitae, but the knowledge he gained during those two years was invaluable. It provided him with an understanding of business culture, which he has applied to his work in coaching. It gave him the chance to learn how a large company structures itself and operates, which is no small benefit considering that a major college football coach is basically the CEO of a multimillion-dollar enterprise. From a personal standpoint, it instilled in him confidence that he could do something else outside of football, which reduced his worry. And when he returned to coaching, he had a much deeper appreciation of how lucky he was to do what he loved, where he could use his empathy to have an impact on young men. He couldn't play anymore, but he sure could talk, and he believed he had something to say.

D abo kept the new house and invited Ervil and his new wife to move into it. Then he packed up his two boys and his pregnant wife and headed for Clemson.

Swinney was an able receivers coach, but his true value was as a recruiter. The task required all the things he was good at—an eye for talent, a willingness to work hard, charm, persistence, and, most of all, a hardwired habit of thinking beyond his circumstances. "I've always considered myself an overbeliever," he says.

He refused to cede the fertile grounds of the South to all those SEC schools (as well as the ACC's Florida State) who were accustomed to plucking the best players like so much low-hanging fruit. Swinney immediately went after the best of the best, guys like C. J. Spiller, a running back from Florida who was a consensus top 10 recruit nationally. Swinney established an early rapport with Spiller, pursuing him even when many people, including folks at Clemson, assured him he was wasting his time. When Spiller promised Swinney that he would visit Clemson, Swinney pulled out his business card and made Spiller sign a "contract" to ensure that he would follow through. Spiller canceled his visit to Alabama to go see Clemson. He eventually became a consensus All-American there as a senior and was the ninth pick in the 2010 NFL draft.

It wasn't long before Swinney started gaining a national reputation. In 2006, Rivals.com, a prominent recruiting website, tapped him as the nation's No. 5 recruiter. The following January, he met with Nick Saban, the recently hired coach at Alabama, who wanted him to come on board as a well-compensated assistant. Swinney was tempted, but considering it was just a few weeks before national signing day for recruits, he didn't feel right ditching kids he had persuaded to come to Clemson, not to mention abandoning Bowden and the school itself, which had given him the opportunity.

Despite those efforts, Clemson continued to languish, leading Bowden to resign halfway through the 2008 season. All of Bowden's assistants were left on the payroll, but it was understood that a new coach would be hired once the season was over. In the meantime, the program needed an interim head coach. The staff included two co-ordinators with previous head coaching experience, but largely based on his recruiting prowess, and partly based on Bowden's recommendation, Swinney got the job. He was all of thirty-three years old.

That decision was widely derided as typifying Clemson's tendency to think small. And in many ways, it was. Swinney didn't care. One of his first acts as head coach was to fire the team's offensive coordinator and take over the offense himself. He also instituted a tradition he called the "Tiger Walk," which involved the entire team walking through the stadium parking lot two hours before kickoff. With Swinney providing a badly needed injection of energy, the Tigers won four of their last six games, including a 31–14 win over rival South Carolina in the season finale. That made Clemson eligible for a bowl game, and it persuaded the administration to give Swinney the job permanently. He had momentum, he showed promise, and he came cheap, accepting an annual salary of $800,000, a paltry sum for an ACC head coach.

Instead of trying to get more money for himself, Swinney put on his businessman's hat and lobbied his board of directors to invest in underfunded areas. He procured higher salaries for assistants as well as commitments to upgrade the woebegone facilities. He also proved unafraid to make big, risky changes. When his second full season ended in a disappointing 6–7 record, he had to concede that his offense was outdated. So he persuaded the school to shell out $1.3 million per season to hire Chad Morris as his offensive coordinator, even though Morris, a longtime high school football coach, had spent just one season in college as the offensive coordinator at Tulsa. Swinney turned the offense over to Morris, who rewarded that faith by helping Clemson to its first 11-win season in thirty-one years. The 2012 season ended with a major breakthrough victory over No. 8 LSU in the Chick-fil-A Bowl.

The blessings of success came with the burdens of expectations. During the three-year period from 2011 to 2014, Clemson lost a total of six games, but every time Swinney's teams were on the verge of greatness, they would suffer a crushing loss. In 2013 the Tigers finished the season by making the Orange Bowl for the first time in twenty years, only to be embarrassed by West Virginia, 70–33. Their national title hopes the following year were derailed in a humiliating 51–14 loss to Florida State. That led to the unfortunate birth of the term "Clemsoning," which the website Urban Dictionary defined as "the act of failing miserably on a grand athletic stage, or when the stakes are high." When the Tigers lost to Florida State even though the Seminoles' star quarterback, Jameis Winston, was sitting out because of a one-game suspension, the *Washington Post* published an online story under the cruel headline "Against Florida State, Clemson's 'Clemsoning' Was the Most 'Clemsoning' Clemson Ever Clemsoned."

Swinney persisted, hauling in five consecutive top 20 recruiting classes, and two that were ranked in the top 10. After the Orange Bowl debacle, he fired his defensive coordinator, Kevin Steele, and replaced him with Brent Venables, whom he plucked from Oklahoma. Swinney's staff payroll grew from $287,118 in Bowden's final season to $1.47 million in 2014. It was a significant capital investment, but one that Swinney knew would produce returns. "Those great businesses out there, those great programs, they don't plateau," he said. "How do you do that? Well, you have to constantly reinvent, reinvest, reset, learn, grow, change."

There have been countless ways, large and small, that Swinney has strived to instill a winning culture. The Tiger Walk was a small but telling early example that he wanted everything done the exact right way. He is a meticulous planner who tells the same stories, uses the same phrases, and harps on the same messages, even if his guys have heard it all a thousand times. "That's something I learned from Coach Stallings," he says. "I spent seven years with him, and every year I'd be like, 'Here comes the Mama Don't Fret story. Here comes the Ben Hogan story.' That's how he protected his culture. When you say it enough so your players can repeat it, that's when you know they're getting it."

At the same time, there are few coaches who are Swinney's equal when it comes to keeping things fresh and fun. He has a fetish for acronyms, like ALL IN (Attitude, Leadership, Legacy, Improvement, New Beginnings), EARN (Effect, Accountability, doing what's Right, Nourishing the concept of team and family), BEST (Belief, Effort, Sense of urgency, and Toughness), and PAW (Passionate About Winning). Before the 2014 game against South Carolina, he heard the Michael Jackson song "Man in the Mirror" and purchased mirrors for all of his players so they could, you know, make that change. On another occasion, Dabo celebrated a big win by asking Kathleen to find a place in town where she could buy big orange foam fingers for all the players.

As the school came to appreciate the correlation between investment and winning, the infrastructure dollars poured in. In early 2017, Clemson completed construction on an obscene $55 million playland for its football players, complete with a laser tag room, arcade, bowling alley, nap room, beach volleyball court, and miniature golf course.

In Dabo Swinney's world, a little extra is a big deal. He is obsessed with the details of football—of life, really. "That's what we live by around here," he says. "Do the common things in an uncommon way, and you can command the attention of the world. That's from George Washington Carver." He knows he can't expect perfection from his players, but he does want them to be as fixated on details as he is, whether it's a particular technique on how to run a route or the precise way they should arrange their lockers. (He provides them with two pictures, one showing the correct way and another the incorrect way.) He insists they clean up after themselves, so much so that when they go to the movies, the team brings its own trash blower. "If you talk to any movie theater manager, they'll tell you that nobody has ever left their theater like we do," Swinney says. "They don't need to send anyone in there. There's no popcorn on the floor. Nobody cleans up after Clemson."

Swinney likes to call Clemson "a relationship-driven program," but it is not easy to foment intimacy with a roster of over a hundred players, not to mention dozens of assistants and staff. Swinney accomplishes this through a communication structure that funnels knowledge his way. He meets every Monday with a leadership group he calls Swinney Council. It includes the senior leaders on the team, but those players will regularly invite younger guys to take part. Then there's the Swinney Huddle, a group of assistants and staffers that meets every Tuesday. Swinney does not attend those gatherings, but the group produces a written report for him so he knows what they discussed.

Between those two days, there are many more gatherings inside the team and around the program, all of which are designed to keep Swinney in the loop. He holds meetings with each player at the beginning and end of each season. And he makes sure he is around his guys as much as possible, from the family nights they have at the facility to the stretching lines, where he can walk up and down the line and exchange words more casually. The system is both efficient and comprehensive, which is not an easy needle to thread.

Every day before practice, Swinney gathers his players in the team meeting room, where he will speak for about ten minutes, give or take, to set the tone for the day. The walls bear signs listing the sixteen team commandments as well as five goals for every season. When the players walk into the room, they are greeted by a slide that shows the view a driver has from behind the wheel of a car. The logo of last week's opponent is in the rearview mirror; the next week's opponent is visible through the windshield. Swinney also brings in two signs, one that reads *BELIEF* and another that shows the word *CAN'T* with the apostrophe and *T* crossed out. A countdown clock hangs on a wall, ticking down to the next opening kickoff. He will say a few words and then show the team a brief video taken from the extensive library he has his staff compile. Then he offers still more words. Swinney rarely prepares his remarks in advance. He may have some idea of what he wants to say, but mostly he speaks from the heart and follows the tangents wherever they lead.

In preparation for all these communication opportunities, Swinney is constantly taking notes. He carries a pen and index cards in his pockets at all times, which he uses to jot down observations and ideas. He frequently invites motivational speakers to address his team and help him hammer home his messages. After he introduces the guest, he will take a seat near the front and take notes during the entire presentation. Then he uses those notes to follow up on what the speaker talked about.

Swinney says he has kept every notebook he ever filled, dating back to his playing days at Alabama. He keeps some in his office, and others in a bunch of boxes at his house. He flips through old notebooks frequently. They bring back happy memories, and they also remind him of small details he may have forgotten along the way.

On top of all the scribbling and hoarding he has done over the years, Swinney has assembled a thick binder that serves as a guide to every aspect of the program. The manual is the result of many years spent jotting and organizing. He still uses the same hole puncher he started with two decades ago. The sections are separated by tabs that cover a comprehensive range of topics: personnel, game-day preparation, recruiting, strength and conditioning, operations, tickets, security, academics, maintenance, travel, administration, and everything in between. There are sections devoted to Swinney's philosophies as well as concepts related to offense, defense, and special teams. No detail is too small to be included.

Every summer, Swinney holes up with his entire staff for five long days, where they read through every single page of the manual and set their plans for the season. He wants the wide receivers coach to know what the janitors do. The secretaries should understand media policy. Everyone needs to study the elements of NCAA compliance. Swinney calls these his "All In" meetings. The manual's cover has a picture of a pointing Uncle Sam alongside the words *I Want You To Be All In*. "That book is a living, breathing thing, man," he says. "We go through it page by page and have such a spirited discussion. I really think it's not fair to hold people accountable to something and not explain very specifically what it is they're supposed to do."

His management style benefited from his experience in the business world. Swinney has figured out how to run a huge operation like Clemson football in a way that allows him to be detail-obsessed without becoming a micromanager. He understands the value of hiring good people and empowering them to do their jobs.

Armed with all of this knowledge, Swinney transformed Clemson football, year by year, class by class, acronym by acronym. It went from being a program that was overly reliant on a handful of flashy skill players to one that was able to slog it out in the trenches with the best of them. That was embodied on October 4, 2015, when the Tigers won an all-time classic at Notre Dame in a downpour, 24–22. When it was over, Swinney stood on the field, mud-splattered, and barked into a television reporter's live microphone, "What I told 'em tonight was, 'Listen, we give ya scholarships, we give ya stipends and meals and a place to live. We give ya nice uniforms. I can't give ya guts and I can't give ya heart.' Tonight it was B.Y.O.G.—*Bring Your Own Guts!*"

As Swinney's public profile began to grow, he was forced to decide whether he should share his family's painful history. The question first arose when he was a wide receiver at Alabama and a local reporter approached him. "We had tried to hide it for so long, and I didn't want to do that anymore," he says. He decided to tell it all. Ervil was not happy. "Sometimes the truth hurts, but me and my dad pushed through that," Swinney says. "It allowed us to have some conversations that we hadn't really been comfortable having."

From that day forward, Swinney has encouraged his family to be just as forthcoming. Says Carol, "For a long time, I didn't want anyone to know because I was protecting my children. So it can become a very lonely world. Now that it's all out in the open, it's probably easier to deal with. I mean, it is what it is." Then she adds with a hearty laugh, "Hey, Seth, I've heard a lot worse!"

It helped that Ervil managed over time to shake his addiction. The impetus was a severe heart attack he suffered shortly before Dabo was hired at Clemson. His doctor told him that if he didn't give up drinking and smoking, he was going to die soon.

So he quit. Just like that. No hypnosis, no medicine, no Alcoholics Anonymous, no twelve steps, no nothing. He just stopped drinking and smoking and never started again. Dabo marveled at the old man's persistence. Unfortunately, Tripp was unable to harvest that same discipline. As Dabo moved up the coaching ladder and Tracy became a well-respected policeman in Pelham, Tripp drifted from place to place, job to job, even from wife to wife. Tripp married in the early 1990s and had three sons, but he later got divorced and remarried three more times. Having been awarded the right to collect social security disability because of his car accident, Tripp has shuttled between homes in Alabama and Georgia. Dabo paid for him to go to rehab a couple of times, but over the years their communication has been sporadic.

In 2003, Kathleen's older sister, Lisa, was diagnosed with breast cancer and underwent a double mastectomy. During the course of her treatments, Lisa learned that she had the BRCA gene, which dramatically increases a woman's chance of developing breast cancer.

That led Kathleen to get tested, and when she discovered she had the gene, she elected to have a double mastectomy as well. Lisa was given a clean bill of health, but the cancer returned in 2012, this time in her lungs and brain. She had brain surgery and battled for two years, eventually withering to eighty-five pounds. Lisa died in April 2014 at the age of forty-nine. Dabo spoke at her funeral.

While Swinney's Christian faith has inspired him to persist despite all the lousy things that have happened, it also imbues him with a desire to keep things joyful. This is a rather uncommon notion in the football world, and in the coaching profession in general. Most coaches barely take time to acknowledge their wins, much less enjoy them, but not Dabo. He'd rather break into goofy dances in the locker room, or lift up ESPN sideline reporter Jeannine Edwards after that bowl game win over LSU. Before the start of the 2015 season, he promised Clemson fans that if their team made the playoff, he would throw the biggest pizza party that town had ever seen. Sure enough, when the Tigers qualified, some 30,000 people gathered in Memorial Stadium and chowed down. "I don't know what happened at the other three schools, but I doubt it was like this," he boasted through a booming sound system. He tries to strike that same work-and-play balance inside his program, scheduling a family night every Wednesday for his coaches. On those nights, he patrols the halls popping his cheeks, kissing babies, and altogether spreading good cheer.

Swinney goes to similar lengths to make sure his own family feels like a priority. Even during the hubbub of the season, he meets Kathleen almost every day for a run at 12:30. As their three sons progressed as high school football players, he rearranged his practice and meeting schedules so he could attend their games.

When I interviewed Swinney in Clemson a few weeks before his team's appearance in the 2016 College Football Playoff semifinal, I asked him if he felt sorry for all those coaches who believe that sustained focus, and sometimes sustained misery, is an important part of the job. It was a thinly veiled reference to Nick Saban, Alabama's famously dyspeptic (and virtually unbeatable) coach, so I assumed he wouldn't take the bait. But he did. "Yeah, I do, because I think life is so short. It's just the blink of an eye, and we're gone," he said. "When people put winning up top, they become miserable. Even when they win, it's a relief. We're never gonna be like that here. We're always gonna have fun."

He continued, "I'm always giving [my players] perspective on life, because I don't want the game to be too big. What's the worst that can happen? You lose a ball game? Hey, let's just put everything into it, and when you look at the man in the mirror, as long as you did your best, you can live with whatever result you got. Sometimes you don't win, and that's okay, you know? The season always starts tomorrow."

Though he is usually one to encourage his guys to flush the past, Swinney wanted them to take one last look into the rearview mirror following their loss to Alabama in the 2016 championship game. So when he met with his team in February, he showed them about a half dozen unforced errors from the game, the kinds of little mistakes that can add up to a loss. Most of the ones he showed were committed by Deshaun Watson. A fumbled exchange with the center. A bad throw to a wide-open receiver because he didn't have his feet set properly. Besides sending a strong message that Swinney intended to hold everyone accountable, including the star quarterback, he hoped that watching them commit those mistakes would make his players more optimistic about the road they could see through the windshield.

"We know we're good enough," he told them. "As long as we don't lose to Clemson, we have a chance to have a special season." To reinforce the message, Swinney had the posters that listed Clemson's opponents and were hung all around the practice facility altered so that every opponent's name read *Clemson*.

Three months after that team meeting, Swinney had a chance to take in a Chicago Cubs game at Wrigley Field as a guest of Cubs manager Joe Maddon. He had never met Maddon before, so he was surprised when he got word that Maddon wanted to visit with him during a rain delay. As they spoke in Maddon's office, he was taken with the words that were printed on the T-shirt Maddon was wearing: *Try not to suck.* Swinney made a note of it.

In preparation for the approaching season, Swinney came up with yet another motivational tactic, which he called the "vision board." He asked each player to complete the sentence "We will get to Tampa this year if I will . . ." The players wrote their answers and placed them on the board, which hung in the front of the team meeting room. Throughout the season, Swinney regularly checked in with the players to see if they were living up to their promises.

Clemson won its first few games out of the gate, but Watson did not look sharp. He had come into the season as one of the faces of the sport, and the sports media was homing in on all the flaws that could potentially trip up the Tigers' season. Swinney could tell Watson wasn't carrying his usual ebullience, so he called his quarterback into his office for a good, long talk.

As they sat and spoke, Swinney reminded Watson of all the good things he had done for Clemson. Somehow, Watson had lost his perspective, and Swinney wanted to get him back to feeling the love. "I could tell it was a good release for him," Swinney says. "He started having fun again."

That set the stage for a pivotal game on October 29 at Florida State. The previous day, Swinney did what he always does the night before a game, which is to put on a coat and tie and speak to the team without any other coaches around. "That's my time with the team," he says. "It gives me a chance to bring 'em all together, tie everything up in a knot, and put 'em to bed in the right frame of mind." That was especially important that evening because Clemson had not won in Tallahassee in ten years.

So after talking again about the importance of love, the need to pay attention to all the little things, the desire to maintain the culture they had worked so hard to build, Swinney started to remove his jacket and tie. Then he unbuttoned his dress shirt and revealed what he was wearing underneath: the same T-shirt Maddon had worn that day at Wrigley Field, with the words *Try not to suck* on the front. The players whooped it up, and the next day they edged Florida State, 37–34.

The Tigers almost blew their chances on November 12, when they lost at home, 43–42, to unranked Pittsburgh. Fortunately, some of the other top teams in the country also lost that day, so their hopes to make the College Football Playoff were still alive. But they could not afford another slip-up. Swinney was concerned about how his team would respond to the setback until he met with his leadership group on Monday to start preparing for their next opponent, Wake Forest. He was blown away by what his leaders had to say. They were angry, but they weren't pointing fingers. There was a high degree of ownership and accountability. He walked out of that meeting and told his assistants, "Boys, Wake Forest is in trouble."

Indeed, the Tigers easily dispatched the Demon Deacons, 35–13. Then they won their final regular season games, defeated Virginia Tech in the ACC championship game, throttled Ohio State 31–0 in the College Football Playoff semifinal, and earned their date with Alabama. By the time Watson led his offense onto the field facing a three-point deficit with 2:07 to play, he was ready to meet the moment. Like all the players, Watson had conducted his own Jon Gordon exercise the previous summer, landing upon the word *legendary*. So when he came into the huddle, he knew the exact right thing to say. "All right, boys," he said. "Let's go be legendary."

Watson put together a drive for the ages, leading the team all the way down to the two-yard line. With one precious second on the clock, he rolled to his right and fired a touchdown pass to Hunter Renfrow to clinch the victory. It was a fitting climax to Dabo Swinney's career, the star quarterback teaming up with the former walk-on to beat his father's favorite team, not to mention his own alma mater. The path to *Us* is never a straight line, but in Swinney's case it was especially circuitous, and it was authentically his own. In the end, his persistence paid off. All those tangents had came full circle.

Alas, Ervil Swinney was not with his son to celebrate his extraordinary triumph. In early 2015, Ervil's lung cancer returned in a bad way. Dabo persuaded him to move into his house in Clemson so he could get his treatments at Greenville Hospital. Not only did that decision provide Ervil with access to first-rate medical care, but it also gave him and Dabo the chance to enjoy long, leisurely talks. Those precious hours would not have happened if Ervil hadn't fallen ill.

The treatments lasted for several months, after which Ervil returned to his job and wife back in Alabama. He seemed to be doing just fine, all things considered. Then one day in early August, a buddy walked into Ervil's store and found him slumped in his chair. "Just quit breathing," Dabo says. Dabo still has some of his dad's voice mails saved on his cell phone. Once in a while, he will touch the screen just so he can hear Ervil's voice. *Just checking in, don't worry about me, everything's fine.*

If there's one thing that bugs Dabo about the way his life story is told, it's the propensity of the narrator to cast Ervil as a villain. That violates Dabo's sense of empathy. "My dad was such a great man. He quit drinking, he quit smoking, he survived cancer. His relationship with my mom towards the end was great," Dabo says. "He had some rough patches along the journey, but who doesn't? What matters is that he finished his race in a great way."

His brother Tripp remains a different, more complicated story. One week before Clemson played Alabama in the 2015 College Football Championship, Tripp was arrested in Florida for aggravated stalking. The incident involved Tripp's fourth wife, who told police that he violated a restraining order by continuing to harass her online and in person. That forced Dabo to address yet again his family's private troubles in public fashion—and at the worst possible time. "Part of what's disappointing is I have to get sucked into his world because of who I am and what my job is," Dabo told me months later. "I understand that comes with the territory. I love Tripp, but I don't always like him. Life is about choices, and he's made a lot of bad ones."

In the months after the loss to Alabama, Dabo had only occasional contact with Tripp. It remains a touchy subject. During the course of our conversations, Dabo was happy to provide me with phone numbers so I could interview friends, colleagues, and members of his family, but he was adamant that he did not want me to call Tripp. "That is not something that he is prepared to handle," he said.

Despite his family's battles with alcohol, Swinney is no teetotaler. He enjoys his red wine, and he especially enjoys the company of people who were with him before he was rich and famous. Woody McCorvey, his old receivers coach at Alabama, is Clemson's associate athletic director for football administration, although Swinney refers to him more accurately as "my national security adviser." Danny Pearman, who served on the staff with Swinney at Alabama, is Clemson's special teams coordinator and tight ends coach. Three other former Alabama teammates have staff positions, and when Swinney holds his annual summer camp for local youngsters, he welcomes in dozens of former players and teammates, as well as his old high school crew from Pelham. "It's amazing how he never changes," says Saia, his childhood friend. "I was just at his camp and he was introducing a bunch of his guys. He's rattling off all these dates and statistics real quick, and I'm thinking, *God almighty, how does he remember all that?* We stay at his lake house a lot, and I just keep thinking, *Same old Dabo, cutting up like we were still in high school.* He's just a great person to be friends with."

When I spoke with Swinney just before the start of the 2017 season, he was in his usual upbeat state of mind, even though he knew he was going to have to replace many of the key starters from his championship team, starting with his quarterback. "My word this year is *appreciation*," he told me. "I just want to have a deep appreciation for the journey because at the end of the day, that's what you love the most. I want my players to have that, I want my staff to have that. Let's don't wait until it's over to appreciate things. The moment we won that game was great, but the best part was the journey getting there."

Swinney's mother was in Tampa the night her son's Tigers came back to beat Alabama. Carol is all for focusing on what's in front of that windshield, but she also believes it's important to check the rearview mirror from time to time as well. That's why she put together three scrapbooks with pictures and photographs that detailed her childhood battles with polio and scoliosis, and included written explanations in the margins. She presented the books to her sons on Mother's Day 2013. "I felt like they really needed to know before something happened to me," she says.

Because her curved spine presses against her organs, Carol experiences shortness of breath on occasion. That aside, she is in fine health for a woman in her seventies. She gets physical therapy on a regular basis and does a variety of exercising throughout the week, including Zumba dance classes for seniors. "I'm very active and very determined," she says. "I do anything that I can to keep moving."

Still, she has her moments of sadness, as all of us do. When they arrive, she finds herself craving time with her son the coach. "It brings me to tears because I get to missing him some days," she says. We are speaking on the phone, and she has to pause to get hold of her emotions. "I'll look at his pictures, or I read his notes that he wrote when we lived together in that apartment. He could always make me see the better outcome."

It isn't easy being apart from her sons while she stays back in Birmingham with her husband. Yet when Carol is feeling like this, she knows that all she has to do is hop in her car and drive for a few hours to Clemson, and she's home again. She's not looking for miracles when she visits Dabo, just a healthy reminder that no matter what losses she might have suffered, the season always starts tomorrow. "If I can just get up there and spend a few days with him, just listen to his little speeches and little sayings, it perks me up," she says. "He can give you a good pep talk, that's for sure."

ACKNOWLEDGMENTS

The genesis for this book occurred during a visit I took to Stanford University in the fall of 2014. I was there to interview David Shaw, the school's football coach, for my Campus Insiders show. After the interview, I went to a campus gymnasium and watched the basketball team practice while sitting with Jeff LaMere, an old friend who was serving as an assistant athletic director at the school. As I explained to Jeff about all the interviews I had been doing, he said to me, "You could write a great book on leadership."

The idea had not occurred to me, but the more interviews I did, the more I realized Jeff was right. So thanks first to him for planting the seed. Beyond that, I'd like to acknowledge the nine men profiled in this book. In order to really delve into how leadership is learned, developed, and implemented, it was imperative that I be able to assess my subjects from a close, even intimate, vantage point. The coaches were all generous with their time. In most cases, I interviewed them on multiple occasions. They were especially helpful in connecting me with friends and family who knew them best. That included their wives, who gave me the best nine interviews of this book, proving yet again that women are much smarter than men.

Thank you to the media relations and sports information folks who helped to facilitate those interviews: Dave Ablauf (Michigan), Tim Bourret (Clemson), Phil Chardis (UConn), Jerry Emig (Ohio State), Jon Jackson (Duke), Matt Larson (Michigan State), and Dennis Rogers (Clippers). I'd like to give special thanks to Celtics assistant coach Micah

Shrewsberry, who not only helped me with my Brad Stevens chapter but also made sure my sons got to meet Jayson Tatum at NBA Summer League in Las Vegas.

This is the second book project that has gotten a major assist from Matt Craig, who as of this writing is finishing up his senior year at Ball State University's Sports Link program. Matt is intelligent, conscientious, hardworking, and definitely headed into the Transcriber Hall of Fame.

This book is ultimately about teamwork, and I was blessed to have two incredible partners throughout the process. Scott Moyers of Penguin Press was a fabulous coach. He was the one who suggested at the outset that I make this a book about coaches, and it was his expert prodding that led me to conceive of the PEAK profile and develop universal themes. David Black has become such a close friend that I tend to forget he is my literary agent. But he's a damn good agent, and his voice in my conversations with Scott was critical in getting us to *Us*.

Speaking of damn good agents, thanks to Sandy Montag, who doubles as my life coach without charging me extra.

I would not have the opportunity to gain access to elusive subjects and write books about them without the incredible platform that Sean Mc-Manus and David Berson have provided me at CBS Sports. If you want to see what a winning team looks like, study the culture those two have established at that company. I will forever be grateful for the twenty-two years I worked at *Sports Illustrated*; so thank you to Stefanie Kaufman for hiring me. Thanks also to Jason Coyle and Josh Wine for creating *The Seth Davis Show* at Campus Insiders. And a huge thanks to Alex Mather and Adam Hansmann for giving me such an exciting opportunity at *The Athletic*. Besides being a great writing gig, running The Fieldhouse is the first chance I have had to lead my own team.

I often joke to people that I have four jobs, three kids, and no life. The truth is I have four jobs, three kids, one dog, and a *wonderful* life. That's due to the greatest life partner a man could ever ask for, Melissa Beth Cohen Davis. There is no question who wears the whistle in our house. Our sons, Zachary, Noah, and Gabriel, are the result of our teamwork. Thanks, guys, for putting up with my long hours spent traveling or hovered over my laptop. I love you more than words can say.

SOURCE NOTES

Urban Meyer

Adelson, Andrea. "Hometown Hero." *Orlando Sentinel*, December 22, 2006.
———. "Leading the Cheers." *Orlando Sentinel*, December 11, 2006.
Bishop, Greg. "Hernandez Among Many Who Found Trouble at Florida in the Meyer Years."
  New York Times, July 6, 2013.
———. "A Mix That's Unmatched." *New York Times*, October 25, 2013.
Caldwell, Dana. "Urban Meyer and Daughter Gigi Strike New Balance in Sports and Family
  Life." *Naples Daily News*, December 3, 2011.
Charlie Rose, October 27, 2015.
Dirocco, Michael. "Meyer's Keys Started Engine." *Florida Times-Union*, January 7, 2009.
Dodd, Dennis. "Meyer's Intensity Has Made Gators Best of Best." CBSSports.com, August 5,
  2010.
Dunstan, Aime. "Shelley Meyer: On Top of Her Game." *Palm Beach Post*, September 1, 2007.
Elliott, Mick. "UF's Meyer a Master Motivator." *Tampa Tribune*, August 17, 2008.
English, Antonya. "Even as a Kid He Was a Coach." *St. Petersburg Times*, August 24, 2005.
———. "For the Kids." *St. Petersburg Times*, December 9, 2010.
———. "UF's Law Run-Ins Drawing Scrutiny." *St. Petersburg Times*, June 27, 2009.
Erardi, John. "Urban Meyer: A Long Way from Cincinnati." *Cincinnati Enquirer*, November
  29, 2011.
Ettinger, Bob. "Ashtabula Natives Pass On Knowledge." *Star Beacon* (Ashtabula, OH), July 6,
  2012.
Frias, Carlos. "An Ohio Son's Emotional Victory." *Palm Beach Post*, January 7, 2007.
———. "Urban Culture." Palm Beach Post, November 26, 2004.
George, Rachel. "Urban Meyer Says 'Enough Is Enough.'" *Orlando Sentinel*, September 17, 2010.
Hope, Dan. "The Evolution of Urban Meyer the Disciplinarian: From Florida Flukes to Ohio
  State Crackdowns." *The Lantern* (Ohio State University), October 23, 2013.
Johnson, Joey. "The New Boss Gator." *Tampa Tribune*, December 4, 2004.
Jones, David. "Urban's Renewal?" *Florida Today*, November 16, 2004.
King, Kelley. "Wild Out West." *Sports Illustrated*, November 1, 2004.
Lesmerises, Doug. "My Dad, the Ohio State Football Coach." *Cleveland Plain Dealer*, June 15,
  2014.
———. "This Is His Home. He's at Peace." *Cleveland Plain Dealer*, May 10, 2015.
Maisel, Evan. "Call It Rolling Green." *Sports Illustrated*, November 4, 2002.
Mandel, Stewart. "The Next Big Thing." *Sports Illustrated*, August 15, 2005.

———. "Urban Knows Defense, Too." *Sports Illustrated*, September 26, 2005.

Markey, Matt. "Urban Legend." *Toledo Blade*, April 10, 2005.

May, Tim. "Finding His Balance." *Columbus Dispatch*, August 26, 2012.

———. "Man with the QB Plan." *Columbus Dispatch*, December 3, 2011.

Meyer, Urban, and Wayne Coffey. *Above the Line: Lessons in Leadership and Life from a Championship Program*. New York: Penguin, 2017.

Miller, Doug. "Baseball Was Meyer's First Love." Associated Press, December 30, 2016.

Murphy, Austin. "Another Urban Renewal." *Sports Illustrated*, April 23, 2012.

Oller, Rob. "Straight Shooter." *Columbus Dispatch*, December 26, 2006.

Porter, Todd. "A New Urban Meyer." *The Repository* (Canton, OH), January 11, 2015.

Price, S. L. "Should I Stay or Should I Go?" *Sports Illustrated*, January 11, 2010.

———. "Urban Meyer." *Sports Illustrated*, December 7, 2009.

Rabinowitz, Bill. "An Abiding Love." *Columbus Dispatch*, September 5, 2016.

Ross, John. "Balancing Act: In-depth Interview with Urban Meyer." *Columbus Monthly*, February 2013.

Sneed, Brandon. "'I'm Not the Lone Wolf.'" *Bleacher Report*, September 13, 2016.

Spencer, Jon. "Excitement Abounds over Meyer's System." *Mansfield* (OH) *News Journal*, August 30, 2012.

———. "A Father's Will." *Mansfield* (OH) *News Journal*, April 4, 2013.

———. "Urban Meyer Twice as Lucky When It Came to Male Influence." *Newark* (OH) *Advocate*, April 6, 2013.

Svoboda, Jeff. "Urban Meyer's First Team at Bowling Green Remains Special to the Ohio State Head Coach." Scout.com, August 29, 2016.

Thamel, Pete. "A Father and a Father Figure Teach Meyer the Rewards of Tough Love." *New York Times*, January 7, 2007.

———. "Florida's Meyer Will Take Leave, Not Resign." *New York Times*, December 27, 2009.

———. "New Game Plan: Smelling the Roses." *New York Times*, December 30, 2011.

———. "O, the Places They'll Go (Just Not This Year)." *Sports Illustrated*, November 19, 2012.

———. "Rested and Ready." *New York Times*, August 29, 2010.

———. "A Winner Built on Family." *New York Times*, November 13, 2004.

———. "The Wired." *Sports Illustrated*, September 30, 2013.

Wilkinson, Jack. "The Sensation of Salt Lake City." *Atlanta Journal-Constitution*, November 22, 2004.

Mike Krzyzewski

Blythe, Will. "Hating Coach." Esquire, March 1, 2006.

Charlie Rose, April 1, 2010.

Chavez, Luciana. "Krzyzewski: Big Man on Campus." *Raleigh News and Observer*, March 3, 2004.

DeCock, Luke. "From the Archives: A Season That Turned Two Coaches' Fates." *Raleigh News and Observer*, January 4, 2017.

Feinstein, John. *A March to Madness: A View from the Floor in the Atlantic Coast Conference*. New York: Little, Brown, 1998.

———. *The Legends Club: Dean Smith, Mike Krzyzewski, Jim Valvano, and an Epic College Basketball Story*. New York: Doubleday, 2016.

Gildea, William. "In Their Quest, Devils Are Possessed." *Washington Post*, March 9, 1999.

Green, Ron Jr. "Coach K's Journey Back." *Charlotte Observer*, March 4, 1999.

———. "Two Elite Coaches Rebuild Their Record-Breaking Bond." *Charlotte Observer*, November 13, 2011.

———. "Dean Smith and Mike Krzyzewski Meet Today in a Rivalry That Grows in Stature— and Draws Closer to the End—with Each Game." *Charlotte Observer*, March 2, 1997.

Jacobs, Barry. "Back Injury, Sitting Out Changed History." *Raleigh News and Observer*, January 4, 2015.

———. "Duke's Krzyzewski Blends Passion, Anger and Adrenaline." *Raleigh News and Observer*, June 5, 2017.

Norwood, Robyn. "Old School Ties." *Los Angeles Times*, November 12, 2004.

O'Neill, Dana. "Mike Krzyzewski Isn't Who You Think He Is." ESPN.com, June 11, 2017.

Sokolove, Michael. "Follow Me." *New York Times*, February 5, 2006.

Tucker, Hank. "The Snarl and the Smile." *The Chronicle* (Duke University), June 5, 2017.

Tysiac, Ken. "Meeting of Two Masters." *Charlotte Observer*, December 19, 2010.

Wolff, Alexander. "Blue Angel." *Sports Illustrated*, March 16, 1992.

———. "Sportsman of the Year." *Sports Illustrated*, December 12, 2011.

Jim Harbaugh

Albom, Mitch. "Bo and Harbaugh: A Strong Bond." *Detroit Free Press*, December 30, 1986.

———. "Inside Harbaugh's Non-Stop, High-Octane World." *Detroit Free Press*, September 3, 2016.

Anderson, Lars. "Why Jim Harbaugh and Michigan May Not Live Happily Ever After." *Bleacher Report*, September 1, 2015.

Bacon, John U. *Endzone: The Rise, Fall and Return of Michigan Football*. New York: St. Martin's Griffin, 2015.

Birkett, Dave. "Off the Hook." *Detroit Free Press*, October 18, 2011.

Chengelis, Angelique S. "Two Brothers, One Devotion." *Detroit News*, January 28, 2013.

Curtis, Jake. "Harbaugh All About Honest, and Football." *San Francisco Chronicle*, August 26, 2007.

Gonzalez, Antonio. "Harbaugh Brothers' Lifelong Competition Hits NFL." Associated Press, September 2, 2011.

Henning, Lynn. "Harbaugh Epitome of Fiery Competitor." *Detroit News*, January 4, 2011.

Hersh, Philip. "According to Jim." *Chicago Tribune*, November 22, 2007.

Kawakami, Tim. "Jim Harbaugh's Tense Relationship with 49ers." *San Jose Mercury News*, February 22, 2014.

Keeler, Sean. "Why Michigan Coach Jim Harbaugh Once Played 5 Games of Racquetball While Recovering from Chicken Pox." Landof10.com.

Lieber, Jill. "Harbaugh Relishes New Life." *USA Today*, September 14, 2005.

Mihoces, Gary. "Football Runs in the Family." *USA Today*, February 12, 2013.

Murphy, Dan. "Jim Harbaugh's Circle of Friends Is Even Cooler Than You Think." ESPN.com, November 24, 2016.

Myers, Gene. "Buckle Up, Football Fans, Harbaugh Mania Is Shifting into High Gear." *Detroit Free Press*, August 30, 2015.

Oates, Bob. "The Three Bears." *Los Angeles Times*, December 25, 1990.

Rabjohns, Jeff. "Captain Coach." *Indianapolis Star*, October 30, 2004.

Rittenberg, Adam. "Jim Harbaugh's Ref Rant Was Peak Harbaugh." ESPN.com, November 28, 2016.

Rosenberg, Michael. "Surrounded by Hype, Jim Harbaugh Motivated by Reality at Michigan." *Sports Illustrated*, May 18, 2015.

Rowland, Kyle. "Trip Takes Coach Back to His Roots." *Toledo Blade*, April 23, 2017.

Seidel, Jeff, and Mick McCabe. "Harbaugh's Wonder Years." *Detroit Free Press*, January 4, 2015.

Snyder, Mark. "Jim Harbaugh Through the Years." *Detroit Free Press*, December 31, 2014.

Strauss, Daniel. "Why Jim Harbaugh Took a Shot at Trump's Budget." *Politico*, March 25, 2017.

Van Walkenburg, Kevin. "Harbaugh Bowl." *Baltimore Sun*, November 24, 2011.

Wagoner, Nick. "Jim Harbaugh: Split Not Mutual." ESPN.com, February 13, 2015.

Walker, Childs, and Mike Klingaman. "Mirror Opposites." *Baltimore Sun*, January 27, 2013.
Wickersham, Seth. "Jim Harbaugh Comfortable in Chaos." *ESPN The Magazine*, October 2, 2014.

Jim Boeheim

Boeheim, Jim, and Jack McCallum. *Bleeding Orange: Fifty Years of Blind Referees, Screaming Fans, Beasts of the East, and Syracuse Basketball*. New York: Harper, 2014.
DelNagro, Mike. "Plenty of Juice in the Orange." *Sports Illustrated*, February 11, 1980.
Diota, Donna. "A Coach's Whistle, Not a Policeman's." *Syracuse Post-Standard*, March 15, 2015.
DiVeronica, Jeff. "Boeheim's Mea Culpa." *Rochester Democrat and Chronicle*, December 4, 2011.
Kornheiser, Tony. "Boeheim Can Predict, but Can He Prevail?" *Washington Post*, April 1, 1996.
McCallum, Jack. "If You Think You Know Syracuse Coach Jim Boeheim . . . Guess Again!" *Sports Illustrated*, December 2, 1996.
Michael, Matt. "900 . . . and Counting." *Syracuse New Times*, December 19, 2012.
Pierce, Charles S. "The Shadow." *Sports Illustrated*, December 16, 1991.
Pitoniak, Scott. "Boeheim Gets His Day in Court." *Rochester Democrat and Chronicle*, February 24, 2002.
———. *Color Him Orange: The Jim Boeheim Story*. Chicago: Triumph Books, 2011.
Rhoden, William C. "His Record of Success Is Sure, but Boeheim Is Still a Mystery." *New York Times*, March 7, 1988.
Thompson, Dick, and Teri Thompson. "Boeheim Gets Loud and Proud." *New York Daily News*, November 30, 2011.
Waters, Mike. "Boeheim's First Class Helped Launch Career." *Syracuse Post-Standard*.

Geno Auriemma

Altavilla, John. "Papa Geno's Heir." Hartford Courant, March 4, 2007.
Auriemma, Geno, and Jackie MacMullan. *Geno: In Pursuit of Perfection*. New York: Warner Books, 2006.
Brady, Erik. "With Pat Summitt and Geno Auriemma, Little Was Ever Out of Bounds." *Daily News Journal* (Murfreesboro, TN), July 10, 2016.
Deford, Frank. "Love, Italian Style." *Sports Illustrated*, November 24, 2003.
Elsberry, Chris. "UConn's Rise to National Prominence." *Connecticut Post*, November 15, 2008.
Fitzpatrick, Frank. "Hide and Peak." *Philadelphia Inquirer*, January 21, 2000.
Garber, Greg. "With His Team Unbeaten in 33 Games, UConn Coach Geno Auriemma Continues His Drive for Perfection." *Hartford Courant*, March 31, 1995.
Jacobs, Jeff. "Geno Still Seeking That Perfect Recipe." *Hartford Courant*, September 9, 2006.
———. "The Marvelous Woman Behind the Coach." *Hartford Courant*, April 1, 2016.
Jenkins, Sally. "Muffet McGraw, Geno Auriemma: These Two Plain Don't Like Each Other." *Washington Post*, April 7, 2014.
Jordan, Pat. "Geno Auriemma, Mr. Women's Basketball." Deadspin.com, March 22, 2012.
Longman, Jere. "Always Pursuing Perfection." *New York Times*, March 18, 2002.
———. "Close to Perfection." *New York Times*, January 17, 2003.
———. "Debating the Male Coach's Role." *New York Times*, March 29, 2002.
MacMullan, Jackie. "Striving Instructor." *Boston Globe*, November 26, 1995.
Tucker, Karen. "Geno Touched by Hall Honor." *New Haven Register*, April 30, 2006.

Doc Rivers

Araton, Harvey. "Willing to Take a Charge, but Not of Nepotism." *New York Times*, March 19, 2015.
Bolch, Ben. "Blunt Force of Nature." *Los Angeles Times*, June 30, 2013.

———. "Doc Is a Shot in the Arm for L.A." *Los Angeles Times*, April 17, 2014.
Bulpett, Steve. "Rolling with the Punches." *Boston Herald*, May 6, 2004.
Howard-Cooper, Scott. "Smooth Operator." *Los Angeles Times*, January 8, 1992.
Lupica, Mike. "Reality Hits Home for Doc." *Newsday*, December 17, 1994.
MacMullan, Jackie. "Family Doc." *Boston Globe*, October 1, 2006.
Massarotti, Tony. "Rivers Runs Through It." *Boston Herald*, December 19, 2007.
O'Donnell, Jim. "Family Doc Makes House Call." *Chicago Sun-Times*, April 24, 2009.
Pierce, Charles L. "Order on the Court." *Boston Globe Magazine*, May 30, 2004.
Povtak, Tim. "Doc Remakes the Magic in His Own Tough Image." *Orlando Sentinel*, October 29, 1999.
———. "The Little Team That Couldn't . . . Almost Did." *Orlando Sentinel*, April 21, 2000.
Raissman, Bob. "Why Rivers Burns Inside." *New York Daily News*, October 26, 1997.
Reid, John. "Austin Rivers Strives to Make It on His Own." *New Orleans Times-Picayune*, October 14, 2012.
Schmitz, Brian. "Magic's Rivers Recalls Bigotry in Milwaukee." *Orlando Sentinel*, April 25, 2001.
Springer, Shira. "Rivers: Rave Reviews." *Boston Globe*, October 12, 2004.
Wertheim, L. Jon. "Sleight of Hands." *Sports Illustrated*, April 10, 2000.

Brad Stevens

Brown, Clifton. "Don't Be Fooled by That Baby Face." *Indianapolis Star*, May 7, 2017.
Grossfeld, Stan. "Floor It." *Boston Globe*, January 8, 2016.
Holmes, Baxter. "Business Decisions." *Boston Globe*, October 28, 2013.
———. "Homecoming King." *Boston Globe*, December 22, 2013.
———. "It Adds Up for Stevens." *Boston Globe*, March 1, 2014.
———. "A Mission, a Method." *Boston Globe*, October 29, 2013.
———. "State of Immersion." *Boston Globe*, October 27, 2013.
Keefer, Zak. "Butler's Magical Run." *Indianapolis Star*, April 2, 2015.
King, Robert. "The Stevens Way." *Indianapolis Star*, May 15, 2011.
Layden, Tim. "Hub Fans Bid Kid . . . What, Exactly?" *Sports Illustrated*, August 26, 2013.
Rehagen, Tony. "How Does Brad Stevens Compete with Big Schools for Star Recruits? He Doesn't." *Indianapolis Monthly Magazine*, December 7, 2012.
Scalzo, Joe. "Not Taking After His Father." *The Repository* (Canton, OH), April 22, 2017.
Springer, Shira. "Firm Foundation." *Boston Globe*, July 23, 2013.
"Talking Teamwork with Celtics Coach Brad Stevens and Angela Duckworth." Heleo.com, May 16, 2016.
Washburn, Gary. "Pull of Indiana Always Looming in Stevens's Case." *Boston Globe*, December 14, 2014.
Winn, Luke. "Homeward Bound: Butler to the Final Four." SI.com, March 28, 2010.
Woods, David. "His Life's Passion." *Indianapolis Star*, April 22, 2007.
———. *Underdawgs: How Brad Stevens and the Butler Bulldogs Marched Their Way to the Brink of College Basketball's National Championship*. New York: Scribner, 2010.

Dabo Swinney

Bamberger, Michael. "Reborn in Death Valley." *Sports Illustrated*, December 16, 2015.
Connolly, Matt. "How Dabo Built Clemson into Nation's No. 1 Team." *The State* (Columbia, SC), December 2, 2015.
"Dabo Swinney Laments Brother's Arrest, Says He Must 'Suffer the Consequences.'" ESPN.com, January 8, 2016.
Eagleton, Rachel, and Elaine Day. "Knowing Your Tigers: Behind the Ball with Dabo Swinney." *Tiger Town Observer* (Clemson, SC), April 23, 2015.

Hale, David M. "There Is Always a Bright Side from Where Dabo Swinney Sits." ESPN.com, November 5, 2015.

Hamilton, Brian. "You Don't Know Dabo." *Sports Illustrated*, November 3, 2015.

McDonald, Zack. "Brother of Clemson's Dabo Swinney Charged with Aggravated Stalking." *News Herald* (Panama City, FL), January 7, 2016.

Morris, Ron. "Making Business Sense of Clemson's Dabo Swinney." *Raleigh News and Observer*, December 2, 2015.

Russo, Ralph D. "Fearlessly, Swinney Has Exceeded Expectations at Clemson." Associated Press, December 3, 2015.

Schlabach, Mark. "Dabo Swinney Overcame Pain and Poverty to Be on the Cusp of History." ESPN.com, January 7, 2016.

Solomon, Jon. "Swinney Faces Beloved Tide." *Birmingham News*, August 27, 2008.

Vandervort, Will. "Clemson's Silver Lining." *Daily Journal-Messenger* (Seneca, SC), December 11, 2008.

Wallace, Greg. "As Tigers Emerge as ACC Power, Phillips' Faith in Dabo Pays Off." *Anderson* (SC) *Independent-Mail*, October 2, 2011.

Wetzel, Dan. "Dabo Swinney Travels Long Road to Restore Clemson to Prominence." Yahoo! Sports, September 19, 2012.

Wolken, Dan. "Clemson Proves It's Ready for Big Time." *USA Today*, October 5, 2015.

———. "Clemson's Swinney Winning His Way." *USA Today*, August 27, 2013.

INDEX

INDEX